Really advanced praise . . .

ANCIENT SELFIES

"A fun read. Sweeping in scope. Quirky and humane."
- *Herodotus, after writing his Histories.*

"Full of intrigue, tragedy and romance."
- *Sophocles after a performance of Oedipus Rex.*

"Inspirational!"
- *Octavian, witnessing Caesar ascend to heaven as a comet.*

"Expands your world. Takes you to new places."
- *Alexander the Great, while conquering the Persians.*

"Intriguing and insightful."
- *Julius Caesar, after meeting Cleopatra.*

"A gorgeous portrayal."
- *Cleopatra, seeing Marc Antony's Cleopatra coin.*

"Revolutionary! Challenges your assumptions."
- *Spartacus, while preparing to fight Rome's legions.*

"Heroes, gods, and conflict! What more could you want."
- *Homer, after writing the Iliad and Odyssey.*

"Innovative approach. Well executed."
- *Hannibal, marching elephants through the Alps.*

"Liberating!"
- *Cassius and Brutus, after assassinating Caesar.*

"Mint condition. As the circumstances require."
- *Croesus after commissioning the first coin.*

"Coins, selfies and social media. What a mix!"
- *Marshall McLuhan, media prophet and scholar.*

"Enlightening. Feeds the soul."
- *Menander, Indo-Greek King and disciple of the Buddha.*

"Perfect! Reveals us warts and all."
- *Phraates IV on seeing his coin.*

... totally fabricated praise.

Ancient Selfies

HISTORY REVEALED THROUGH THE WORLD'S
FIRST SOCIAL MEDIA: ANCIENT COINS

Clinton Richardson

Read Janus LLC
Atlanta, Georgia

Why Ancient Selfies?

More than 2,500 years ago, rulers in Greece and Lydia created the first social media when they began stamping images on their newly invented coins. Distributed widely, these coins survive today with striking images that let us experience our past in an immediate way. *Ancient Selfies* uses these images to bring you closer to the leaders and artists who built empires, created great art, and invented both science and democracy.

What's in the book?

Ancient Selfies will introduce you to the ancient Persians, Greeks, Phoenicians, Celts and Carthaginians. You will follow Alexander the Great on his campaigns and Rome as it grows into an empire. You will watch as ambitious men tear apart the Roman Republic. And you will witness, with the ancients, the formation of Rome, Greek rebellion against Rome, the genius of Homer and much more.

What can you learn?

How did Cleopatra and Marc Antony appear to their contemporaries? How did the Greeks inspire revolt against the Romans with coins? Did an ancient coin embolden Caesar's assassins? These are just a few of the questions answered in *Ancient Selfies*. Check out the Contents and Introduction for more.

Copyright © 2017 by Clinton Richardson
ISBN: 978-0-9912475-3-0
Also from the author:
Richardson's Growth Company Guide 5.0
The Venture Magazine Compete Guide to Venture Capital
Check out www.ancientselfies.com

Contents

Preface..1

Introduction...3

The Ancients 13

From 561 BC. Lydia's King Croesus invents coins, loses his empire and escapes death on a funeral pyre; the Buddha awakens; Thales and the Milesians anticipate the Big Bang Theory; Cyrus builds a Persian Empire and puts his likeness on coins; Darius steals the Persian throne and invades Greece; Xerxes attacks but fails to subdue Athens; Herodotus travels and writes the Western world's first history; a flashing bronze helmet from Troy; the first Alexander thwarts the Persians; the Sarmatians, descended from Amazon women and Sythian men, arrive from Central Asia; the Thracians expand; Athens has a Golden Age; the Corinthians and Spartans thwart Athens' siege of Syracuse; the Phoenicians colonize, invent an alphabet and command the Mediterranean Sea; Darius succeeds Artaxeres in Persia; the Phoenician Abd' Ashtart suffers at the hand of his nurse; Philip of Macedonia sets the stage for Alexander the Great; the gods Athena and Pan; the Celts trade with the Greeks and displace the Etruscans; fish coins from China; and more. Introduction, timeline and list of featured coins. The coins and their stories.

Greek Empire...57

From 336 BC. A 20-year-old Alexander takes the Macedonian throne and leads his army against the Persians; Darius and the Persians defeated at Gaugamela; the impact of Aristotle and Homer's *Iliad* on Alexander; Greek victories in Egypt and India; Ptolemy steals Alexander's body to secure his claim to Egypt; Greece rules an empire; the Celts and others reflect on Alexander's renown; Ephesus and the Temple of Artemis; the Thracian Seuthes opposes Alexander's general; Lysimachus as king; the potter Agathocles rules Sicily; Seleucus and the Persian princess Apama; the "one-eyed" Antigonus and his son Demetrius, besieger of cities; Philetairos; Iona's tribute to Homer; Ptolemy's dynasty in Egypt; Antiochus and his father's bride Stratonice; Antigonus rules Greece; Hieron and Archimedes of Syracuse; the costly victories of Pyrrhus; the children of Mars spark the Punic Wars; Hannibal's campaign, the Bretti and Rome's near destruction; Castulo, the sphinx and Hannibal's brother Hasdrubal; Antiochus III, a Roman line in the sand and battlefield ghosts; Saba and the land of Sheba; Halicarnassus, home to Herodotus and Artemesia; Dyrrachion, Qin Shi Huangdi and Masinissa; the Thrace of Spartacus; Heracles, son of Zeus; the first Cleopatra and the Rosetta Stone; the Celtiberians and the Parthian Mithradates; the Eastern Greek empire of Menander; and more. Introduction, timeline and list of featured coins. The coins and their stories.

Republican Rome..135

From 149 BC. What Spartacus, Kirk Douglas and Joe McCarthy have in common; Rome's Republican Monetales and their coins; the goddess Tanit, Carthage and Roman destruction; a Roman oath scene; the two-faced Janus;

Roman vote by ballot; Africanus defeats Hannibal to save Rome; the Delsutors and their riding skills; Jugurtha and a Roman legionnaire; a Caesar's take on Mars, Venus and Cupid; a victorious Gaius Marius; a crushed Tarpeia and the Sabine War; Pergamon and Rome's Senators; Mithradates of Pontus; the Greek gods and Mithradates' call to arms; Dionysus, Gorgon and Nike; Athena, Perseus and Medusa; Ariarathes and the challenge of ruling Cappodica; Clodianus and Spartacus; Norbanus and Sulla; Sulla's triumph over the Marians; Censorinus, Marsysas and a severed head; Limetanus, Odysseus and the dog Argus; Cicero's Rome; Cupid and the Venus Gens; Rome's Vestal Virgins; Perseus and wars with Rome; Numidia's Juba I; Scarus and the Nabateans; the Remi; Viridovix and the Unelli; the wealthy and ruthless Crassus; Orodes and the violent death of Crassus; Pompey's ring and his triumphs; Cassius Longinus; Brutus and his storied Republican past; Rufus and Sulla; and more. Introduction, timeline and list of featured coins. The coins and their stories.

Caesar's Legacy..227

From 48 BC. Julius Caesar crosses the Rubicon, conquers Rome, woos Cleopatra and dies at the hands of assassins; the civil wars that follow; Antony and Cleopatra's rise; Octavian schemes and succeeds; Decimus Brutus serves and betrays Caesar; Celtic warrior-chieftain Vercingetorix from a Roman prison; the eventful year of 48 BC; Caesar as conqueror; Cato in black; the great Magnus Pompey; Cleopatra in exile; Cleopatra as queen; the last Pharaohs; Juno Monetas and

Roman coins; Caesar's great Roman Triumph; victory at the Battle of Munda; Julius Caesar as dictator; the coin that killed Caesar; Fulvia, Marc Antony's wife and first woman on a Roman coin; Ariobarzanes and the peril of ruling Cappadocia after Caesar's death; Antioch and Philadelphos; Brutus and his Ides of March coin; Cassius and the final battle at Philippi; Octavian at Philippi; victory over Brutus celebrated; Ahenobarbus, general and pirate; Sextus Pompey commands the sea; Marc Antony, Octavia and an uneasy truce; the Parthian Phraates defeats Antony's legions; a cut coin and Roman fatherhood; Cleopatra as Aphrodite; Marc Antony's legionary coin; Caesarion, son of Caesar and Cleopatra; Octavian defeats Antony and Cleopatra at Actium; the great Marcus Agrippa; Agrippa and Octavian celebrate Egypt's defeat; Juba II and Cleopatra Selene; and more. Introduction, timeline and list of featured coins. The coins and their stories.

Afterwords..307
Aristotle's Influence, the Roman Senate, the Egyptian Factor and Fulvia's Revenge.

Book II Preview: Imperial Rome................................315
Appendix and Index...323
About the Author...335

To the curious, who wonder how we became who we are.

Preface

THIS BOOK CELEBRATES a unique resource that few people know much about - ancient coins. Hand stamped from dies engraved by artisans more than 2,000 years ago, these ancient art miniatures opened up commerce by replacing barter and in so doing became, with their ability to deliver images, the world's first social media.

Ancient rulers quickly realized the power coins had to broadcast images that could shape impressions and deliver messages to their subjects and trading partners. With carefully selected images, they used their coins to convey messages of strength and power, to celebrate accomplishments and beliefs and, sometimes, to deceive. In so doing, they left a permanent record of images that let us see the ancient world as the ancients themselves saw it.

This book invites you to join the author on a personal journey to the distant past, one assisted by the hand stamped coins ancient rulers issued to support their economies and convey their messages. The images on these coins say something direct about our ancient ancestors, who they were, how they acted, and what they did to shape the world we live in. Like modern day selfies, they provide unique, first-person glimpses into the lives and times of the rulers who produced them.

You hold a piece of history when you examine an ancient coin. You hold an artifact from a world of city states, republics, empires, noble aspirations and conflict. It is a world that included Alexander the Great, Aristotle, Hannibal, Homer, Spartacus, Julius Caesar, Cicero, Brutus, Marc Antony, Cleopatra and more. It is a world that refined art and literature and built the institutional foundations that support our 21st century way of living.

But it was also a world of physical hardship where even the wealthy lived without the modern conveniences we take for granted. There was no electricity or Internet. There were no combustion engines, fire arms, light bulbs, or telephones. Roads, when they existed, were aggregations of cut stones. Even necessities like soap had yet to be invented. Chocolate and coffee were hundreds of years in the future.

Come visit this fascinating and important world. Experience it in new and tangible way. Spend time with the coins our ancient forbearers left behind. Contemplate their world as they saw it. Hear their stories, celebrate their victories and learn about their values and gods. Experience it all through the telling images their leaders commissioned for their coins.

Introduction

THE REMARKABLE STORY OF CROESUS, wealthy and powerful king of the Lydians more than 500 years before Christ, comes to us from *The Histories* of Herodotus, written in the fifth century BC. Misunderstanding the oracle's words and wanting to expand his empire, Croesus launches an attack against the Persian ruler Cyrus the Great. He expects a great victory but, instead, loses his empire.

Captured, he is made Cyrus' prisoner and seated atop a funeral pyre that is set on fire. Reflecting on his life while the flames grow, Croesus repeats the name of the wise Solon three times and catches the attention of Cyrus. While responding to questions about his behavior, Croesus reveals his humanity in a way that moves Cyrus to instruct his servants to douse the fire. But it is too late. The fire rages out of control and Croesus faces imminent death.

Weeping, Croesus appeals to the god Apollo for help. Clouds quickly gather and release a torrent of rain that douses the fire and spares Croesus' life. Croesus lives on to serve Cyrus as his trusted counsel and becomes guardian to Cambyses, son and heir to Cyrus.

The fantastic details of this ancient story challenge the modern reader to believe in its veracity or the reality of the man. But Croesus was a very real and powerful man, one who left very tangible evidence of his tenure and influence on this planet. Like other ancient rulers who would follow, Croesus left his mark on the coins he issued to fuel the commerce of his realm.

In fact, while still in control of his vast empire, he issued one of the first coins to be recognized as a ready medium of exchange between cultures. Unmistakable in their design and consistent in their quality and weight, the silver coins of Croesus showed other rulers how to leave their words and images in permanent form as irrefutable evidence of their existence and influence.

The images of many great figures appear on the pages that follow, along with their very human stories. They are the images ancient rulers chose to circulate in the most wide spread media of the time - coins. That many of them are also strikingly precise and beautiful is a testament to the skills of the ancient celators who engraved the dies used to hand stamp these coins. The incredible art miniatures their work created provide us with unique glimpses into the lives and times of our ancient ancestors.

Included here are coins and stories from 550 BC to 4 BC, beginning with the Lydians of Croesus and their Persians conquerors. The Greeks held off the Persians and colonized the Mediterranean. The Romans fought and conquered until they turned the Mediterranean into a Roman sea. Both are represented in the coins presented here.

So too are the Phoenicians, Egyptians, Seleucids, Carthaginians, Parthians, and Thracians. All played important roles in the ancient world, as did the Celts, Sarmatians, Numidians, Mamertini, and Mauretanians. The coins they issued take us back in tangible ways and give us unique windows into their times.

The great Persian rulers Cyrus, Xerxes and Darius stamped their coins with heroic images of the Persian king in action, wearing a crown and bearing weapons. The Macedonian King Philip II and his son Alexander the Great both put their profiles on coins. Alexander added the lion headdress of the Greek hero Heracles to his profile and placed the greatest of the Greek gods, Zeus, on the back.

The Alexander Mosaic at the Naples Archaeological Museum

Alexander's general Ptolemy, who founded a dynasty that ruled Egypt for three centuries, issued coins with similar profiles. His most famous descendant Cleopatra VII influenced the direction of Western history by captivating, in turn, both Julius Caesar and Mark Antony while ruling the wealthiest empire on the planet. Her profile graces three different coins included in these pages from very different stages of her eventful life.

Also here is the ancient artisan's portrait of a Greek king in Afghanistan, at the far eastern edge of Alexander's conquest, who attained the highest stage of sanctification and died a Buddhist monk. Other coins portray the author of Greek epics, the founding of Rome, the first vote by ballot and the touching story of Odysseus' return to his beloved Penelope.

The lives and times of Spartacus, who lead an army of 120,000 slaves against Republican Rome, are captured on coins of the time - first on a coin from the native Thrace where Spartacus was born and taken captive and second on a Roman coin celebrating his eventual defeat at the hands of the Roman generals Crassus and Pompey. The unfortunate Senator Lentulus Clodianus, whose Roman legions were defeated by Spartacus, also appears here with a coin he issued.

Ancient Mosaic from the Roman Coliseum

The Parthian general Surenas, who defeated the Romans, put Crassus to death and sent his severed head to his king, Orodes, as a prize. Crassus left a coin from his term as Governor of Antioch, just before his death. Orodes and his son Phraates both issued coins with imposing profiles that include a prominent forehead wart, something that distinguished Parthian royalty.

The great Celts of Europe later battled Julius Caesar and displayed a unique abstract style on their coins. The Celtic chieftain Vercingetorix brought together several tribes in southern France to give Julius Caesar his greatest challenge. He is here not on a Celtic coin but, instead, on a Roman coin with a haunting portrait commissioned while he sat imprisoned in a Roman jail. So too is a Celtic coin that mimics the coin of Philip II, the father of Alexander the Great, but with a stylized horse and rider that look more like the work of a modern artist than that of an ancient artisan.

The Iliad from a fifth century AD manuscript page

Intriguing coins and stories from the chaos that followed the assassination of Julius Caesar in 44 BC also fill these pages. Did

Brutus, an assassin of Julius Caesar, flaunt his act by minting a coin depicting daggers of the very sort used to put Caesar to death? Did the son of Caesar's adversary Lucius Ahenobarbus really become a pirate and later reconcile with Caesar's close friend Mark Antony?

Contemplate, on the pages that follow, the only attributed portrait of Marcus Brutus on a coin he issued to pay his armies as he fought Octavian and Marc Antony to succeed Caesar as Rome's ruler. And consider the coin of Decimus Brutus, the cousin to Brutus who convinced Caesar to ignore his foreboding and go to the Senate on the morning he was killed. See too how Marc Antony celebrated a short-lived truce with Octavian with a unique coin. It bears his profile on one side and the image of his wife Octavia, renowned beauty and sister to Octavian, on the other poised between two opposed snakes.

In today's entertainment-saturated world, it can often be hard to separate reality from fiction. What follows, however, is the real thing, hand engraved, hand stamped coins minted by real people that provide unique glimpses into the lives and times of our very real predecessors. No fictional characters or movie action figures here. Instead, contemporary images of Alexander the Great and the generals who helped him conquer much of the known world. Here too you will find the coin of Hannibal, the great Carthaginian general who crossed the Alps to attack and subdue Rome's best legions.

See history reflected in the dramatic images that have been preserved through time on the coins ancient rulers issued in their names. See the coin that Socrates and Plato used for their purchases. Reflect, with their contemporaries, on the impact of Homer's *Iliad* and *Odyssey* on the Greek and Roman world. And see through their coins how Octavian, Agrippa, Marc Antony and Cleopatra aligned, maneuvered and fought to reestablish an empire out of the chaos that followed Caesar's assassination.

The actions of the leaders portrayed on these pages created the world we live in today. Their successes and failures touch every aspect of our lives. Reflect on their lives and stories while considering the incredible and telling images they left on their coins. Enjoy the opportunity this first and permanent social media gives us to see the ancients as they saw themselves.

And look for the future volumes of this *Ancient Selfies* adventure. Hand stamped coins continued to mark the accomplishments, beliefs and challenges of ancient rulers who changed our world after Octavian consolidated his hold on Rome and became known as Emperor Augustus. As the first social media, these coins continued to serve ancient rulers as a means for communicating with their subjects and others.

In our next book, Roman emperors will expand Roman predominance throughout the Mediterranean and beyond. Augustus, Tiberius, Caligula, Claudius, Nero, Trajan, Hadrian, Commodus and others will rule into the second century AD. Nero will persecute Christians and Vespasian will put down a Jewish revolt in Jerusalem. But Christianity will take hold and the Jews will survive.

A third century of instability will follow with emperors and challengers galore, including the first African emperor, the first woman to openly rule the Roman Empire and the only vestal virgin to serve as an empress. The empire will split and run through a succession of short term emperors until

Aurelian finally reunites Rome under one ruler. Diocletian will follow with a successful reign that is marred by Christian persecutions that give rise to legends like those of Saint George and the dragon.

And then Constantine will change everything by consolidating the empire and legitimizing Christianity after receiving a vision from the Christian god. His mother will find the Holy Grail and other Christian artifacts while the Church grows in influence. Emperor Justinian will follow later and codify Roman law while fighting a growing Persian threat and one brought on the backs of fleas, a plague that will change everything and open the empire to later assault from a new threat - the nation of Islam.

Raphael Imagines Aeneas (Rome's forefather) Escaping Troy
Detail from the *Fire in the Borgo* fresco at the Vatican Museum

[1]

The Ancients

WE WELCOME YOU with a puzzle.[1] Is this encrusted metal fish one of the oldest coins known to man? Or is it something else?

Authorities date this fish-shaped object to the Chinese Chou Dynasty from the 8th century BC. Metallic and small enough to fit easily in your hand, these tokens are found in large enough numbers to suggest that they may have served some purpose in commerce. Many of these pieces have been discovered in Chinese tombs, where they may have served as funerary objects.

But with no contemporary writings describing how this piece was used, archeologists can only speculate about whether or not this small metal fish from more than 2,500 years ago was one of the first coins used in commerce or something else. And, whether or not this abundant artifact is money, what can it tell us about the people who made it and their times?

---

[1] China Chou Dynasty fish money produced from 770 to 476 BC. Their abundant numbers suggest they may have been used as an early form of money. Acquired from ECIN Associates, O'Fallon, Missouri in December 2007.

Welcome to the fascinating world of ancient history and ancient coins where records can be sketchy, nonexistent, or conflicting and where some of best evidence about the people and their lives is found on the coins they used in trade. On the pages that follow are the images of ancient coins fashioned by the artists of their times to reflect the people, the events, and the gods of their worlds.

Artisans, who the Romans called celators, were commissioned by ancient rulers to engrave images into dies that were then used to hand stamp their coins. Despite the lack of modern equipment or mechanical stamping processes, the coins produced by these celators contain images that are often exquisitely detailed.

These metallic art miniatures circulated throughout ancient realms in everyday commerce and provide us with a unique opportunity to see and touch very real and tangible evidence of the ancients themselves and, in the process, to understand more about their times and how they saw themselves.

This first chapter contains some of the oldest coins issued by leaders of the ancient world. In it you will find coins from the mid-sixth to the mid-fourth century BC. They come from the Mediterranean cradle of Western civilization, the more "barbaric" civilizations to the north, and the land of the Buddha far to the east. They include coins from the Lydians of Croesus, the Persians of Darius and Xerxes, the Phoenicians, the Greeks of democratic Athens, and the Macedonians of Philip II, father to Alexander the Great.

Around 550 BC, coins produced by the wealthy and powerful Lydian King Croesus emerged as a medium of international exchange to facilitate commerce and convey messages to a large and widespread population. His coins portray a roaring lion confronting a bull, images undoubtedly chosen to communicate the king's power. They were remarkable for their consistent purity and weight.

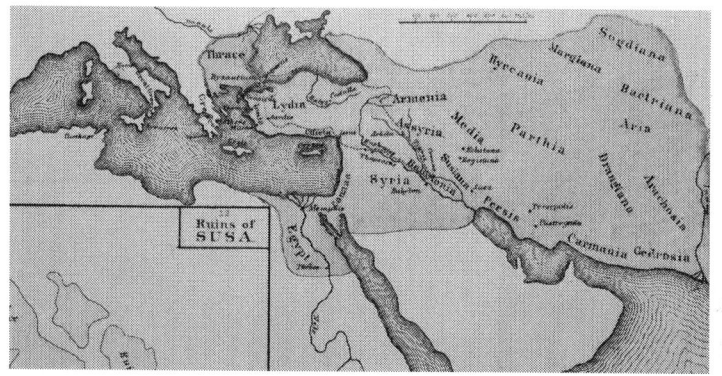

Persian Empire
Labberton's Historical Atlas (1884)

The Persian ruler Cyrus the Great had no coinage of his own when he conquered Croesus and his Lydian armies. After his conquest, Cyrus adopted coins as a tool of commerce and method of communicating with his subjects. The coins he commissioned included profiles of the king himself. His successors Darius, Xerxes, and Codomannus (aka Darius III) continued making similar coins until Alexander the Great appeared in the fourth century BC and turned the Persian Empire into a new Greek Empire.

To the north of the Lydians, Persians and Greeks, in what is now Russia, the Ukraine and Central Asia, the Sarmatians were also issuing coins to support their commerce. Theirs include no engraved images but, instead, are shaped in the image of a dolphin. Considered "barbarian", a term meaning non-Greek to the Greeks, these Sarmatians were described by the Greek historian Herodotus as being a blond, stout, and tanned people who had descended from the Scythians and Amazons.

To the east, the great religious leader Siddhartha Gautama Buddha was traveling and teaching in the Magadha region of India south of the Ganges River. He was a contemporary of both Croesus and the Sarmatians. And, although he did not issue coinage because his domain was spiritual and not political, we have here a coin of his realm, issued by Bimbasara, who ruled the region and became an important disciple of the Buddha.

The golden age of Greece occurred while the Persians ruled the East. The signature coin from the unofficial Greek capital of that era, Athens, portrays a helmeted portrait of the goddess Athena with a distinctive archaic eye on one side and the symbolic Athenian owl with an olive branch on the other.

The Death of Socrates by Jacques-Louis David (1787)

This coin circulated for more than 30 years while Athens was the leading cultural, intellectual, and commercial center of the

Western world. Dramatists Sophocles, Aeschylus, Euripides, and Aristophanes all walked the streets of Athens while this coin was in circulation. Philosophers Socrates and Plato, historians Herodotus and Thucydides, and physician Hippocrates all lived in or visited Athens during this period, likely using the coin to purchase goods.

Also here are coins from city-states in Thrace, Syracuse and Phoenicia that bear the images of contemporary gods, battlefield armor, and animals. Here too is the coin of Philip of Macedonia, the father of Alexander the Great, who consolidated power in Greece to such an extent that Alexander could strike out on his conquest of the East.

These ancient coins represent the first mass produced and widely distributed art. Their invention provided rulers with a powerful medium for commerce and political expression. Through these coins, rulers were able to portray themselves and their messages in the manner they chose to the broader population.

Contemporary portraits of the great ancient rulers first appear on coins during this period. As time passes, rulers get more and more sophisticated about the images they strike onto their coins, conveying overt and subtle messages to their people. As you flip through these pages, pause and consider how close these remarkable coin images bring you to the ancients, their ways and world.

PARTIAL TIMELINE.

753 BC Founding of Rome.
700 BC Sabines and Romans jointly rule Rome.

653 BC Rise of the Persians.
563 BC Siddhartha Gautama Buddha is born.
561 BC Croesus becomes king of the Lydians.
551 BC Confucius is born.
550 BC Cyrus the Great founds the Persian Empire.
547 BC Cyrus defeats Croesus.
539 BC Babylonians fall. Cyrus liberates the Jews.
512 BC Darius I expands Persian Empire.
509 BC Lucius Brutus defeats Tarquinius, Roman King.
508 BC Democracy in Athens begins.
490 BC Greeks defeat the Persians at Marathon.
480 BC Xerxes defeated at Salamis.
469 BC Socrates is born.
460 BC Greek city-states begin Peloponnesian war.
449 BC Athens golden age begins.
414 BC Athenians fail to take Syracuse.
404 BC Peloponnesian war ends.
338 BC Codomannus (Darius III) rules Persia.
336 BC Philip II prepares to invade Persia.

COINS FEATURED IN THIS CHAPTER.

Chou Dynasty Fish Money, 770 to 476 BC
Croesus, 561 to 515 BC
Magadha Region of the Buddha, 550 to 470 BC
The Milesians, 550 to 377 BC
Cyrus & Darius, 505 to 480 BC
Xerxes I, 485 to 420 BC
Alexander I, 498 to 454 BC
The Sarmatians, 6th to 5th century BC

Thracian Chersonese, 480 to 350 BC
Thrace, Mesembria, 450 to 350 BC
Athens Golden Age, 449 to 413 BC
Syracuse, circa 380 BC
Phoenicia, Arados, 380 to 352 BC
Artaxerxes & Darius, 375 to 340 BC
'Abd 'ashtart I, 372 to 361 BC
Panticapaeum, 4th century BC
Philip II, 359 to 336 BC
The Celts, 2nd century BC

The answer both oracles gave to the question were perfectly consistent with each other: they told Croesus that if he made war on the Persians, he would destroy a great empire.

The Histories by Herodotus
Chapter 1, Book 53

Lydian King Croesus
561 to 515 BC

This is the coin that started it all. First issued more than 550 years before the birth of Christ by a Lydian king with global aspirations, it introduced coins to the conquering Persians and triggered the growth of a new international medium of exchange and communication. Greek city-states had issued coins before but none gained the international acceptance of this Lydian coin.

This silver siglos with its distinctive image of a confronted lion and bull was issued by the great Lydian King Croesus who conquered much of Greece in the sixth century BC. The consistent quality of its silver and weight made it an ideal medium for international exchange. Its striking image proclaimed the ancient ruler's power and attested to the remarkable skill of the artisans who engraved and stamped the coins by hand.

We know about Croesus and his eventful life through accounts of his life in the Western world's first written history, *The Histories* of Herodotus. Composed more than a century later using stories remembered by local inhabitants, the Greek historian from Halicarnassus paints a colorful picture of this ancient Lydian ruler whose wealth was so great that it gave rise to the phrase "rich as Croesus."

After subduing Greece, King Croesus consulted with two oracles and set his sights on expanding to the east. Encouraged by the words of the oracles, he attacked the new Persian King Cyrus in 547 BC expecting to destroy the Persian Empire only to lose his own.

Following the battle, the Persians forced Croesus to climb atop a funeral pyre to die. According to Herodotus, Croesus cried out from the flames in remorse, understanding for the first time the wisdom of the Athenian sage Solon who had belittled his wealth and power years before.

On hearing the cries of Croesus, Cyrus took pity and ordered the flames to be put out. But the fire had grown too intense and raged on. Croesus prayed to the gods and clouds appeared miraculously in the sky, sending down a torrential rainstorm that quickly quenched the blazing pyre.

Croesus survived and went on to become a trusted advisor to his new master Cyrus. His method of coinage was adopted by the Persians and spread throughout the ancient world.

Coin details and provenance: Croesus, King of Lydia. 561 to 515 BC. Silver half-siglos. Minted in Lydia. Obverse: Confronted foreparts of roaring lion and bull. Reverse: Double incuse punch. 5.55 grams. References: SNG Copenhagen 456; SNG von Aulock 2875. Acquired from Tom Vossen Antiquities, Kerkrade, Netherlands in March of 2004.

Magadha Region of the Buddha
550 to 470 BC

Far to the east of Lydia at this same time, a great spiritual leader lived and spread his word in the Magadha region of India south of the Ganges River. This coin, with its symbolic images, circulated in this region while Siddhartha Gautama Buddha, the spiritual leader and founder of Buddhism, lived and taught in the area.

Believed to have lived from 563 to 483 BC while rulers Bimbasara and Ajatashatru ruled the Magadha region, the Buddha began his spiritual quest at the age of 29 when he left his palace to meet his subjects and came upon an old man, a diseased man, a decaying corpse, and an aesthetic. Siddhartha later abandoned his palace to become a monk and practice near total deprivation of worldly goods in search of enlightenment.

He eventually discovered what Buddhists refer to as the middle way and, at age 35, following 49 days of meditation, achieved enlightenment. It was from this point on that he became known as the Buddha, or "Awakened One." For the remaining 45 years of his life, the Buddha traveled and taught in the Gangetic plain where this coin circulated.

Bimbasara, who ruled the region from 545 to 493 BC and first met the Buddha before his enlightenment, became an important disciple of the Buddha and attained the sotapanna status reserved to those who eradicate the first three fetters of the mind. Bimbasara was succeeded by his son and murderer Ajatashatru, who ruled the region until 461 BC.

The date when these coins started being issued is obscure. It is believed this coin type was first issued around 550 BC and that it was replaced by 470 BC with a smaller and thicker coin of the same weight. These dates coincide with the reigns of both Bimbasara and Ajatashatru.

Coin details and provenance: Bimbasara and Ajatashatru. Circa 550 to 470 BC. Silver karshapana. Minted in the Magadha region. Obverse: Five various punch marks. Reverse: Bankers marks. 3.25 grams. 25 x 19 mm. References: Gupta and Hadraker I VI C 34 (#55). This type has an unpublished variety of the 6-arm symbol from the lifetime of the Buddha. First issue karshapanas are rare and hard to find. More precise attribution of these coins is impossible at this point. Acquired from Ancient Coins Canada, Ontario, Canada in March of 2007.

Symbols on the Coin:

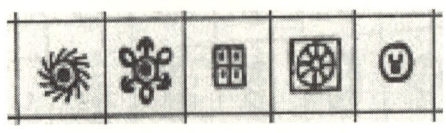

THE MILESIANS
500 TO 377 BC

About the same time the Buddha was finding spiritual revelation in the Gangetic plains of India, a very different tradition was taking root among the Greeks. In Ionian Miletus on the western coast of Anatolia (present day Turkey), a group of thinkers began speculating about the causes of natural phenomena and the origins of the universe in a new way.

The Milesian philosopher Thales, from the era in which this coin was issued, is now widely regarded as the father of western philosophy. During his life, he counseled Croesus and helped the city of Miletus avoid entanglement in the Lydian conflict with the Persia. This resulted in a long period of independence for Miletus and much of Greece. Thales' most lasting contribution, however, was the way he thought and the school of thinkers he established in Miletus.

Among those who participated in his Milesian school were Anaximander and Pythagorus. Thales and his followers were the first to search for and define general principles that accounted for natural phenomena and the first to offer hypotheses for why things occurred as they did. Members of his school focused on discovering the mechanisms that created the cosmos and explained natural phenomena instead looking to mythology or spirituality for explanations.

Anaximander, for example, speculated that the universe began as an undifferentiated concentration of material that began to spin and separate in a way that brought like materials together. The earth fell from this to the center, surrounded by water and then air. The fourth element, fire, formed the stars. Essential portions of this remarkable ancient theory are very similar to the big bang theory that modern scientists believe describes the creation of the universe.

The Melisians were the first to apply deductive reasoning to geometry. Thales theorem, that posits the necessary creation of a right angle from connecting three points on a circle, was discovered by the Melisians. They were among the first to inquire about the world in a scientific manner and created a tradition that has lead to the modern scientific tradition.

The Melisian coin from 500 BC depicts the head of a roaring lion and an ornamental star. The star is a fitting symbol for the city that turned the study of the cosmos into scientific deliberation.

Coin details and provenance: Miletus. Satraps of Caria, Iona. 500-377 BC. 1/12 obo. Obverse: Lion head facing left. Reverse: Ornamental Star. References: Sim-SNGCOP 953, Sim McClean pl 284/16, Iona. 1.25 gram. 10.25 mm. Acquired from Topcoins and Fine Art, Czech Republic, in April 2011.

Cyrus & Darius
505 TO 480 BC

The figure of the Persian king drawing his bow on the front of this coin identifies it as the first of the coins minted by the Persians after they defeated Croesus and went on to assemble the greatest empire of their time. Like the Lydian coin it succeeded, this silver siglos proclaims the power of its issuer with a bold image.

Both this coin and the Lydian coins that preceded it were produced by placing a metal flan beneath a hand engraved die and then striking the die with a hammer. The incuse punch on the reverse of the coin came from an elevation on the platform that held the metal flan during the minting process.

The Persians burst onto the world scene in the sixth century BC when Cyrus merged the Medes and Persians to create a single great Achaemenid dynasty. His decisive victory over Croesus in 547 BC expanded Persian territory and made the new empire the dominant force in the region.

The next great Persian king, Darius I, took the throne through murder and deception. As related in *The Histories* of Herodotus, Darius plotted the removal of the rightful heir Smerdis in 522 BC with six high ranking Persian conspirators. Together, they accused Smerdis of being an imposter, claiming that the real Smerdis had been murdered earlier by Cambyses, the successor to Cyrus. Cambyses conveniently died before Darius launched his deception and was unable to foil the plot.

Once enthroned, Darius organized and expanded the Persian Empire with great success. It would be nearly 30 years before he would meet with a major military defeat.

Attempting to expand westward after putting down a revolt of Greek city-states in Asia Minor, Darius invaded mainland Greece. He met with much success until his massive army met the Athenians at the Battle of Marathon in 490 BC just 25 miles from Athens. The Athenian's won the battle and stopped the Persians expansion into Greece, preserving Greek independence.

Darius died five years later and was succeeded by his son Xerxes.

Coin details and provenance: Persia. Achaemenid Empire. Circa 505 to 480 BC. AR siglos. Obverse: Persian king or hero in kneeling/ running stance right, drawing bow. Reverse: Incuse punch. 5.44 grams. 14 mm. References: Carradice Type II, 12-13. Carradice, NumChron 1998, 79-88 (same reverse punch). Toned VF. Scarce issue. Acquired from Barry P. Murphy Coins, Willow Street, Pennsylvania in January 2006.

XERXES I

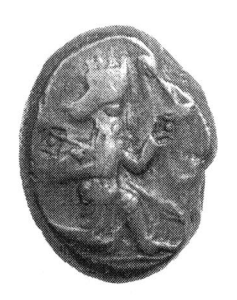

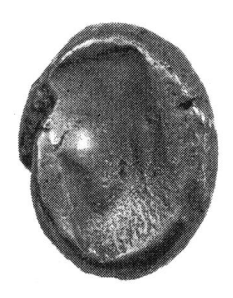

485 TO 420 BC

The Persians minted coins like these for nearly 200 years, changing the design of the king's image on the front only a few times. The details of this coin, with its running king carrying a spear and bow, identify it as being minted from 485 to 420 BC. This puts the coin's issuance into the reigns of Xerxes I and his son Artaxerxes I.

Xerxes' reign began in 485 BC, the year Darius died and the great Greek historian Herodotus was born. Just two years later, in 483 BC, Xerxes began preparations for the great task left undone by his father – punishing the Athenians for supporting rebellion among Persia's Ionian possessions.

After securing an alliance with Carthage three years later, Xerxes launched his large fleet and army from Sardis. His forces advanced quickly into mainland Greece.

A Greek alliance led by Athens, Sparta and Corinth formed to confront the threat. The Athenian general Themistocles persuaded the Greeks to make their stand against the Persian army at the narrow pass of Thermopylae. The Persian fleet was to be confronted at the straits of Artemisium.

Notwithstanding large losses to their fleet from a storm, the Persians easily dispatched the smaller Greek fleet. Their massive army, however, fought for seven days against just 7,000 Greeks at the narrow pass at Thermopylae before executing a successful rear guard action that ended the battle.

This left the route to Athens undefended and the conquest of the Greeks all but sealed. The Athenians, in their desperation, deserted to the nearby island of Salamis to watch their city burn and prepare to meet the Persians in a last-stand naval battle.

The battle that ensued matched just 371 Greek ships against 1207 Persian ships, including Persian ships under command of Artemisia, the female tyrant of Halicarnassus. Confident of his ultimate success, Xerxes sat ashore on a golden throne to watch his navy complete the Greeks' destruction.

Instead, the smaller but more agile Greek fleet outflanked and defeated the Persian navy in full view of a disappointed Xerxes. With the loss of much of his navy, Xerxes withdrew his forces to Asia. The unexpected Greek victory marked a turning point in the Persian wars and preserved the Greek homeland for the Greeks.

Coin details and provenance: Achaemenid Kings of Persia. Xerxes I, King of Persia. 485 to 420 BC. Silver Siglos. Minted in Lydia, Asia Minor. Obverse: King in guise of a kneeling and running archer wearing a kidaris (gown) and a kandys (crown) with a bow in left hand, spear in right. Reverse: Oblong punch. 5.56 grams. 13 mm. References: Carradice Type IIIb. Choice VF. Acquired from Glenn W. Woods Numismatist, Dallas, Texas in December 2004.

ALEXANDER I
498 TO 454 BC

Alexander I, who claimed descent from the Argive Greeks and the hero Heracles, was the first Macedonian ruler to put his name on his coins. This example has images on both sides, with a cantering horse on one and the profile of a Greek battle helmet on the other.

The helmet depicted fits the description given by the poet Homer of the helmet worn by the great Trojan hero Hector in the *Iliad*. As the poet describes Hector's last meeting with his wife and infant son before leaving to defend Troy, Hector's child screamed out "terrified by the flashing bronze, the horsehair crest, and the great ridge of the helmet nodding, bristling terror - so it struck his eyes." Hector and his wife laughed and Hector lifted the helmet from his head and set it down, "fiery in the sunlight," to pick up and console his son.

Alexander would have known this passage from the *Iliad* and, like his Macedonian contemporaries, he would have aspired to the heroic values portrayed in the Greek classic. But Alexander did more than aspire to the Greek heroic ideal. He also supported the Ionian Greeks during their revolts against Persia in the early fifth century BC, going so far as to murder envoys of the Persian Emperor Darius who were sent to his court.

When Xerxes invaded Greece in 480 BC, however, Alexander was forced to submit and represent Persian governor Mardonius during peace negotiations after the Battle of Salamis. While so constrained, however, he surreptitiously gave aid to Greek city-states who were battling the Persians, even warning them of the Persian governor's plans before the Battle of Plataea.

Alexander escaped his servitude when the Greeks prevailed at Plataea. As the Persians retreated, Alexander led troops to harass them, killing many at the estuary of the Strymon River in 479 BC.

After the Persians were expelled, Alexander reasserted Macedonian independence and modeled his court on the court of Athens. Poets Pindar and Bacchylides both dedicated poems to their patron Alexander.

Some Greek city-states considered Macedonia a non-Greek state. But a court of Olympic judges, the *Elean Hellanodikai*, confirmed Alexander's claim of descent from the Argive Greeks and included the Macedonians in the Olympic Games. Alexander's accomplishments set the stage for future expansion of Macedonian influence within and outside the Greek world.

Coin details and provenance: Alexander I. 498 to 454 BC. Silver tetrobol (heavy). Obverse: Horse cantering right. Reverse: Crested Illyrian helmet right within single lined incuse square. 2.06 grams. 15 mm. Acquired from Hixenbavgh Ancient Art, New York, New York in August 2009.

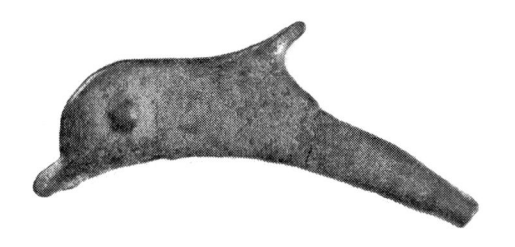

The Sarmatians
6ᵀᴴ TO 5ᵀᴴ CENTURY BC

The Sarmatians' domain stretched from the Caspian Sea west to the Vistula River and covered parts of modern day Russia, Ukraine, the Baltic States, and Central Asia. A collection of independent tribes, they moved west from the Central Asian steppes into Europe between the sixth and fourth centuries BC. This dolphin shaped object was their coin.

Greek historian Herodotus described the Sarmatians as blond, stout and tanned and believed them to be descended from the Scythians and Amazons. This, he reported, accounted for their Iranian-type language and the unusual freedoms of their women, who participated in warfare.

As recorded by Herodotus, the Greeks defeated the Amazons at the Battle of Thermodon and sailed away with three ships of captured Amazon warriors. While at sea, the women overpowered and killed their Greek captors and then drifted at sea because they did not know how to navigate. They eventually landed in an area populated by Scythians and, after skirmishing with them, reconciled with a group of young Sythian men.

Rather than assimilate with the Scythians, whose women did not hunt or make war, this new group of Amazon women and Scythian men traveled east and north for six days to a new territory where they settled and became known as the Sauromatae or Sarmatians. The Greeks and Romans widely accepted the analysis of Herodotus and his reports of an ancient Amazon nation ruled by female warriors.

That the Sarmatian women served as warriors is undisputed. Modern archaeological evidence shows why the Scythian and Sarmatian culture may have given rise to the stories about the Amazons. Graves of armed females have been found in Sarmatian territory. In ancient warrior graves excavated on the lower Don and Volga rivers, one in five is a female dressed for battle.

Comparisons of genetic evidence taken from the sites have found genetic links to the Kazaks, a Turkish-Mongol people from north central Asia. Some ancient historians portrayed them as a separate nomadic people who did little trading but glass beads at the excavated sites suggest they had meaningful ties to other cultures.

Coin details and provenance: Olbia, Sarmatia. Circa 6th to 5th century BC. Bronze dolphin-shaped coin with raised spine. 23 mm long. As cast with dark green and brown patina. References: SNG BM Black Sea 362; SNG Stancombe 334. Acquired from Ancient Coins Canada, Ontario, Canada in January 2006.

Thracian Chersonese

480 to 350 BC

The Chersonese peninsula, what is now the Gallipoli peninsula of Turkey, was part an ancient Thracian kingdom that encompassed much of modern-day Bulgaria, northern Greece and parts of Turkey, Serbia, and Macedonia. The Thracians settled 12 cities on the Chersonese peninsula during the seventh century BC.

This coin from a Greek settlement on the peninsula was issued in the fifth and fourth centuries BC. It portrays both a lion and a lizard. At the time it was issued, the peninsula was controlled by the Athenians who had established a number of colonies on the peninsula and enrolled them in the Delian League to resist Persian expansion into Greece. Sparta gained control between 431 BC and 404 BC but the peninsula reverted to the Athenians until it was ceded to the Macedonian Philip II in 338 BC.

The wealthy Miltiades the Elder, who opposed the Athenian tyrant Pisistratus, founded a major Athenian settlement on the peninsula around 550 BC, 70 years before this coin was first issued. Eventually, he took control of the entire Chersonese and built defenses to protect the peninsula against invasion.

His step-nephew Miltialdes the Younger seized control of the peninsula in 516 BC and married the daughter of Thracian King Olorus. He later became a vassal of the Persian King Darius I but joined the Greek Ionian revolt against the Persians in 499 BC, establishing relations with Athens and taking the Islands of Lemnos and Imbros.

When the revolt failed, Miltiades escaped to Athens, where he was elected one of the ten Athenian's strategio (generals) in 490 BC. In that role he served as a leader at the Battle of Marathon. According to Herodotus, he was responsible for devising the battle plan used by the Greeks to defeat the Persians in the battle.

Just one year after his great success, however, Miltialdes led an unsuccessful naval battle and suffered a leg wound. When he returned to Athens, his rivals charged him with treason. He died in prison, probably from gangrene.

Coin details and provenance: Thracian Chersonese. 480 to 350 BC. AR Hemidrachm. Obverse: Forepart of lion right, head turned back. Reverse: Quadripartite incuse square, monogram, pellet and lizard in sunken quarters. 2.2 grams. 18.67 mm. References: SNGCop 830. Acquired from Inclinatioroma Ancient Coins, New York, New York in January 2007.

Thrace, Mesembria
450 TO 350 BC

This coin comes from Mesembria, a city established at the end of the seventh century BC on the southeastern coast of Thrace, in what is now the Black Sea coast of Bulgaria. The coin bears the image of a crested Corinthian helmet and the initials META between four spokes of a wheel. This reverse image has been interpreted as a reference to solar worship with the radiate wheel representing the midday sun.

The Corinthian helmet, which originated in ancient Greece, was made of bronze and covered both the head and neck. It was the most popular and widely depicted helmet of antiquity and was worn by both Greek and Roman armies into the first century AD. The Greek hoplites and the later Roman legionnaires would wear the helmet tipped up for comfort between battles.

The Thracians who populated Mesembria were, by the time this coin was issued, the second most populous people in the world, at least according to Herodotus. They were an Indo-European people who were considered rural and barbaric by their more urban Greek neighbors. They were ruled for nearly half a century by the Persians in the sixth and fifth centuries BC and later conquered by Philip II of Macedonia in the fourth century BC.

Mesembria flourished during the fifth and fourth centuries BC when this coin was issued but declined after Macedonian occupation. Herodotus referred to the Thracian city of Mesembria, where this coin was minted, as a Samothracian stronghold but otherwise there are few references to this ancient city.

The site of the city has been located and has supported an active archeological dig since excavations began in 1966. The site is administered by the Hellenic Ministry of Culture and is designated by the Ministry as Mesembria-Zone to reflect archeological finds that identify the city site as a colony of Samothrace.

The foundations for fortified walls with towers have been excavated. City streets and houses within the walls, two public buildings, a sanctuary of Demeter, and a temple to Apollo have also been uncovered.

Coin details and provenance: Thrace, Mesembria. 450 to 350 BC. Obverse: Crested war helmet facing. Reverse: 'META' in 4 quarters of wheel. 1.14 grams. 11.72 mm. References: Seaby 1673. Nearly extremely fine. An old collection piece with deep toning. Acquired from Lodge Antiquities, Grantham, United Kingdom in August 2005

ATHENS' GOLDEN AGE
449 TO 413 BC

This is one of the most famous of ancient coins. It is one of the earliest fully sculpted, double-sided coins minted with a portrait on one side and an animal on the other. The portrait on the front is of the goddess Pallas Athena, protector of the city, wearing a helmet. A large-eyed Athenian owl, symbolizing wisdom, graces the reverse with an olive branch and a small crescent in the field.

The images on this coin reflect the foundational myth of the city. According to tradition, Athena claimed dominion over Athens by causing an olive tree to spring up next to a salt water well Poseidon had created by driving his trident into the soil. The Olympic deities were called together to determine Athena or Poseidon would have dominion over the area. They sided with Athena after hearing the testimony of Cecrops, first King of Athens, who had witnessed Athena's gift of the olive tree.

This coin was first issued in Athens after hostilities ended with Persia. It remained Athens' principle medium of exchange for 36 years. While this coin was being issued, the Athenians put together the Delian League of Greek city-states to contend with the continuing threat from the Persians. Over this period, with the help of the league, many Greek city-states in Asia Minor and the Aegean Islands were freed of their Persian overlord.

This was the golden age of Greece, when Athens was the leading cultural, intellectual, and commercial center of the Western world. It was a period during which the Parthenon was constructed and the best and brightest of the Greeks were attracted to the city, unleashing a unprecedented period of artistic and theatrical creativity.

Dramatists Sophocles, Aeschylus, Euripides, and Aristophanes all walked the streets of Athens while this coin was in circulation. Philosophers Socrates and Plato, physician Hippocrates, and historians Herodotus and Thucydides all lived in or visited Athens during this period. Sophocles' Oedipus the King saw its first performance in 430 BC, while the coin was in circulation.

Democracy also thrived at the time, with political heavyweight Pericles dominating politics for much of the period. The Peloponnesian War with Sparta began in 431 BC and continued until the end of the period. The Spartans and their allies eventually prevailed, ending Athens' golden age and its dominance throughout the Greek world.

Coin details and provenance: Athens, Attica. 449 to 413 BC. Silver tetradrachm. Obverse: Helmeted head of Athena, with signature 'archaic eye' facing right. Reverse: Athenian owl with an olive branch and crescent, AOE legend to the right. Acquired from the Robert Johnson Coin Co., London, United Kingdom in 2000.

SYRACUSE
380 BC

Located on the eastern heel of Sicily, Syracuse was a Greek colony that witnessed the battle that effectively ended Athenian predominance in the Peloponnesian war. The failure of Athenian forces to take control of Syracuse in the year 414 BC and the losses that Athens sustained in the final battle for that control changed the balance of power in the Greek world.

This coin, minted years later in 380 BC, pays homage to the city's Corinthian heritage by portraying the Greek goddess Athena in a Corinthian helmet. The goddess wears her helmet tipped up in this portrait, as was the practice of the Greek hoplite who wore them in this fashion between battles. The reverse side of the coin features a sea star surrounded by two dolphins.

Originally founded by Greek Corinthians and allied with Corinth and Sparta during the Peloponnesian War, Syracuse found itself besieged in 414 BC by Athenian forces commanded by Nicias. The city was on the brink of surrender when eleven triremes manned by Corinthians and their allies under command of the Corinthian general Gongylus slipped through the Athenian naval blockade. Spartan forces lead by Glyippus arrived shortly after by land.

Both the Athenian commander Nicias and his general Demosthenes, who lead the Athenian land force, were captured and executed. Most of the surviving Athenian soldiers were enslaved and made to work in the Sicilian quarries. Few escaped or survived.

The failed Athenian siege devastated the Athenian war effort. Thousands of soldiers and hundreds of ships were lost, a significant portion of Athens' military. Athens enemies elsewhere were emboldened and rebellions broke out throughout the Aegean. Athen's dominion over Greek affairs came to an end.

Coin details and provenance: Sicily, Syracuse. Circa 380 BC. Æ drachma. Obverse: Head of Athena left, wearing Corinthian helmet decorated with an olive wreath. Reverse: Sea star between two dolphins. 33.03 grams. Green and brown patina. References: SNG ANS 454ff; Calciati II pg. 111, 62ff; SNG Copenhagen 720; SNG Morcom 697ff; Favorito 14; Laffaille 218; Virzi 1422ff. Acquired from Barry P. Murphy Coins, Willow Street, Pennsylvania in August 2003.

The Phoenicians of Arados
380 to 352 BC

This coin was issued by the Phoenician population of Arados, a tiny island in the Mediterranean Sea about 30 miles north of Tripoli. It was first settled in the second millennium BC by the Phoenicians, who constructed an artificial harbor and turned the island into a trading city protected by their powerful navy. When this coin was issued in the fourth century BC, Arados was ruled by the Persians.

The coin bears the image of an unidentified male deity and the prow of a naval vessel. So powerful was the Phoenician navy in ancient times that it's ships are mentioned on Egyptian monuments. Assyrian King Tiglath-pileser I reported sailing in Phoenician ships from Arados, then called Arvad or Arwad, around 1,000 BC.

The Phoenicians were inventors of the phonetic alphabet and descendants of the ancient Canaanites mentioned in the Book of Genesis. They formed a federation of city-states on the eastern Mediterranean coast in the 16th century BC and became a great merchant sea power.

Cambyses, the great Persian ruler, enlisted Phoenician ships in his conquest of Egypt in 525 BC. Phoenicians participated in the Greco-Persian wars, shuttling Persian troops to battles including those at Miletus (494 BC) and Salamis (480 BC). Xerxes' Persian forces crossed into Greece on a pontoon bridge constructed, in part, by Phoenicians.

In 350 BC, while this coin was in circulation, the Phoenician city-states rebelled against Persia only to be put down violently by King Artaxerxes III and his more than 300,000 Persian troops. The Phoenician city of Sidon was destroyed in the course of the rebellion and more than 40,000 Phoenicians are said to have perished.

Sixteen years later, when the 35,000 man Macedonian army crossed the Hellispont into Phoenicia under command of the 20-year-old Alexander of Macedonia, Arados' King Strabo submitted without a struggle and lent his Phoenician navy to Alexander for the Battle of Tyre.

Coin details and provenance: Phoenicia, Arados. 380 to 352 BC. Silver stater. Obverse: Head of male deity, laureate, hair and whiskers dotted, pointed beard represented by lines, full eye, and border of dots. Reverse: Prow of galley above waves. 10.27 grams. 18.1 mm. References: BMC Phoenicia, page 10, 61. From Glenn W. Woods Numismatist, Dallas, Texas in December 2004.

Artaxeres & Darius
375 to 340 BC

This coin was issued during the reign of Persian Emperor Artaxeres III and circulated widely during the reign of his successor Darius III. The coin shows the Persian king in a running position with a dagger and a bow.

Artaxeres was reportedly poisoned by his Viser, the wealthy and powerful eunuch Bagaos, in 338 BC. After dispatching Artaxeres direct heirs, Bagaos recruited a a distant cousin of Artaxeres named Codomannus and installed him as the Persian Shah. He chose Codomannus believing he would be easy to control.

Codomannus took the name Darius III and immediately struck his own course over a large but unstable empire. When Bagaos tried to regain control by poisoning Darius, the king learned of the plot and forced Bagaos to drink the poison himself.

Before long, Darius had to deal with an even greater threat. In 333 BC, Alexander the Great and his Greek hoplites invaded Persia and defeated his army at the Battle of Granicus. A year later, Darius led his armies in battle against Alexander at Issus but was again defeat after his chariot driver was killed and he was seen to be vulnerable after being knocked off of his feet.

Following the battle, Darius worked to rebuild his army but with little success. When Alexander and his troops later approached the Persian army near the city of Ecbatana in 330 BC, Darius withdrew to Bactria to begin a rear-guard action.

This emboldened the Persian satrap Bessus of Bactria who captured Darius while the Greeks pursued and had Darius bound in a wagon. When Alexander's forces unexpectedly approached the captive Darius, his captors panicked and wounded Darius with their spears. Darius was found dead or dying in the wagon.

When Alexander saw the corpse, he removed Darius' signet ring and ordered his body to be transported to Persepolis where Darius was accorded a magnificent funeral and buried in the Persian royal tombs. Five years later, Alexander married one of Darius' daughters in a mass marriage to help consolidate his power over his conquered empire.

Bessus, who declared himself King of Asia after capturing Darius, was tracked down and captured by Alexander's general Ptolemy. Alexander had him mutilated and killed.

Coin details and provenance: Artaxeres and Darius III. Achaemenid Kings. Circa 375 to 340 BC. AR siglos. Obverse: Persian hero-king right, in running kneeling position holding dagger and bow. Reverse: Oblong incuse. 5.49 grams. 15 mm. References: Carradice, Taf. XV, 46. Acquired from Tom Vossen Antiquities, Kirkrade, Netherlands in October 2006.

'ABD' ASHTART I

372 TO 361 BC

'Abd' ashtart was King of Sidon, the leading state in the fifth satrapy of the Persian Empire during the first half of the fourth century BC. The city, located on the southern Mediterranean coast of present day Lebanon, was renowned for the purple dyes and glass produced by its craftsmen.

Sidon was one of Phoenicia's oldest cities, having been inhabited since 4,000 BC and possibly earlier. Its history illustrates the expansion of the Phoenician trading empire.

Sidon colonized the city of Tyre in the second millenium BC which, in turn, colonized Carthage in the ninth century BC. According to the Roman Virgil, Tyre's Queen Dido fled her home city after her brother King Pygmalion murdered her husband.

'Abd' ashtart's coin, minted in Sidon between 371 and 361 BC, shows a galley rowing to the left with a Phoenician B above, an unmistakable reference to the seafaring prowess of the Phoenicians. On the back is a depiction of the king standing and confronting an upright lion. The images proclaim the power of the ruler and the scope of his influence.

At the time, the Phoenician's were considered loyal Persian subjects whose fleet ranked second only to that Xerxes himself. 'Abd' ashtart cultivated friendly relations with Athens and ruled over a court known for its luxury and appreciation for Hellenistic art and culture.

According to the writings of Menander of Ephesus as quoted by the first century historian Josephus, 'Abd' ashtart came to power at the age of 20 just seven years after the death of his grandfather Hiram I when his father Beleazarus died at the age of 43. He ruled for just nine years.

During his short reign, the Persians lost Cyprus and the city of Tyre to Evagoras, the King of Salamis, in what came to be known as the great revolt of the satraps. Through association with Evagoras' son Nicocles, 'Abd' ashtart became vulnerable to claims that he was conspiring with the disloyal satraps. Four sons of his nurse plotted his death and killed him.

Coin details and provenance: Phoenicia Sidon. 'Abd' Ashtart I (also, Straton I or Bod 'ashtart). 372 to 361. AR 1/16 shekel. Obverse: Galley rowing left, Phoenician 'B' above, waves below. Reverse: King standing right, confronting lion, which he holds by its mane; small 'o/o' between. 0.78 gram. 10 mm. References: Betylon 32; BMC Phoenicia pg. 147, 34; SNG Copenhagen 197ff. Dark toning. Exceptional detail, strike and grade for type. Mild roughness, particularly on obverse. Acquired from Civitas Galleries Numismatics & Philately, Middleton, Wisconsin in April 2005.

PANTICAPAEUM
325 TO 310 BC

This coin is from the ancient city of Panticapaeum, an important port city on the Kerch Strait that separates the Black Sea from the Sea of Azov to the north. When this coin was issued in the fourth century BC, the city was governed by the Spartocids, a dynasty of the Thracian kings of the Bosphorus. At the time, Panticapaeum was facing growing commercial competition from Egypt for the grain it supplied to foreign markets. Conflict over territory with the Sarmatians also occupied the Thracians.

The coin issued by these Thracians bears no witness to these two growing pressures. Instead, it contains a distinctive image of the god Pan on the front and a griffin above a sturgeon on the back. Pan is the Greek god of mountain wilds, flocks and sheep, hunting and rustic music.

Pan was also known to inspire fear, or panic, in crowds. According to mythology, he claimed credit for the victory of the gods over the Olympians because of the disorder and panic he spread among the Olympians. Greeks also believed he assisted the Athenians in their victory at Marathon by spreading panic among the Persians.

The griffin was a legendary king of the beasts that combined the forepart of an eagle with the body of a lion. To the ancients, the griffin was a symbol and guardian of the divine. The griffin protected against evil, witchcraft and slander.

By combining these two powerful images, the Thracians conveyed a message of strength and power to their citizens and trading partners. Notwithstanding the message, however, Thracian power and influence declined in Panticapaeum over the fourth and third centuries BC.

In 107 BC, Mithradates VI of Pontus dispatched a general to persuade King Paerisades V of Panticapaeum to cede his kingdom to Mithrades. While Mithradates' general was there, the Sythians revolted and killed King Paerisades. Escaping back to Pontus, Mithradates' general returned with a large fleet and ended the revolt, reducing Panticapaeum to a dependency.

Many years later, when his Greek resistance to Roman rule was coming to an end, Mithradates fled to the city to avoid capture by Magnus Pompey and the pursuing Romans. There he reportedly died from self-inflicted poison while his son Phraates laid siege to the city. Pharnaces sent his body to Pompey as proof of his death.

Coin details and provenance: Thrace Panticapaeum. 325-310 BC. Æ21 bronze. Obverse: Head of Pan facing left, wreathed in ivy. Reverse: Forepart of Griffin facing left, sturgeon below, Π-A-N in field. 7.55 grams. 21.57 mm. Reference: SNG BM Black Sea 869-71. Acquired from Ancient Imports, Grand Marais, Minnesota in March 2011.

PHILIP OF MACEDONIA
359 TO 336 BC

The great ruler from northern Greece, Philip II, made Macedonia the predominate power in Greece through a series of military and diplomatic conquests. His success in growing Macedonia and subduing the other Greek city-states set the stage for the great Persian conquest of his son Alexander III.

On his coin, Philip chose the images of Apollo and a prancing horse ridden by a naked youth. Apollo was one of the great Olympian deities, son of Zeus and deity of the Delphic Oracle. Among the ancient Greeks, his name was associated with the verb for destruction, apollymi, and with medicine and dominion over colonists. The horse was associated with Philip's name and, in this image, reminds one of the legendary taming of the wild steed Bucephalus by Philip's son Alexander in his youth.

Before his reign, Philip was held hostage in Thebes for three years. When he was released to Macedonia, he used what he observed while a captive to assist his brother, King Perdiccas III, to reorganize and strengthen the Macedonian army.

In 359 BC, Philip became king of a declining Macedonia, most recently defeated by the neighboring Illyrians. Within a year he neutralized Athens with concessions and a treaty, retook territory from the Illyrians in a battle that saw the Illyrian soldiers flee in panic, and convinced the neighboring Thracian king to execute a pretender to the Macedonian throne.

During his lifetime, Philip extended Macedonian control east and west from the Black Sea to the Adriatic and as far north as the Danube. At Chaeronea in central Greece he defeated a Greek army that included Athenians, Thebans and Achaeans to impose his will south into the southern half of Peloponnesia.

Ruling Greece through the League of Corinth and with his borders safe, Philip used the League to appoint himself general of a Pan-Hellenic crusade against the Persian Empire in 336 BC. With his troops already encamped in Persian territory, however, Philip was assassinated while participating in the wedding procession for his daughter Cleopatra. After his death, Philip's son Alexander seized the throne and was elected to succeed his father as general of the Pan-Hellenic campaign.

Coin details and provenance: Philip II of Macedonia. 359 to 336 BC. AE. Obverse: Head of Apollo facing right, hair bound with tainia. Reverse: ΦΙΛΙΠΠΟΥ, naked youth on horse prancing, facing right. 7.08 grams. 17mm. References: Muller 129. Acquired from Herakles Numismatics, Charlotte, North Carolina in December 2004.

THE CELTS
2ND CENTURY BC

It is believed that some seven thousand years ago, a people who would eventually cover the European continent began travelling west from the Black Sea, driven by rising waters and global warming. By the fourth century BC, when Philip II ruled Macedonia and began expanding his influence throughout Greece and elsewhere, diverse tribes of these people, the Celts, occupied the territories north and west of Macedonia.

Trade and conflict between the Macedonians and the adjoining Celtic tribes was inevitable. This coin, and others like it, provide some of the best surviving evidence of this interaction and of the creativity of ancient Celtic artisans.

Obvious in its reference to the horse and rider motif of Philip's coin, this Celtic coin from the second century BC also displays the unique abstract artistic temperament common to Celtic coins. The front of this coin also mimics the Philip coin with an abstract profile of a man, though on this example the image is obscured by time and wear.

So too is much of our understanding of the early Celts, much of which must be extrapolated from archaeological finds and evidence of neighboring Greek and Roman societies who interacted with the Celts. One of the first recorded encounters with the Celts occurred around 400 BC, when a Celtic tribe displaced the Etruscans from the Po Valley in northern Italy and Rome sent three envoys to the Etruscans to evaluate the situation.

Later battles between the Celtic tribes of continental Europe and Julius Caesar would be recorded in notes Caesar published while on campaign. Celts in the British Isles would resist Roman invasion by Caesar and his successors, at one time even destroying the city of Londinium in an uprising. The Picts in Scotland would prove so resistant that Emperor Hadrian would order the construction of a wall across northern England to keep them at bay.

Many Celtic coins, like the one above, are masterful miniatures of surreal art. They depict an artistic temperament and perspective of a proud people who were quite different from their Greek and Roman neighbors to the south.

Coin details and provenance: Celtic Tetradrachm Imitating Philip II of Macedonia. 2nd Century BC. Obverse: Celtic style bust of Philip facing right. Reverse: Celtic style horse and rider facing right. 7.3 grams. 24.71 mm. References: DLT 9618. Acquired from Ancient Imports, Grand Marias, Minnesota in May 2005.

Temple of Athena at the Greek colony of Paestum

[2]

Greek Empire

ALEXANDER THE GREAT RETURNED to the city of Ecbatana in the fall of 324 BC for a three-month binge of drinking and entertainment. The city was an appropriate cite for a celebration. Alexander had first been there after the Battle of Gaugamela. And, it was outside the city where Darius III had been captured and Alexander secured his claim to the Persian Empire. The victory sealed Alexander's reputation and opened the east as far as India to his conquest.

The city was also where this coin, in the style of most of Alexander's coins, was minted.[2] It shows the great Greek hero Heracles on the front, fashioned in the image of Alexander himself, wearing a lion's head for a headdress. On the back is Zeus, the greatest of the Greek gods and father to Heracles seated on a throne holding an eagle and a scepter.

---

[2] Alexander at Ecbatana. Silver obol of Alexander the Great minted between 336 and 326 BC. 10.3 grams. 67 mm. Acquired from Forum Ancient Coins, Morehead City, North Carolina in 2006.

To mark his conquest, Alexander had 3,000 entertainers and artists brought from Greece. But tragedy struck during the celebration. Alexander's closest companion and suspected lover, Hephaestion, fell ill and died after drinking heavily and eating a fowl. Glaucus, his doctor, was at the theater and unable to help. Distraught, Alexander ordered the doctor crucified and the tails and manes of all the horses to be cut.

Alexander the Great astride Bucephalus at the Battle of Isus
Detail from the Alexander Mosaic from Pompeii

The coin depicted above, and others like it, were valuable tools Alexander used to consolidate his victories and portray himself as a god-like ruler. The lion's headdress and portrayal of his profile as the hero Heracles provided a powerful graphic image to everyday citizens that the new ruler was to be respected and obeyed. The portrait of Zeus' on a throne with an eagle on his hand, reinforces the message of power and connects Alexander to the greatest of the Greek gods.

These carefully chosen images, carried to every corner of his vast empire, reinforced the message Alexander wanted conveyed to his charges. They represent an early and powerful use of art in a widely distributed media for propaganda purposes.

The ancient times reflected on the coins that follow saw great conflicts between civilizations, where battles won and battles lost determined whose culture and ideas would shape the development of Western civilization. We are fortunate that these times also saw the development of coins depicting images of the rulers, gods and heroes of the time, providing us with a unique source of contemporary images.

Alexander would die from disease a year after his interrupted celebration at Ecbatana but the influence of his Greece would continue through the Greek rulers who would rule his empire for centuries. Alexander's lieutenants divided his empire among them shortly after he died.

A period of conflict, called the Diadochi, quickly ensued between these new empires as one lieutenant after another strove to increase his territory or defend if from another. It was Alexander's conquests followed by Greek rule for centuries that marks the Hellenistic period during which the ways of the Greeks began to be adopted by large populations that were not Greek themselves.

Alexander's lieutenants Ptolemy, Lysimachus, and Seleucus all ruled large empires taken from the conquests of Alexander. Each issued coins that appear in this chapter. Ptolemy, who ruled Egypt, appears in full profile on a coin issued by his son Ptolemy II. Lysimachus leaves us a heroic portrait of himself with his personal emblem on the back – a lion of the sort he reputedly killed with his bare hands while on a hunt with Alexander. Seleucus appears with two coins, one that bears his profile and another that pays homage to Alexander with the images of an elephant (of the sort confronted by Alexander in India) and a regal horse like the famous stallion Bucephalas that Alexander tamed as a boy and rode through his conquests.

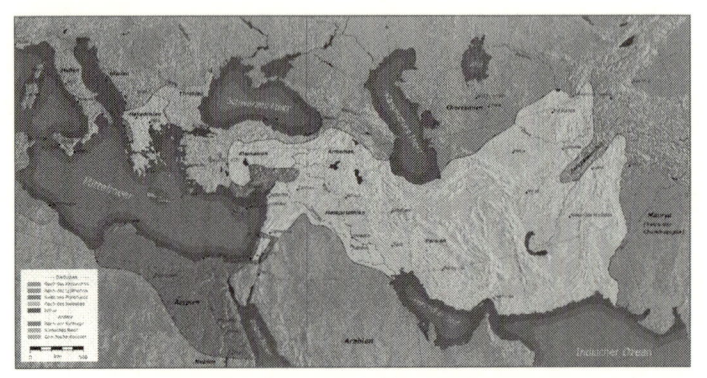

Map of the Diadoch Kingdoms

Thracians, Sarmatians, Parthians, Phoenicians, Egyptians and Celts are also represented on these pages. So too are the Parthians, Seleucids, Carthaginians, Indo-Greeks and Celtiberians. The Mamertini who triggered the Punic wars between Rome and Carthage have their coin as well. Also here as is a coin from the ancient land of Sheba, home to the queen who visited Israel's King Solomon sometime in the 10th century BC.

Other famous figures walked the world stage during the two centuries covered by this chapter. Homer, father of modern literature and author of the *Iliad* and the *Odyssey*, is honored here with a portrait on an ancient coin from Ionia.

Alexander's general Ptolemy built a dynasty in Egypt that ruled for centuries after Alexander's death. His coins and those of his successors are here as well. One, Cleopatra I, is here in full profile. Her husband's coronation was the subject of the writing on the Rosetta Stone that enabled linguists, centuries later, to decipher Egyptian hieroglyphics. Ptolemy's descendants also included the more famous Cleopatra VII who would capture the hearts of Julius Caesar and then Marc Antony and influence the history of Rome and Egypt.

Antiochus IV, the Seleucid emperor whose encounter with the Romans outside Alexandria gave rise to the phrase "line in the sand" is here on a coin that shows him in profile. This is the same Antiochus mentioned in the Bible, who ordered the city of Jerusalem and its Temple destroyed when the Jews refused his order to worship Zeus. The biblical account of Maccabees describes Antiochus' violent response to the Jews revolt:

> Raging like a wild animal, he set out from Egypt and took Jerusalem by storm. He ordered his soldiers to cut down without mercy those whom they met and to slay those who took refuge in their houses. There was a massacre of young and old, a killing of women and children, a slaughter of virgins and infants. In the space of three days, eighty thousand were lost, forty thousand meeting a violent death, and the same number being sold into slavery.

Here too are coins of great Greek rulers from Sicily like Agathocles and Hieron. Agathocles is perhaps most famous from his mention in Machiavelli's *The Prince*, where he is described as an example of "those who by their crimes become princes." Hieron served with the great Greek general Pyrrhus (also here) whose victories against the Romans so depleted his armies that his name became synonymous with costly or "pyrrhic" victories.

The eunuch Philetairos is also here. This competent administrator deftly switched allegiances from Alexander's lieutenant Lysimachus to Seleucus to become the ruler of Pergamon. So too is the Indo-Greek king Menander who was born a commoner but obtained attained Arhatship, the last stage of Buddhist sanctification.

The Carthaginian Hannibal issued coins from the Italian peninsula after crossing the Alps and putting the Romans to their ultimate test. The Mamertini, or "children of Mars," helped trigger the Punic wars between Rome and Carthage and left their coin. Also here are coins and stories about the Celts, Iberians, Thracians, Parthians and Ethiopians from Saba.

Welcome to an ancient world that is both familiar and strange. Turn the page to journey through the ancient past of the Hellenistic Greeks and the others who shared the world stage at the time. Consider the stories of ancient leaders whose decisions, victories and defeats shaped Western civilization.

And take your time with the remarkable images on the coins. With consummate skill, ancient artisans created images from their world that grace the coins on these pages.

PARTIAL TIMELINE.

336 BC Alexander III becomes ruler of Macedonia.
334 BC Alexander crosses the Hellispont into Turkey.
331 BC Alexander defeats Darius III of Persia at Gaugamela.
326 BC Alexander defeats Indian King Porus at Hydapses.
326 BC Alexander dies at Babylon.

323 BC Lysimachus becomes King of Thrace.
323 BC Ptolemy forms dynasty in Egypt.
317 BC Potter's son Agathocles subdues Syracuse.
312 BC Seleucus begins Seleucid Empire.
288 BC Mamertini seize Messene in Sicily.
282 BC Eunuch Philetairos becomes ruler of Pergamon.
280 BC Pyrrhus wins victory over Romans at Heraclea.
275 BC Hieron II takes command of Syracuse.
218 BC Hannibal crosses the Alps to attack Rome.
202 BC Silk road opens.

Coins featured in this chapter

Alexander at Ecbatana, 324 BC
Alexander of Macedonia, 336 to 323 BC
Alexander the Great, 336 to 323 BC
Celtic Alexander, unknown
Ephesus, 305 to 228 BC
Seuthes, 324 BC
Lysimachus, 323 to 281 BC
Agathocles, 317 to 289 BC
Seleucus, 312 to 280 BC
Philetairos, 282 to 263 BC
Ionia's Homer, 301 to 288 BC
Ptolemy, 285 to 246 BC
Antigonus II, 277 to 239 BC
Hieron II, 274 to 216 BC
Epirus & Pyrrhus, before 238 BC
The Mamertini, 220 to 210 BC
Hannibal, 213 to 207

Castulo & Hasdrubal, 2nd century BC
Antiochus III, 223 to 187 BC
Saba, Land of Sheba, 3rd to 2nd century BC
Halicarnassus, 3rd to 2nd century BC
Dyrrhachion, Illyria. 229 to 100 BC
Qin Shi Huangdi, 220-180 BC
Masinissa, King of Numidia, 208 to 148 BC
Thrace of Spartacus, 196 to 88 BC
Cleopatra I & Ptolemy VI, 180 to 145 BC
The Celtiberians, 180 to 20 BC
Antiochus IV, 175 to 164 BC
Mithradates I, Parthian King, 171 to 138 BC
Menander, Indo-Greek King, 160 to 145 BC

To survive in the midst of so many enemies on the northern fringes of the Greek world, the Macedonians held fast to the heroic warrior code of Homer's *Iliad* and *Odyssey*. In battles, brawls and drinking bouts, the Macedonians measured a man from king to commoner by the implacable standards of Achilles and Agamemnon.

Alexander the Great and the Mystery of the Elephant Medallions

ALEXANDER OF MACEDONIA
336 TO 323 BC

Alexander III, the son of Macedonian King Philip II and Queen Olympia, was born on July 20, 356 BC. He came to power after his father was assassinated at the wedding of Alexander's sister Cleopatra. Alexander was just 20 years old at the time.

This coin from Macedonia was issued during Alexander's 13-year reign and features him posing as Heracles in a lion skin headdress. The choice of imagery was deliberate. Heracles was the Greek archetype for bravery and manliness and the greatest of their heroes. On the back of the coin is a bow case, a club, and an ear of grain with the Greek legend Alexander between.

Despite his young age at his ascension, Alexander had already shown signs of brilliance. He was just 16 when he served as regent for Macedonia in his father's absence. And he was only 18 when troops he commanded broke through the Theban line in Philip's great victory over the combined forces of Athens and Thebes at the Battle of Chaeronea. The victory secured Philip's place as the leading power in Greece, helping to set the stage for Alexander's later conquests.

After Philip's death, Alexander secured Macedonia's borders and put down revolts from competing Greek city-states to the south. This included laying waste to the city of Thebes. Then he assumed command of the army his father Philip had assembled in Persia.

In the spring of 334 BC, Alexander and an army of more than 40,000 soldiers and cavalry crossed the Hellespont into northwest Turkey. During the next 11 years, Alexander would conquer most of the known world east and south of Macedonia, defeating the great Persian King Darius III at Gaugamela in 331 BC and Indian forces of the Rajah of Pauravas at Hydaspes in 326 BC. His conquests would include the Levant, Egypt, modern-day Iraq and Iran, and parts of Afghanistan, Pakistan and India.

Considered one of the finest military leaders in history, Alexander's campaigns of conquest were rewarded with vast territorial acquisitions and enormous wealth, including precious metals that were minted into his coins. They also resulted in the extension of Greek culture throughout the eastern Mediterranean, Middle East and into Pakistan and India.

Coin details and provenance: Alexander III. 336 to 323 BC. Uncertain mint in Macedonia, probably lifetime strike. Obverse: Heracles facing right, wearing lion's skin headdress. Reverse: ALEXANDROU between bow in case and club with Δ above and grain ear below. 5.84 grams. Drama Hoard 108. Acquired from Atlantis Quality Ancient Coins, United Kingdom, December 2003.

ALEXANDER THE GREAT
336 TO 323 BC

Alexander grew up as heir apparent in an expanding Macedonia, the most powerful kingdom in Greece. This coin, like the first, shows Alexander as Heracles wearing a lion headdress but with the greatest of the Greek gods Zeus on the reverse, enthroned and holding an eagle and a scepter. This coin and its imagery would become the staple coin of Alexander's vast realm.

Tutored with other young men in the Macedonian court by Aristotle, Alexander acquired an appreciation for Greek art and literature that would stay with him throughout his life. He carried a copy of Homer's *Iliad* with him on his military campaigns that was personally edited by Aristotle. He reportedly referred to it often, even sleeping with it at his side.

When he was only 12, Alexander tamed a wild stallion in a scene that became renowned later to his compatriots and those he conquered. The horse, Bucephalas, was given to him after taming and served as his personal mount throughout his military campaigns. During his reign, Alexander established many cities named Alexandria and one named Bucephalas. This helped to establish Greek culture and influence throughout the region he conquered.

Alexander's campaigns took him first through modern-day Turkey and then down the Mediterranean coast to Egypt. After conquering the Persians, Alexander attacked Egypt and added that territory to his spoils. While there, he was proclaimed Pharaoh of Egypt and, after a consultation with the oracle at Siwah in the Ammon Oasis, declared to be descended from the Egyptian god Ammon. He also conquered territories east of Persia, leaving Greeks in charge as far east as India.

His life was cut short in June of 323 BC when he succumbed to illness just weeks before this 33rd birthday. He was preparing for his Arabian campaign at the time. The campaign was abandoned after his death.

His lieutenants soon began to maneuver and fight, dividing his empire between them. The resulting kingdoms would keep most of the territory conquered by Alexander under Greek rule for hundreds of years. The Egyptian kingdom of Ptolemy would survive for three centuries until the death of Cleopatra VII in 30 BC.

Coin details and provenance: Alexander III, the Great. 336 to 323 BC. Obverse: Head of Heracles facing right, wearing a lion's skin headdress. Reverse: Zeus enthroned facing left and. holding eagle and scepter. Acquired from the Robert Johnson Coin Co., Little Russel Street, London, United Kingdom in 2000.

CELTIC ALEXANDER
DATE UNKNOWN

Attesting to the widespread influence of Alexander the Great is this ancient Celtic coin from the Danube valley north of Macedonia. Undated, but minted sometime during or after the reign of Alexander, this coin provides a unique Celtic depiction of Alexander in his lion headdress and of the Greek god Zeus, holding an eagle and a scepter.

By the time of Alexander's conquests, the Celts had spread west from the Danube valley through most of continental Europe. By 390 BC, a group of Celts had expanded as far west and south as northern Italy. After encountering the Etruscans there and being brought into contact with Roman soldiers, they traveled south and sacked Rome itself.

It was not until more than a century and a half later that the Romans would exert control over the Celts residing in northern Italy and even then their control did not prevent Celtic tribes from assisting Hannibal when he crossed the Alps into Italy and attacked the Romans in 218 BC.

Although we do not know which Celtic tribe produced this coin, it does reflect the powerful influence that Alexander and his memory exerted over the ancient world. Later Greek and Roman rulers would revere the memory of Alexander and frequently used it for their own purposes.

Ptolemy I, for example, stole Alexander's body to support his claim of legitimacy to the Egyptian throne. Placing Alexander's tomb in Egypt helped to validate Ptolemy's sovereignty and the rule of his successors for centuries to follow. More than 250 years after Alexander's death, the greatest Greek challenger to Roman domination, Mithradates of Pontus, copied Alexander's appearance and issued coins that mimicked the coins of Alexander. Magnus Pompey interrupted his campaign against Mithradates to search for Alexander's cape. He later wore the cape he found to enhance his image.

Even Cleopatra VII, who secured her rule with a politically astute romance with Julius Caesar, relied on her family's association with Alexander. Her son by Julius Caesar, Caesarion, gave Egypt a ruler-in-waiting who could claim legitimacy from both Caesar and Alexander. Even her adversary Octavian took time to visit Alexander's tomb when he was in Egypt.

And 200 years later still, more than 500 years after Alexander's death, the erratic Roman emperor Commodus emulated Alexander and copied his coins. Such was Alexander's enormous influence on the ancient world.

Coin details and provenance: Celtic imitation of Alexander III. Drachm. Obverse: Stylized head of Heracles right. Reverse: Zeus seated left with eagle and scepter, amphora left in field. 2.9 grams. 19 mm. Acquired from Gitbud & Nauman, Münchun, Germany, in February 2010.

Ephesus
305 TO 288 BC

This coin is from the Ionian city of Ephesus at the turn of the third century BC. It bears the image of a bee on the front and a kneeling stag on the back. To the Greeks, the bee symbolized Demeter, the goddess of the harvest who presided over crops, the earth's fertility and the seasons. Her priestesses were called Melissae, which translates to bees.

The bee symbol was also emblematic of Artemis and a symbol of virginity. At the time this coin was issued, Ephesus was home to the Temple of Artemis, one of the seven wonders of the ancient world. Dedicated to the Greek goddess of the hunt, the temple rested on a temenos, or holy ground, whose origin was attributed to the Amazons.

The temple was completed around 550 BC with funding from the Lydian monarch Croesus. Throughout its history it provided refuge to those in need of protection. Tradition held that the Amazons had taken refuge there from Heracles and Dionysus.

On or about July 20 of 356 BC, a young man named Herostratus set fire to the temple and destroyed it. Ephesian authorities executed him and forbid the further mention of his name as punishment.

Plutarch later noted that the fire coincided with the birth of Alexander the Great, speculating that the goddess Artemis was too preoccupied with the great man's birth to save her own temple from fire. Alexander later offered to rebuild the temple but the Ephesians declined and restored it on their own in 323 BC.

Other conquerors were not so respectful of the temple. In 40 BC, shortly after Cleopatra secured her political and romantic ties with Marc Antony, her sister Arsinoe took refuge in the temple to escape Cleopatra's schemes. Antony's henchmen tracked her down, dragged her onto the temple steps and executed her.

The city of Ephesus also became an important outpost for the early Christian church, being noted as home to one of the seven churches of Asia in the Book of Revelations. According to the Book of Acts, however, Ephesians first showed resistance to the new faith, fearing that the Christian message would cause the goddess of the temple to be despised.

Coin details and provenance: Ephesus, Ionia. 305-288 BC. Bronze AE 15. Ephesus mint. Obverse: Bee, E - ϕ in upper fields. Reverse: Stag kneeling left looking back, astragalos (knuckle bone used for divination) above, uncertain magistrate name left. 2.324 grams. 14.0 mm. References: Ionia, p. 54, 58 ff; SNG Cop 245 ff (various magistrates). Acquired from Forum Ancient Coins, Morehead City, North Carolina in March 2010.

SEUTHES
328 BC

Ruling one of the last surviving kingdoms of the Odrysian Thracians, Seuthes III ruled from the small town of Seuthopolis in what is now Bulgaria from a palace whose structure suggests that Seuthes may have been both a king and high priest of his tribe. This bronze coin from 324 BC shows a laureate head of Zeus, likely bearing the profile of Seuthes, and a rider on a cantering horse.

The Odrysian kingdom was made up of a union of Thracian tribes. It began in the fifth century BC and continued into the third century BC. At its height, the Ordysian domain stretched from present day Bulgaria to parts of Romania, northern Greece and Turkey. Herodotus claimed the Thracians were more numerous than any people in the known world other than the Indians.

During the time of Philip II, the Thracians were ruled by the Macedonians. After his death, the Thracians revolted against Alexander but were again subdued, eventually providing troops for Alexander's army. Seuthes is believed to have led the

Thracians when they were defeated by Alexander's general Antipater in 325 BC.

After Alexander's death, the Thracians again took up arms against the Macedonians, who were led by Alexander's successor Lysimachus. In this conflict, Seuthes served as a general under the Getae ruler Dromichaetes, His responsibility was to keep Lysimachus from defeating the Thracians north of the Danube. Somehow, Seuthes managed to join the army of Lysimachus during this time and use his infiltration to help the Getae defeat the Macedonians.

The Gatae ruler Dromichaetes then used diplomacy to turn Lysimachus into an ally by treating him well after his capture. He is reputed to have impressed Lysimachus by serving him a lavish meal on silver plates while his Getae ate more modest food off wooden plates.

Ultimately, Seuthes and the Odrysian kingdom were forced to submit to the authority of Lysimachus. Not surprisingly, however, Seuthes took arms against Lysimachus once again in 313 BC when he supported the unsuccessful attempt of Antigonus I to overthrow his rival. The time and circumstances of Seuthes death are unknown.

Coin details and provenance: Thracian King Seuthes III, King of the Odrysians. 324 BC. Bronze AE 16. Obverse: Laureate head of Zeus. Reverse: [SEUQOU] Horseman cantering, star below; scarce. 4.68 grams. 16.2 mm. References: S 1725, SNG Cop 1073. Acquired from Forum Ancient Coins, Morehead City, North Carolina in May 2006.

Lysimachus

323 TO 281 BC

This coin was issued by Alexander's general Lysimachus while he was ruling Thrace. The front shows a helmeted Athena in profile. The reverse shows a running lion with a legend declaring Lysimachus as king. The lion and its strength served as Lysimachus' personal emblem following an incident where he killed a lion with his bare hands while hunting with Alexander.

Lysimachus was a boyhood friend of Alexander and a trusted member of his personal bodyguard. He was one of the close cadre of Macedonian boys in the court of King Philip II who studied under Aristotle and then helped Alexander create an empire that encompassed Greece, Egypt, Persia and parts of India.

After Alexander died in 323 BC, Lysimachus and Alexander's other generals Seleucus, Ptolemy, Cassander and Antigonus, carved up the conquered empire. Antipater, a contemporary of Philip who had defended the home front during Alexander's conquests, remained in control of Greece.

Lysimachus became governor of Thrace, a region that no longer recognized Macedonian rule, and began a long series of wars with the Thracian King Seuthes. While occupying himself with pacifying Thrace and defending it against coastal Greek cities, Lysimachus married Antipater's daughter Nicaea.

In 315 BC, he joined a coalition with Seleucus, Ptolemy, and Cassander to battle Antigonus and Demetrius as the Third Diodach War began. A decade later, he launched an offensive into Asia Minor and joined forces with Seleucus to defeat and kill Antigonus.

After the victory, Lysimachus received Asia Minor as his bounty. To help secure the southern border of his expanded territory, he took Arsinoe II, the daughter of Ptolemy, as his wife. Years later, in 288 BC, he conquered Macedonia with the help of Pyrrhus and added it to his domain.

Lysimachus eventually lost his empire and life in February of 281 BC at the Battle of Corupenium in Asia Minor. The 80-year-old Lysimachus body was found on the battlefield days later protected by his faithful dog. The 77-year-old victor, Seleucus, was assassinated soon afterward.

Their deaths marked the end of Alexander's successors. Ptolemy, Demetrius and the others had already passed away.

Coin details and provenance: Lysimachus, King of Thrace. 323 to 281 BC. Obverse: Helmeted head of Athena facing right. Reverse: ΒΑΣΙΛΕΩΣ ΛΥΣΙΜΑΧΟΥ, bounding lion; spearhead below. 2.6 grams. 20 mm. Acquired from Ancient Caesar Classical Numismatics, Wichita, Kansas in May 2005.

Agathocles

317 TO 289 BC

As Alexander's lieutenants divided and governed the vast territories he conquered, the island of Sicily was overrun by the ambitious son of a potter. This coin, issued by Agathocles while he was tyrant of Syracuse, betrays nothing of his humble beginnings. The front shows Artemis, the virgin goddess of the hunt, and the back shows a thunderbolt, associated with the greatest of the Greek gods, Jupiter.

Agathocles was born in the town of Thermae Himeraeae in Sicily and moved with his family to Syracuse in 343 BC. There he learned the potters trade and later joined the army. In 333 BC, he married the wealthy widow of his patron and advanced in Syracuse society.

An ambitious man, Agathocles was twice banished from Syracuse for plotting the overthrow of the ruling party. In 317 BC, while still banished, he assembled an army of mercenaries and overran Syracuse. After his conquest, in which as many as 10,000 are said to have been murdered or banished, Agathocles made himself tyrant and set about building a strong army and navy.

Once he was securely in control, Agathocles used Syracuse as a base from which to subdue most of the island of Sicily.

A disastrous war with Carthage followed. By 311 BC, the Carthaginians besieged Syracuse and defeated Agathocles at the Battle of Himera. The next year, Agathocles broke through Carthaginian lines into Africa and scored several victories before being completely defeated in 307 BC. He then secreted himself back to Syracuse and concluded a peace treaty with the Carthaginians.

Once secure from further Carthaginian intervention, an emboldened Agathocles ruled the Greek cities on Sicily more firmly than ever. As he grew older, however, his health declined and he had to battle political agitation instigated by his grandson. In his later years, he also secured important political alliances by marrying a stepdaughter of Egypt's Ptolemy I and wedding a daughter to Pyrrhus of Epirus.

Agathocles became more moderate as he grew older. On this deathbed, he even restored democracy to Syracuse, refusing to be succeeded by his children. Machiavelli later identified Agathocles in *The Prince* as an example of "those who by their crimes become princes."

Coin details and provenance: Agathocles. 317 to 289 BC. Sicily, Syracuse. Obverse: Head of Artemis with quiver. Reverse: Thunderbolt. 8.18 grams. Reference: Calciati 142. Acquired from Pegasi Numismatics, Ann Arbor, Michigan in June 2007.

SELEUCUS
312 TO 280 BC

Seleucus was an officer in Alexander's army and one of the Diadochi who divided Alexander's empire after his death. His first position after Alexander's death was as satrap of Babylon but after many conflicts among the Diadochi, Seleucus emerged as the ruler of a vast empire that included much of the Middle East to India. The territory he consolidated survived as the Seleucid Empire for hundreds of years.

The images on his coin remind the observer of Seleucus' conquests and his association with Alexander the Great. The front depicts an elephant of the sort Alexander's troops confronted and defeated in the critical battles of Gaugamela and Hydaspes. It also reminds us of the 500-elephant tribute paid to Seleucus by his Indian adversary Chandragupta in 303 BC. The back shows a great steed, like the famous Bucephalus that accompanied Alexander on his campaigns. It also contains an anchor of the sort ancient legend said proved Seleucus descended from the god Apollo.

Seleucus was born to Antiochus and Laodike of Europos in Macedonia sometime between 358 and 354 BC. Both he and his father were part of the military aristocracy that helped Philip II establish Macedonian preeminence among the Greeks and then helped Alexander conquer the Persians. Seleucus served Alexander in both his Persian and Indian campaigns, rising to prominence in Afghanistan and commanding Alexander's elite infantry corps in the victorious Indian campaigns of 327 BC.

It was widely circulated during and after Seleucus' life that Seleucus was told by his father before the Persian campaigns that Seleucus' real father was Apollo. The god was said to have left his son a ring with the image of an anchor. Proof of the legendary family history was said to be confirmed by a birthmark in the shape of an anchor that Seleucus and future family members had. A similar story circulated in ancient times about Alexander the Great.

After Seleucus was assassinated in 281 BC, his son Antiochus started a cult to worship his father. One surviving inscription from the time instructs priests of the cult to sacrifice to the god Apollo. The name Nicator, often associated with Seleucus, was given to him after his death. It means victorious.

Coin details and provenance: 312 to 280 BC. Seleucus I Nicator. Obverse: Elephant standing right. Reverse: Horned horse's head facing left, anchor below.

SELEUCUS
312 TO 281 BC

    This coin was issued in Antioch during the reign of Seleucus, the founding ruler of the Selucid Empire. The profile is reminiscent of those on the coins of Alexander the Great but with the profile showing the wings of a Gorgon instead of a lion headdress. The reverse depicts a rutting bull and declares Seleucus as king.

    Seleucus was an officer in Alexander's army when it pursued the remnants of Darius' Persian army into Afghanistan. They met with fierce resistance there from a Persian army led by the satrap Bessus, who had murdered Darius before retreating to Bactria. Through conquest and betrayal, Alexander captured Bessus and had him tortured and executed. Spitamenes, a Persian courtier in Sogdiana, continued the resistance for a time before surrendering to Alexander's general Ptolemy and ending Bactrian resistance.

    Sometime after this, Seleucus claimed the Persian princess Apama and took her with him as he traveled with Alexander's army. Within a year, Seleucus married Apama in a mass marriage ceremony of Alexander's officers in the city of Susa. Apama, who ancient sources tell us was Spitamanes' daughter, soon bore Seleucus a son named Antiochus who would later succeed Seleucus as the second emperor of the Seleucid Empire.

Before Alexander could fully secure his Bactrian conquests, however, Seleucus' new Persian father-in-law rallied a new resistance that nearly proved fatal to Alexander's plans. Led by Spitamenes and other regional leaders, the resisting fighters used local knowledge and the harsh terrain of Afghanistan to cut off Greek supplies and stage successful ambushes.

In this lethal guerilla war, Alexander's army was reduced to eating its baggage animals to survive. Somehow, however, Alexander and his army persevered. Eventually Alexander's general Coenus met and defeated Spitamenes at the Battle of Gabai. Afterwards, Spitamenes' allies sent his severed head to Alexander's camp to sue for peace.

Notwithstanding the rebellion, Seleucus remained loyal to Apama and went on to have two daughters and another son with her. While most of Alexander's other officers later unloaded the women they were wedded to in the mass marriage, Seleucus retained Apama and made her his queen. In 300 BC, Seleucus fortified the city of Pharmake in Syria and renamed it Ampamea to honor his wife.

Coin details and provenance: Seleucus I. 312 to 281 BC. Bronze AE 19. Antioch mint. Obverse: Winged Gorgon head facing right. Reverse: BASILEWS SELEUKOU, bull butting right, X in exergue. 7.994 grams. 10.2 mm. References: Newdll WSM 925, SNG Spaer 23. Acquired from Forum Ancient Coins, Morehead City, North Carolina in August 2008.

DEMETRIUS
294 TO 288 BC

Demetrius Poliorcetes was the son of Antigonus the "one-eyed" and his wife Stratonice. He was born in 336 BC, the same year Alexander the Great came to power.

By the time Demetrius reached maturity, Alexander was dead and his generals were fighting one another to control the great empire the Greeks had conquered. As the son of one of Alexander's most powerful generals, Demetrius was thrown into the fray. Over time, he came to be known throughout the Greek world as the besieger of cities.

His coin is from Macedonia and bears a depiction of Athena on the front wearing a crested Corinthian helmet. On the back is the prow of a battle ship and a double headed axe, proclaiming Demetrius' military and naval prowess.

At the age of 22, Demetrius led his armies against the Egyptian forces of Ptolemy while defending Syria. Five years later, in 310 BC, he confronted the forces of Seleucus in Babylon. Each of these battles resulted in defeat. With other setbacks suffered by his father, the Macedonian kingdom they ruled was reduced by two-thirds.

Not all of his campaigns were unsuccessful, however. After several naval campaigns against Ptolemy, Demetrius sailed a fleet of 250 battleships to Athens and freed the city from Ptolemy and Cassander. The Athenians were elated and welcomed Demetrius as their ruler. Some even worshiped him as a deity. Demetrius scored more victories against Ptolemy but was unable to subdue Rhodes after an extended siege.

Lysimachus, Cassander and Seleucus eventually joined forces to defeat Antigonus and Demetrius. In 301 BC, their combined forces defeated the Macedonians and killed Antigonus at the Battle of Ipsus.

The defeat emboldened Demetrius' critics. The Athenians refused him entrance into the city. His earlier behavior as ruler had made him many enemies. While in power, he had transformed the Parthenon into a personal residence and stocked it with a large harem. Many Athenians had been offended by his licentiousness, made famous when a young boy jumped to his death in a cauldron of hot water to escape Demetrius' advances.

Eventually, by 294 BC, Demetrius regained control of Athens and Macedonia. He ruled for six years until he was ousted. Demetrius died later while a captive of Seleucus.

Coin details and provenance: Demetrius Poilorcetes. Macedonia. 294 to 288 BC. Obverse: Athena facing right in crested Corinthian helmet. Reverse: Ship's prow with double headed axe (a bipennis) to left, BA above prow, AP below. 3.56 grams. 15 mm. Reference: SNGCop. 1185. Acquired from Wayne C. Philips Rare Coins, Diamond Bar, California in July of 2011.

Philetairos
282 to 263 BC

Said to be a clean-shaven, heavy-looking man with short, curly hair, Philetairos was a eunuch who became ruler of Pergamon. This rare coin struck in his name shows a helmeted Athena on the front. On the back is a thrysos, or giant staff of fennel, of the sort carried by the goddess Dionysus and used as a sacred instrument in religious rituals.

Like many Greeks of his generation, Philetairos became embroiled in the conflicts of Diadochi after the death of Alexander the Great. He first served Antigonus and then Lysimachus as treasurer of Pergamon until 282 BC. For reasons unknown, he then changed allegiance to Seleucus, who defeated Lysimachus in the following year. After Seleucus died later that same year, Philetairos' autonomy over the affairs of Pergamon increased.

Pergamon flourished under Philetairos' rule, becoming a political and cultural center. Eventually, as Seleucid control over the region lessened, Pergamon came to be an independent kingdom ruled by Philetairos. During his 40 years in power, Philetairos constructed an acropolis, Pergamon's first palace and temples to Demeter and Athena.

Being a eunuch, Philetarios had no children and so adopted his nephew Eumenes I as his heir. When Philetairos died, his nephew succeeded him and ruled for many years. His nephew's successor, Attalos I, defeated the Galations in 238 or 237 BC and became recognized as the ruler of a new Attalid dynasty.

Pergamon became an ally of Rome and served as buffer state between Rome and the Seleucid Empire. When conflict arose between Pergamon and the Seleucids, Rome would intervene to support Pergamon. After 189 BC, Pergamon extended its influence over most of western Anatolia, much of which is now contained in modern-day Turkey.

One hundred and fifty years after Philetairos first issued this coin, the eccentric Attalos III "bequeathed" Pergamon to Rome. Although the bequest was opposed and suspected to be a Roman deception, Pergamon was suppressed by Rome four years later and in 129 BC became Rome's Asian province.

Coin details and provenance: Philetairos of Pergamon. 282 to 263 BC. Pergamon mint. Rare coin struck in his own name. Obverse: Head of Athena right. Reverse: Thyrsos, monogram in the left field, ΨΙΛΕΤΑΙΡΟΥ. 3.70 grams. 17 mm. Reference: SGN France 1673. When Lysimachus established the mint of Pergamon, he entrusted its treasury to the eunuch Philetairos. In the latter 280s BC, Philetairos changed his allegiance to Seleucus, striking these rare Alexandrian style tetradrachms. Acquired from Ancient Coins Canada, Richmond Hill, Ontario in January 2009.

Ionia's Homer
301 TO 288 BC

This coin from Smyrna, in the western coastal region of Anatolia (modern day Turkey), bears the image of the Greek poet Homer seated and holding a scroll. The front of the coin shows a profile of the god Apollo.

Minted after the region's conquest by Alexander, the coin pays homage to the poet who is credited with creating both the *Iliad* and the *Odyssey*. Two centuries after this coin was minted, the city continued to celebrate the great poet. The first century BC geographer and historian Strabo confirmed this with a description of Smyrna that included a library and a shrine with a wooden statute of Homer.

One tradition holds that Homer was a blind poet who was born in an Ionian city such as Smyrna. One theory posits that the poems were dictated by a non-literate Homer to a scribe around the sixth century BC. Another suggests that the poet only became blind in later life.

Most scholars, however, believe the *Iliad* and *Odyssey* were oral poems that were refined over generations until they were eventually committed to writing. In fact, the evidence suggests there were many versions of the poems. Ancient authors quote lines from Homer that no longer appear in the accepted texts. Greek cities such as Athens, Cyprus, Crete, Chios and even the western colony of Massalia had versions of their own. Aristotle had a version different from Plato's and even created a version for Alexander the Great.

The versions we celebrate today appear to have taken shape between the third and second centuries BC when Alexandrian scholars from the city's great library compiled monumental manuscripts of the poems, known to scholars as Venetus A, complete with marginal notes and commentary. Funded by the Greek Ptolemaic dynasty that ruled Egypt for centuries, the work of these scholars assembled the basic text we know today.

The ancients themselves appear to believe Homer was more than a man. Aristotle is quoted from a lost text called *On Poets* as believing Homer's mother was made pregnant by a spirit who danced with the muses. Like Achilles, this Homer was half man and half god. Writings attributed to the ancient historian Plutarch claim that Homer's ancestors came from heaven.

In truth, little is actually known about Homer. A common joke posits that the poems were not written by Homer at all but by another man with the same name.

Coin details and provenance: Ionia's Homer. Ionia, Smyrna. 301 to 288 BC. Obverse: Apollo laureate facing right. Reverse: Homer seated, holding roll, legend ΕΥΜΗΛΟΣ ΙΩΠΥΡΟΥ, scepter behind. 8.01 grams. 20.54 mm. Reference: BMC 104. Acquired from Tom Vossen, Kerkrade, Netherlands in December 2004.

Ptolemy

285 to 246 BC

The Greek general Ptolemy I, whose image appears on this coin, took control of Egypt after the death of Alexander the Great in 323 BC and established a dynasty that would rule Egypt for three centuries. This coin bearing his image was issued by his son and successor Ptolemy II Philadelphus. The eagle on the back was the traditional symbol for Egypt.

The melding of a Greek ruler's profile with the very Egyptian eagle became the standard imagery on the Ptolemys' Egyptian coinage for three centuries of Greek rule. The symbolism and length of Greek rule attest to how successful the Greeks were at assimilating to Egyptian customs while retaining essential Greek.

Ptolemy was a close friend of Alexander from childhood and one of his most trusted generals. When Alexander died in 323 BC, Ptolemy participated in the Partition of Babylon, where the recently conquered empire was divided into satrapies with a regent assigned to rule the satraps for Alexander's infant son.

Ptolemy became satrap of Egypt and Libya and quickly moved the body of Alexander to Memphis for internment to strengthen his claim to the region. He soon joined a coalition against Perdiccas, who had been appointed the imperial regent after Alexander's death. Perdiccas likely believed Ptolemy meant to succeed to all of Alexander's empire because of the Macedonian custom of kings burying their predecessor to claim their throne.

An attack on Ptolemy in Egypt followed, with Perdiccas suffering a decisive defeat that took his life. Ptolemy was offered the regency but declined, preferring to focus his efforts on establishing a defensible empire in Egypt.

Ptolemy lived a long life, surviving Alexander by 40 years and living to the age of 84. Throughout his life, he supported the arts, writing a history of Alexander's campaigns, starting the great library of Alexandria and sponsoring the mathematician Euclid.

His capital of Alexandria became the cultural wonder of the ancient world. Its library became the largest in the world and supported a university of scholars and scientists for centuries. So great and wealthy did the city become, that when Julius Caesar followed Pompey there during the Roman civil wars in 48 BC, Alexandria made Rome look like a backwater city.

Coin details and provenance: Ptolemy II of Egypt. 285 to 246 BC. Tetradrachm of Year 10, 274 - 273 BC. Tyre, Phoenicia. Obverse: Head of Ptolemy I facing right and wearing a fillet. Reverse: BASILEWS PTOLEMAIOU around eagle standing on a thunderbolt. 13.67 grams. Reference: SNG Cop 477. Acquired from Malter Galleries, Encino, California in January 2003.

Antiochus I
281 to 261 BC

This coin was issued in Tigris during the reign of Antiochus I and bears a diademed portrait of the king on its front. The back shows Apollo seated on an omphalos holding a bow and arrow. The omphalos was a sacred stone believed to represent the center, or navel, of the world. The most famous omphalos was at the Temple of Apollo at Delphi.

Antiochus was the son of Greek Emperor Seleucus and his Persian wife Apama, whom Seleucus acquired in Afghanistan while on campaign with Alexander the Great. Apama was the daughter of a Sogdian baron named Spitamenes.

The couple were married in Susa in a mass marriage of Greek officers ordered by Alexander. Seleucus retained Apama as his wife and made her his queen after most of Alexander's officers discarded their wives following Alexander's death in 323 BC.

In 300 BC, while Antiochus was a young man, his elderly father solicited the hand of the young daughter of the Macedonian King Demetrius. The 17-year-old maiden Stratonice was given to Seleucus in marriage and despite a substantial age difference seemed content. The couple lived together harmoniously and had one child, a daughter.

Over time, however, Antiochus became obsessed with the young Stratonice. His passion was such that the emperor could not help but notice. Fearing for his son's health, Seleucus made a surprising decision.

Six years after they were wed, he released Stratonice from their marriage and betrothed her to his son. At the same time, he appointed Antiochus to rule his eastern provinces. Antiochus' marriage to Stratonice produced five children including a successor, Antiochus II Theos.

Antiochus became emperor 13 years after his marriage to Stratonice when Seleucus was murdered by Ptolemy's son Keranous. The empire Antiochus inherited was fragile and faced great challenges. In fact, the threat from Egypt was so serious he was compelled to make peace with his father's assassin just to secure his border.

A few years later, the Gauls invaded and threatened the very existence of the Seleucid Empire until Antiochus finally subdued them. After that, war broke out with the Egyptians.

Antiochus managed to rule for 20 years. He died in 262 BC after losing a battle to the armies of Pergamon.

Coin details and provenance: Antiochus I, Soter. Seleucid King. 281 to 261 BC. Tigris Mint. AE 17. Obverse: Laureate head right, BASILEWS ANTIOXOY. Reverse: Apollo seated left on omphalos holding bow and arrow. 4.66 grams. 18.5 mm. Reference: SNG Spaer 209. Acquired from Holyland Numismatics, West Bloomfield, Michigan in May of 2011.

Antigonus II

285 to 239 BC

Antigonus II Gonatas, the son of Demetrius and grandson of Antigonus Monophthalmus, ruled greater Greece for 40 years. His coin depicts a helmeted Athena looking right with Pan standing on the reverse erecting a trophy. Pan was the Greek god of mountain wilds, hunting and rustic music.

Antigonus' grandfather served under Philip II and then as a satrap under Alexander the Great. As one of the Diadochi after Alexander's death in 323 BC, he was assigned territories and battled with the other Diadochi in the disputes that ensued. He wound up ruling all of Greece and much of Ionia. Antigonus' maternal grandfather was Antipater, who had been appointed regent over all of Alexander's conquests in 320 BC.

When Antigonus Monophthalmus was defeated and killed at the Battle of Ipsus in 301 BC, his son Demetrius escaped with 9,000 troops and enlisted the 18-year-old Antigonus II into his army. Demetrius continued to look for opportunities to expand what remained of his empire until he was forced to surrender to Seleucus in 285 BC following an unsuccessful campaign into Asia that saw Demetrius fall into the hands of Seleucus.

Antigonus II offered to exchange himself as a hostage for his father's release but was rebuffed. When his father later died in a Syrian prison, Antigonus assembled his entire fleet to recover his father's remains from the Seleucid fleet at Cyclades.

Antigonus II would go on to rule Greece for more than 45 years, successfully defending his empire from foreign incursions but not venturing to challenge other successors to Alexander for the Asian territory taken from his grandfather. His victories included defeating Pyrrhus, one of the great generals of the day, who repeatedly attempted to expand into Macedonia. It was Antigonus' army that trapped Pyrrhus in the Peloponnesian city of Argos in 272 BC where the famous general lost his life.

Throughout his reign, Antigonus was recognized as a man of letters who surrounded himself with poets, philosophers and historians. When he died in 239 BC at the age of 80, his son Demetrius II succeeded to his throne.

Coin details and provenance: Kings of Macedonia. Antigonus II Gonatas. 285 BC to 239 BC. Coin struck between 271 and 239 BC. Pella or Amphipolis mint. Obverse: Helmeted head of Athena right. Reverse: Pan standing right, erecting trophy; monogram A between legs. 2.89 grams. References: SNG München; SNG Alpha Bank 1017. Acquired from Marc Walter Ancient Coins, Vienna, Austria in December 2010.

HIERON II
274 TO 216 BC

While Ptolemy II was ruling his empire in Egypt, the city of Syracuse on the island of Sicily came under the rule of the illegitimate son of Heirocles, a native nobleman. This son, named Heiron, is pictured on the front of this coin wearing a diadem, the ancient world's equivalent of a crown. The back features a warrior on horseback carrying spear.

Heiron came to rule Syracuse after serving in the army of Pyrrhus of Epirus. The citizens of Syracuse appointed him to command their troops after Pyrrhus departed the city in 275 BC. Five years later, Heiron defeated the Mamertini and became king of Syracuse.

Six years later, he attacked the Mamertini and laid siege to their city of Messana. The Roman's intervened and defeated Heiron. He managed, nonetheless, to conclude a treaty with Rome that enabled him to continue ruling over parts of Sicily until his death in 215 BC. As their ally, Heiron frequently assisted the Romans during the Punic Wars.

Heiron was a contemporary and kinsman of the great Archimedes. As told by the historian Vitruvius, Heiron once gave Archimedes a golden crown to determine whether the gold was real. The assignment led Archimedes to discover the principle of displacement that enabled him to measure the density of the crown and answer his ruler's question. Upon making the discovery, Archimedes reportedly became so excited that he ran through the streets of Syracuse naked yelling "eureka, eureka!"

Archimedes brought fame and tactical advantage to Syracuse. Not only was he one of the leading scientists of antiquity credited with advancements in physics, he also invented novel machines such as siege engines and the screw pump. The later moved water uphill and was used to move water into irrigation ditches. He was also a master mathematician, although his contemporaries knew little of this.

Archimedes died during a Roman siege of Syracuse four years after the last of these coins were minted. So great was Archimedes' fame that the Roman senator Cicero visited his tomb hundreds of years later and described his visit. He found, on top of the tomb a sphere inside a cylinder, a testament to Archimedes' discovery that the volume and surface area of the sphere was two thirds that of the cylinder.

Coin details and provenance: Hieron II. 274 to 216 BC. Syracuse, Sicily. Bronze AE26. Obverse: Diademed head of Hieron facing left. Reverse: IEPONOE - Horseman facing right and holding spear, sigma monogram in lower right field. 16.55 grams. 26.6 mm. Reference SNG ANS-995. Acquired from Glenn W. Woods Numismatist, Dallas, Texas in August 2007. Accompanied with an Italian coin dealer's ticket.

Epirus & Pyrrhus
Before 238 BC

From the ancient Greek State of Epirus in the western Balkans comes this coin depicting the laureate head of Zeus. On the back is a rendering of a thunderbolt and a cornucopia. Issued before 238 BC, this coin was in circulation during or shortly after the life of Pyrrhus, one of the most famous and successful generals of ancient Greece. The State of Epirus, located on the western coast of Greece, was his home.

Pyrrhus, son of Aeacides and Phthia and second cousin to Alexander the Great, was renown in the ancient world for his skills and success on the battlefield. He reigned as king of Epirus from 306 BC to 301 BC and, then again, from 297 BC to 272 BC, taking power the second time with the support of Ptolemy I. In between, Pyrrhus was held hostage in Ptolemy's court during which time he married Ptolemy's stepdaughter Antigone. In 286 BC, Pyrrhus took control of Macedonia for two years before being driven out by Lysimachus.

Pyrrhus was most famous for his victories on the Italian peninsula where he led a successful war against the Romans at the behest of the Greek city of Tarentum, which was located in southern Italy. He entered Italy with 3,000 cavalry, 2,000 archers, 20,000 slingers and 19 war elephants and defeated the Romans at the Battle of Heraclea in 280 BC. Casualties were great on both sides.

The next year the armies again fought at Asculum where Pyrrhus won another battle whose casualties were so high that they prevented him from pursuing his campaign further and inspired the term "pyrrhic victory" as a description of a victory won at too great a cost.

Pyrrhus died in 272 BC while trying to expand his empire in Greece. While attacking Sparta at the request of Cleonymus, Pyrrhus was invited to intervene in a civic dispute in Argos. After entering Argos with his army, he found himself and his troops fighting in the city's narrow streets. During the in-city fighting, an Argive woman dropped a roofing tile on his head. While he stood stunned from the blow to his head, Pyrrhus was decapitated by an Argive soldier.

Coin details and provenance: Epirus. Epirote Republic. Home of Pyrrhus. Before 238 BC. Obverse: Laureate head of Zeus facing right. Reverse: Thunderbolt, monogram above, cornucopia below; all within oak-wreath. 9.08 grams. 24 mm. References: France pg. 127; V33/R?; SNG Copenhagen 85 (Pandosia). From Barry P. Murphy, Lancaster, Pennsylvania in January 2008.

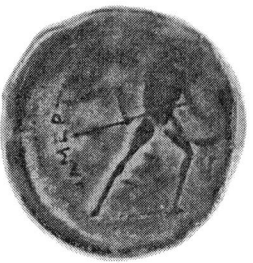

The Mamertini
220 TO 210 BC

How did a band of highland mercenaries from the Italian peninsula spark the beginning of the Punic Wars between Rome and Carthage?

The Mamertini, or "children of Mars," were a band of Campanian mercenaries hired in 288 BC by Agathocles of Syracuse to defend the Greek town of Messana in northern Sicily. The Mamertini took the commission but, instead of defending the town, seized Messana and held it for more than 20 years.

Their coin, struck between 220 BC and 210 BC, depicts the laureate head of Zeus on the front and a nude warrior in a crested helmet advancing right with a shield and spear. The choice of images reflects the aggressive inclinations of its issuer.

Under Mamertini rule, the farming and trading town of Messana became a base for raiding and plundering Sicily. Like the outlaws that they were, the Mamertini looted nearby cities, took hostages, demanded tribute and pirated ships on the nearby seas. Their exploits made them rich, feared and powerful.

Around 270 BC, Heiron II of Syracuse gathered an army of citizens to confront the Mamertini and rescue their Greek compatriots in Messana. The next year Heiron met and defeated the Mamertini on the Mylaen Plain north of Syracuse. However, when he besieged Messana in 265 BC, a Carthaginian fleet came to the Mamertinis' aid.

The Mamertini had petitioned for Carthaginian aid but became uneasy with their Carthaginian allies and appealed to Rome for assistance. Fearing the possible consequences of Carthaginian dominance of Sicily, the Romans intervened. The convergence of these two great powers in Sicily precipitated the first of three Punic Wars that would eventually destroy the Carthaginian Empire and make the Romans the sole rulers of the Italian peninsula.

Once the conflict expanded beyond Messana, the fate of the Mamertini was lost to history. As late as the first century BC, however, inhabitants of Messana were still known as the Mamertines.

Coin details and provenance: The Mamertinoi. 220 to 210 BC. Bronze pentonkion from Sicily. Obverse: Laureate head of Zeus. Reverse: MAMERTINWN with nude warrior in crested helmet, advancing with shield and long spear, P in right field. 12.3 grams. References: Calciati 40/1, BMC 25ff; SNG Cop 458. SNG ANS 447ff. 12.3 grams. Acquired from Melqart in April 2005.

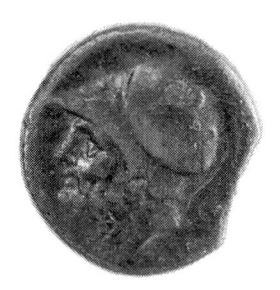

HANNIBAL
213 TO 207 BC

This coin was issued by the Bretti of southern Italy between 213 and 207 BC during Hannibal's long occupation of the Italian peninsula. Its front bears the profile of Ares wearing a Corinthian helmet. Its reverse shows Nike crowning a military trophy, a reference to Hannibal's victories over the Romans.

In the winter of 218 BC, the great Carthaginian general marched from Spain through southern Gaul and across the Alps to attack Rome on the Italian peninsula. A master strategist and tactician, Hannibal proceeded to defeat three separate Roman armies. In the last of these battles, at Cannae in 216 BC, Hannibal destroyed eight Roman legions sent to confront him.

Livy reported Rome's losses at 45,500 infantry and 2,700 horsemen compared with 8,000 Carthaginians. It was a catastrophe for Rome. Over the course of Hannibal's campaign, Rome lost one-fifth of its adult male population and most of its allies in southern Italy. And it lay vulnerable to further attack.

Rome's citizens, in their desperation, resorted to human sacrifice to appease the gods. They buried-alive two Gauls and two Greeks in the city's marketplace and then abandoned a baby in the Adriatic Sea.

Hannibal, for his part, chose not to attack Rome and moved his armies into southern Italy. Following his victory, Greek cities in Sicily revolted against Roman control and an independent Syracuse aligned with Hannibal's Carthaginians.

The Romans survived this dark hour in their history to fight another day. Hannibal departed Italy after being called back to Africa in 203 BC. In the following year, Roman Scipio Africanus led his legions into Africa where they met and defeated Hannibal decisively at Zama near Carthage.

Following the conclusion of a peace treaty that stripped Carthage of its empire, Hannibal retired to private life. Before long, however, he reemerged as a leader of peacetime Carthage.

Rome grew concerned with his rising power and demanded his surrender. Hannibal, instead, went into exile. His travels took him east to the court of the Seleucid emperor Antiochus III where, as a military advisor, he assisted the Seleucids in their resistance to Rome.

Coin details and provenance: Bruttium, the Bretti. 213 to 207 BC. Issued Under Hannibal Barca in Bruttium. Æ sextans. Obverse: Head of Ares wearing crested Corinthian helmet; two pellets. Reverse: Nike crowning military trophy, star above, cornucopia before, BPETTIΩN. 14.40 grams. 27 mm. References: SNG ANS 29. Includes attractive classical circular ticket. Acquired from Herakles Numismatics, Charlotte, North Carolina in February 2010.

Castulo & Hasdrubal
Early 2ND century BC

This coin from the second century BC is from the town of Castulo in south central Spain. It comes from an area settled by the Oretans, an Iberian people who came to the area in the sixth century BC. The coin bears the image of a man facing right on the front and a winged sphinx on the back with a raised forepaw facing a star.

The sphinx in Greek lore was a creature with the body of a lion, the wings of an eagle and the head and breasts of a woman. She was merciless and hungry for human flesh. In the Greek tradition, the sphinx was sent from Ethiopia to guard the entrance to the city of Thebes. She is said to have asked travelers a riddle before allowing them passage into the city. Those who could not answer were devoured by sphinx.

According to tradition, the riddle asked what creature had four legs in the morning, two in the afternoon and three at night. Oedipus is said to have answered the riddle correctly by responding "man" whereupon the sphinx threw herself from a high rock and died. The image on this coin would have called up this story to Greeks and Romans alike and may have been intended as a warning to those who might do harm to the city.

In the years before this coin was minted, Castulo came under Carthaginian control. By tradition, a local princess named Himilce married the Carthaginian general Hannibal to seal the alliance.

In late 212 BC, the city was witness to one of the great victories of the Carthaginians over the Romans. Under the command of Hannibal's brother Hasdrubal Barca, combined Carthaginian and Numidian forces routed the Roman legions and allies commanded by Publius Cornelius Scipio in the area near Castulo. The Numidian general Masinissa, who would later become a client king of Rome, lead the light cavalry for the Carthaginian forces.

Coin details and provenance: Castulo, Spain. Early 2nd century BC. AE 27. Obverse: Male head facing right. Reverse: Sphinx standing right, forepaw raised with star in foreground. 12.76 grams. 27 mm. Reference: CNH 23. Acquired from Jencek Historical Enterprise, San Mateo, California in February 2011.

Antiochus III
223 TO 187 BC

Antiochus III was one of the most successful of the Seleucid monarchs. During his long reign from 222 BC to 187 BC he conquered much of Persia and expanded his empire all the way to India.

His coin features a profile of Apollo on the front with the features of Antiochus. On the back, Apollo sits on a sacred stone, called an omphalos, examining an arrow resting on a grounded bow.

In 199 BC and 198 BC Antiochus defeated the Ptolemies to take their Syrian, Phoenician and Judean provinces. Then he invaded Greece with the assistance of the great Carthaginian general Hannibal who had fled east after the Romans destroyed his army in 195 BC.

The invasion brought Antiochus into conflict with the Romans, which ended in the rout of his army by the Roman general Glabrio at Thermopylae in 192 BC. The defeat gave Rome control of what would become their Asian province.

Macabre reports from Thermopylae, however, would circulate throughout the region and embolden later Eastern monarchs to attack the Romans. According to those reports, a Syrian cavalry officer named Bouplagos rose from the dead while Rome's legionnaires were looting the battlefield.

In a rasping whisper, he warned the Romans that Zeus would send a "bold-hearted tribe" to punish Rome. The next day, Roman general Publius fell into a trance and began raving about wars and gory atrocities to come. As his soldiers watched with horror, Publius was reportedly consumed by a wolf while his severed head ranted about a great king from the east who would obliterate Rome.

The great Mithradates of Pontus, who would retake Rome's Asian province one hundred years later, used legends like this one from Thermopylae to help rally the Greeks to resist the incursions of Rome. He would succeed for decades in thwarting Roman ambitions in the area until a young and ambitious Roman general named Pompey finally defeated his armies in the field.

Coin details and provenance: Seleucid Kingdom, Antiochus III. 223 to 187 BC. Antioch on the Orontes mint. Obverse: Laureate head of Apollo with features of Antiochus III facing right. Reverse: ΒΑΣΙΛΕΩΣ ΑΝΤΙΟΧΟΥ, Apollo seated on omphalos, examining arrow in right, rest-ing left on grounded bow, symbols left. 11.499 grams. 24.9mm. References: Houghton 1048(1), SNG Spaer 561. Acquired from Forum Ancient Coins, Morehead City, North Carolina in February 2010.

SABA, LAND OF SHEBA
3ʳᵈ TO 2ⁿᵈ CENTURY BC

Looking very much on its reverse like the classical Athenian drachm but with a distinctly un-Greek profile on the front, this coin comes from the ancient country of Saba, also known as Sheba. It was issued sometime in the third to second century BC.

Located on the Red Sea in the vicinity of modern Yemen and Ethiopia, Saba was a wealthy country with advanced irrigation techniques and a thriving agriculture. It was also rich in precious metals and spices and engaged in active caravan trading. For centuries, the country sent caravans north along the Red Sea as far as Israel trading frankincense, myrrh, saffron, cumin, aloe and galbanum.

It is reported in the both the Bible and Ethiopian sources, that Makeda, Queen of Sheba, visited Israel's King Solomon sometime in the tenth century BC to test his legendary wisdom. After Solomon answered Makeda's riddles, the queen showered him with gifts. The Biblical Book of Kings reports that the Queen of Sheba was "overcome with amazement" when she observed the wisdom of Solomon and the great palace he had built. Ethiopian tradition completes the story with the queen returning to Saba to bear the son of Solomon, Menelik I, who began an Ethiopian royal dynasty.

A much earlier reference to Saba is found in the works of the Jewish-Roman historian Josephus. He describes a nearly impenetrable royal city named Saba in ancient Ethiopia that was encircled with a wall.

It, Josephus reports, was conquered when the daughter of its king fell in love with an Egyptian prince whose army was besieging the city. She sent her servants to discuss marriage, which the prince accepted on condition that she deliver up the city. When she did, he gave thanks to God and married the princess.

The Egyptian prince was Moses. After leading his troops back to Egypt, Josephus reports, Moses took flight into the desert to escape his Egyptian enemies. There he encountered a bush burning with a fire that did not consume its leaves or branches. From the bush he heard the voice of God, who instructed him to return to Egypt and bring the Hebrews out of the land of Egypt.

Coin details and provenance: 3rd to 2nd Century BC. Sabean imitation of Athens attic drachm. Saba. Obverse: Head of Athena with Sabean letter "N" on cheek. Reverse: Owl facing right, AOE and crescent in Athenian style. 4.5 grams. Acquired from the Time Machine Co., Flushing, New York in August 2005.

Halicarnassus

3rd to 2nd century BC

This tiny coin from the third century BC comes from the Ionian city-state of Halicarnassus situated on the eastern coast of the Mediterranean Sea. The coin, which is less than one third the size of a penny, bears the images of Apollo and an eagle.

The city of Halicarnassus was part of a six city Dorian federation called the Doric Hexapolis. At times Halicarnassus was ruled by the Persians and participated with the Persians in battles against the Athenians and other mainland Greek city-states.

Halicarnassus was also home to the female tyrant Artemisia who ruled as a client of the Persians and commanded five Persian ships against the Athenians at the battle of Salamis in 480 BC. She is said to have convinced the Persian King Xerxes to retreat back to Asia Minor after the defeat. Later, she was summoned to Ephesus to care for Xerxes' sons.

Halicarnassus was also home to the fifth century BC historian Herodotus who wrote the Western world's first epic history. He fled the city after the poet Panysis, possibly his cousin or uncle, was executed by the city's tyrant Lygdamis. His travels afterwards provided the stories and descriptions that fill his *Histories*.

Those *Histories* describe the epic war between the Greek city-states and the Persian Empire and the events, in Greece and Persia that led to the conflict. In so doing, it describes not only the conflict that concluded successfully for the Greeks in the early days of his lifetime but also the rise of two new empires a century before, the Lydians and the Medes, who competed with Babylon for dominance in the Near East. The success of Persian leader Cyrus, who seized Median power and then defeated the Lydian King Croesus, set the stage for Persian dominance and eventual war with the Greeks.

Herodotus' description of those events, and much more, created a new literary genre that takes its name from the title of his book. From his work, Herodotus earned the epitaph "father of Western history."

Coin details and provenance: Ionia, Halicarnassus. Home of Herodotus. 3rd to 2nd century BC. Obverse: Apollo laureate facing left. Reverse: Eagle standing in front of lyre, ΑΛΥ. 1.78 grams. 11.21 mm. References: SNG Copenhagen 348. From Tom Vossen, Kerkrade, Netherlands in January 2005.

Dyrrachion
229 TO 100 BC

This coin with its pastoral image of a cow and suckling calf comes from an Illyrian province of Rome in the second century BC. In the background are a Greek legend and a celestial body.

Founded in 627 BC on the Adriatic coast by Greek colonists from Corinth and Corcyra, the city of Dyrrachion, then called Epidamnos, became noted as an advanced political society and was praised by Aristotle.

The Illyrian King Glaukias conquered the city in 317 BC but pledged allegiance to Macedonia after being defeated by Alexander the Great's successor Cassander in 314 BC. The great general Pyrrhus grew up in the city. He was a child when Glaukias ruled, joining the household of Glaukias when his father Aeacides of Epirus was dethroned.

The Roman's conquered Epidamnos and defeated the Illyrians in 229 BC. It was then that the city was renamed Dyrrachion and coins like this were issued. The Romans objected to the name Epidamnos because of its similarity to the Latin word damnu, meaning loss or harm.

As newly named, the city prospered and became the western end of the Via Egnatia, the Roman highway that led to Thessalonica and Constantinople. Pompey the Great, rival to Julius Caesar, made a stand here in 48 BC before fleeing to Greece. Octavian later proclaimed the city a free town, or civitas libera, and made it a colony for veterans of his legions after his victory over Marc Antony and Cleopatra at the battle of Actium.

Coin details and provenance: Dyrrhachion, Illyria. 229-100 BC. AR silver drachm. Obverse: A cow stands left with her head looking down at a calf, bunch of grapes in the exergue ΦΙΛΩΤΑΣ above, club to left and corn ear to right. Reverse: Double stellite pattern, wreath/star above. 2.91 grams. 17 mm. From Zeus Coins, Kent, Great Britain in January 2008.

QIN SHI HUANGDI

220 TO 180 BC

Far to the east at this same time, King Ying Zheng of the State of Qin ended the 250-year Warring States Period in China by consolidating the seven states of Qin, Han, Wei, Zhao, Qi, Chu and Yan into one Chinese kingdom. He took the name Qin Shi Huangdi, or Great August First Emperor of Qin, and undertook a number of major economic and political reforms.

He built roads to connect his kingdom and ordered construction of the first great wall. He also standardized weights and measurements, currency, and even the length of axels for carts using the imperial roads.

In stark contrast to Roman conquerors in the West, however, Qin Shi Huangdi suppressed the knowledge of those he conquered rather than emulating their achievements. As a means of control, he also eliminated the Hundred Schools of Thought that reflected the great flowering of free thought and philosophy, including the teachings of Confucianism and Daoism that had flourished in China during the Warring States Period. Beginning in 213 BC, he ordered the burning of many books and had some 460 scholars buried alive for possessing forbidden books.

Today, however, Qin Shi Huangdi is remembered more for his pivotal role in unifying China and for his city-size mausoleum, begun at the beginning of his reign, which contains thousands of life-size terracotta warriors buried in the ground to guard his elaborate tomb. The mausoleum is encased in an artificial hill that has the shape of a truncated pyramid with bushes and trees on its sides and top.

Coin details and provenance: 220-180 BC. Qin dynasty. Emperor Qin Shi Huangdi, 1st emperor of China. Obverse: Two Chinese characters – Ban Liang ("Half ounce"). Reverse: Blank. 4.17 grams. 29 mm. References: BM Chinese coins (Poole) #(1632); Schjoth 79ff; Hartill #7.7. The "History of Han" says: When Qin united the world, it made ... [the currency] of bronze, which . . . bore an inscription Ban Liang and was equal in weight to its inscription. Qin Shi Huangdi (259 BC – 210 BC), personal name Ying Zheng, is a pivotal figure in Chinese history. He was king of the Chinese State of Qin from 246 BC to 221 BC during the Warring States Period. He became the first emperor of a unified China in 221 BC. He ruled until his death in 210 BC at the age of 50. From Kenneth W. Dorney Ancient Coins, Redding, California in July 2016.

Masinissa

208 TO 148 BC

This coin is from the son of an African king who deployed his military skills in the Punic Wars for both Carthage and Rome and wound up ruling all of Numidia as a Roman client-king. It depicts a determined and bearded Masinissa wearing a laureate crown on the front with a galloping horse on the back. The horse likely refers to Masinissa's great success as a cavalry commander during the Punic Wars.

Masinissa was the second son of the king of Massyli in eastern Numidia. During much of his youth, he was held hostage by the Carthaginians to insure his father's loyalty.

When the Second Punic War began, Masinissa fought for Carthage against Syphax, who was ruler of the Masaesyles in western Numidia and ally to the Romans. He became respected for his success as a warrior. At the age of 17, he won a decisive victory over Syphax's army.

Afterwards he advanced to command the Numidian cavalry against the Romans in Spain. When Hannibal's brother Hasdrubal Barca departed for Italy, Masinissa took command of all the Carthaginian cavalry in Spain and engaged the Roman commander Scipio Africanus in a guerilla war. After the Carthaginians were defeated at the Battle of Ilpia in 207 BC, Masinissa defected to join the Romans. Meanwhile, Spyhax realigned himself with Hasdrubal and the Carthaginians.

Masinissa's defection paid him benefits. He became the cavalry commander for the Roman general Africanus and was instrumental in securing Roman victory in the pivotal Battle of Zama five years later. That decisive victory hastened the collapse of Hannibal's army and set the stage for Masinissa's further advancement.

In recognition of his service, Masinissa received the kingdom of Syphax and became the king of Numidia. For the rest of his life, Masinissa worked to extend his borders and remained a staunch and compliant ally of Rome.

Coin details and provenance: Masinissa. North Africa King of Numidia. 208 to 148 BC. Obverse: Laureate bust facing left. Reverse: Horse galloping left. Acquired from Ancient Byways, Wethersfield, Connecticut in December 2007.

THRACE & SPARTACUS
196 TO 88 BC

This coin was issued from Thrace during the lifetime of Spartacus, a freeborn Thracian who became a Roman soldier and was later condemned to slavery for reasons no longer known. Thrace was an area east and north of mainland Greece that was populated by several tribes known to the Greeks as Thracians. They appear as Trojan allies in Homer's *Iliad* and were known to accompany Alexander the Great when he crossed the Hellespont to invade Persia.

The front of this coin from Thrace bears a profile of Darsalas, the Thracian god of health and spiritual vitality. On the back, the great god appears on horseback carrying a cornucopia above a Greek legend.

Spartacus, one of the most famous Thracians, was trained to be a gladiator at the gladiatorial school of Lentulus Batiatus in Capua after his enslavement. In 73 BC, he and about 70 of his fellow trainees plotted to escape. When their plans were discovered, they grabbed kitchen implements and fought their way free, seizing weapons and wagons as they escaped. They defeated a small force sent after them and plundered the region.

Over time their force grew to more than 120,000. Slaves throughout the Italian peninsula escaped their masters to fight with Spartacus and his co-leaders Crixus and Oenomaus. For more than two years, the slave army roamed the Italian countryside from their base on Mt. Vesuvius defeating every Roman legion sent to confront them.

Their presence and their success against Roman legions threatened the very existence of Rome. In 71 BC, Rome sent eight legions under the command of Marcus Crassus to deal with Spartacus. As he approached from the north, Magnus Pompey and his battle hardened legions approached from the south. Crassus met Spartacus in southern Italy near the headwaters of the Siler River and overwhelmed the slave army. Spartacus is believed to have died in this battle. Julius Caesar was among those who fought in this campaign.

After the battle, Crassus marched the defeated slaves up the Appian Way 350 miles to Rome, crucifying 6,000 of them along the way. Their rotting bodies were left hanging on their crosses, sending a message of deterrence to the millions of slaves on the Italian peninsula.

Coin details and provenance: Roman occupied Thrace, Odessos. 196 to 88 BC. Obverse: Laureate head of Darsalas facing right. Reverse: ΟΔΗΣΙΤΩΝ, Darsalas on horseback holding cornucopia in right hand, reins of horse in left; monogram below. References: Topalov 24, cp. p. 179 for monogram on this issue; SNG BM 290-3 var. (monogram); SNG Stancomb 261ff var. (same). Acquired from Atlantis Quality Ancient Coins in February 2004

Heracles
190 TO 167 BC

This coin from the beginning of the second century BC comes from the Island of Kos off the coast of Turkey in the Carpathian Sea. The ancient community that inhabited this island is known for sending a contingent to the Trojan War and, later, for being the home to the fifth century BC physician Hippocrates.

The haunting image on the front of the coin is of Heracles, the greatest of the Greek heroes who was famous for completing the Twelve Labors. His tools of the trade, a bow in a case and a club appear on the back.

Believed to be the son of Zeus and the mortal Alkmene, Heracles was the ancient archetype for bravery and manliness. He was revered by both the Greeks and the Romans, who called him Hercules.

Emperor Commodus, in the second century AD, was so obsessed with him that he portrayed himself as Hercules on statues and coins. Homer's *Odyssey* reports that Odysseus recognized Heracles' during his visit to the underworld along with Achilles, Ajax and Minos, son of Zeus.

When the gods punished Prometheus for giving fire to humans, it was Heracles who freed him from his torture and bondage. Heracles ended his mortal existence before the sack of Troy in pain from being poisoned. The Greek warrior Philoketetes is said to have received his bow, pictured on the coin with his club, and used it in the siege of Troy.

The Twelve Labors completed by Heracles required him to slay the mythical Nemean Lion and the nine headed Lernaean Hydra. They included capturing the Ceryneian Hind (deer) and Erymanthian Boar. Labors five and six required cleaning the enormous Augean stables in one day and slaying the man-eating Stymphalina birds. The seventh and eighth labors required Heracles to capture the Cretan Bull and steal the man-eating Mares of Diomedes. Next, he had to steal the magical girdle of Hippolyta, the queen of the Amazons. His final three labors required him to take cattle from the monster Geryon, steal apples from the Hesperides nymphs, and capture the three-headed Ceberus that guarded the gates of Hades.

Coin details and provenance: Heracles. Islands off Caria, Kos. Circa 190 to 167 BC. Uncertain magistrate. Obverse: Three-quarter facing head of Heracles, wearing lion's skin, head turned slightly right. Reverse: Bow in case and club; ...ICTO. References: SNG Copenhagen 678ff var. (magistrate); BMC Caria pg. 209, 156ff var. (same). Acquired from the David Herman Collection. Ex CNG with original sales ticket from Inclinatioroma Ancient Coins, New York, New York in September 2006.

CLEOPATRA I
180 TO 145 BC

This coin from the reign of the sixth Greek ruler of Egypt, Ptolemy VI, bears an idealized portrait of his mother, Cleopatra I. She is portrayed on this coin from 180 BC as Isis, the Egyptian goddess of motherhood, fertility and magic. The eagle on the back symbolized Egypt and remains symbolic of the country to this day.

Cleopatra ruled Egypt as regent for her young son. She was the first Ptolemy queen to rule Egypt openly and the first to issue coins in her own name. The daughter of Seleucid ruler Antiochus III, Cleopatra was known to her contemporaries in Alexandria as the Syrian because of a region of Syria that was included in her dowry.

Cleopatra officially came to power when she was named a vizier in 187 BC during the reign of her husband Ptolemy V. It was when her husband died seven years later, that she began ruling Egypt as regent for her six-year-old son.

This same son, Ptolemy VI Philometor, was later married to his sister Cleopatra II. He is remembered for leaving Alexandria in 164 BC to live in Rome as member of the working class. He was summoned back to Alexandria just one year later, however, because of displeasure with his younger brother, who ruled in his absence. Returning in 163 BC, Philometer and his brother Physcon divided responsibilities for the empire, with Philometer ruling Egypt.

The first Cleopatra may also have witnessed the creation of one of the great relics of antiquity. While her husband ruled, a trilingual inscription describing the coronation of her husband Ptolemy V and the establishment of a divine cult in his honor was engraved into stone. The stone was inscribed in Egyptian hieroglyphics, Egyptian demonic script and Greek by a congress of priests in Memphis during the ninth year of Ptolemy V's reign.

When this stone was later discovered by archeologists, scholars were able for the first time to decipher Egyptian hieroglyphics, by comparing it to the accompanying Egyptian demonic and Greek texts. Because of this relic created in Cleopatra's time, scholars were able to greatly expand our knowledge and understanding of ancient Egypt and its civilization. This relic is called the Rosetta Stone.

Coin details and provenance: Egypt, Ptolemy VI: Cleopatra I. 180 to 145 BC. Struck at Paphos in Cyprus. Obverse: Head of Cleopatra I as Isis facing right. Reverse: Eagle standing left, monogram in field to left. 26 mm. Reference: SG 7903. Acquired from Wayne G. Sales Antiquarian, New Providence, Pennsylvania in March 2005.

THE CELTIBERIANS
180 TO 20 BC

The Celts first migrated to the Iberian Peninsula in the tenth century BC, settling mostly in the south. A second major wave of migration, further north, occurred five centuries later. By the third century BC, these Iberian Celts lived in political units with defined territories supported by fortified cities.

When this coin was issued, between 180 BC and 20 BC, the Celts had moved deep into northern Spain and Portugal and merged with the native Iberians. They had also submitted to the Romans after years of brutal conflict in a long and bitterly contested war that the Roman senator Cicero described as "with deadly enemies, not to determine which would be supreme, but which would survive."

Before submitting to the Romans in the early second century BC, the Celtiberians joined forces with the Carthaginian general Hannibal during the Second Punic War. Thousands of their troops joined Hannibal in his famous journey through southern France and over the Alps to attack the Romans on the Italian peninsula. Hannibal nearly vanquished Rome, which lost nearly one-fifth of its adult male population in the war. Ancient accounts report Rome losing more than 45,000 infantry and 2,500 horsemen in the struggle.

Without completely destroying the Romans, Hannibal and his Iberian allies retired to southern Italy, after which Hannibal was recalled to Carthage. After regrouping, the Romans later succeeded in driving Hannibal and his Celtiberian allies off the Italian peninsula. It was not until Rome successfully concluded the Second Punic War that it turned its attention to the Iberian Peninsula and, after vicious fighting, subdued the Celtiberians.

The coin above bears the image of a bearded man on one side and a mounted cavalry officer on the other. The legend below translates to Turiasu, where the coin was minted. The lance depicted on the coin as well as the two-edged sword are both believed to have originated with the Celtiberians.

Coin details and provenance: 180 to 20 BC. Celtiberian, Silver denarius. Turiasu, Spain mint. Obverse: Bearded male head right, Iberian "Ka-S-Tu" below. Reverse: Horseman holding lance and galloping right, Iberian legend "Turiasu" below. 3.8 grams. 17.9 mm. References: Villaronga pg. 266, 33; Burgos 1911. Acquired from Forum Ancient Coins, Morehead City, North Carolina in June 2006.

ANTIOCHUS IV
175 TO 164 BC

Antiochus IV ruled the Seleucid Empire from 175 BC until his death in 164 BC. He came to power by ousting Heliodorus, a usurper of King Seleucus IV, and seizing the throne while the true heir Demetrius I was being held hostage in Rome. His coin shows him wearing a crown on the front with a goddess holding a long scepter or torch on the back.

In 170 BC, Antiochus conquered all of Egypt except Alexandria in a preemptive strike after Egypt demanded the return of Syria. Two years later, he launched a second attack that was thwarted before it reached Alexandria by an ambassador of the Roman Senate, Gaius Popillius Laenas.

When confronted with the ambassador's demand that he withdraw or face war with Rome, Antiochus played for time. Popillius is reported to have drawn a circle in the sand around Antiochus and demanded a decision before Antiochus left the circle. Antiochus conceded and the phrase "line in the sand" came into being.

While he was in Egypt, a rumor spread that Antiochus had died. This emboldened the deposed Jewish high priest Jason to assemble an army and attack Jerusalem. Menelaus, the high priest of Jerusalem appointed by Antiochus, fled the city.

Enraged by the defeat, Antiochus attacked and took back the city. In retribution for the rebellion, he ordered the execution of many Jews, outlawed Judaism and ordered the worship of Zeus as the supreme god.

When the Jews resisted, Antiochus destroyed the city, slaughtering many, and established a fortress on a hill above the Temple that was garrisoned with Greek soldiers. For the atrocities he inflicted on the Jews, Antiochus is remembered as a persecutor in the Jewish traditions of Hanukkah and the Books of the Maccabees.

While Antiochus succeeded in expanding Seleucid territory and influence, his rule also brought with it the seeds of decline. His status as a usurper led to a series of civil wars after his son Antiochus V Eupator succeeded to the throne. This ultimately weakened the empire.

Coin details and provenance: Antiochus IV. 175 to 164 BC. Seleucid Kingdom. Bronze serrated ake. Ptolemais mint. Obverse: Diademed and radiate head of Antiochus right, fillet border. Reverse: BASILEWS ANTOCOU, veiled and draped goddess (Hera or Demeter) standing facing holding long scepter or torch. 2.70 grams. 15.1 mm. 0°. References: AE 14. SGCV II 6994, SNG Spaer 1130-1138. Acquired from Forum Ancient Coins, Morehead City, North Carolina in August 2008.

Mithradates
171 to 138 BC

The fifth and most powerful king of the eastern empire of Parthia was the son of Phriaapatius and father to Phraates II. His coin shows him wearing a bashlyk, or cone shaped hood. The reverse depicts a beardless archer seated on an omphalos, a religious stone believed to enable direct communication with the gods.

Mithradates inherited a small kingdom from his brother Phraates around 171 BC and transformed it during his 37-year rule into a great empire and world power. His efforts expanded Parthian territory to include Hyrcania, Media, Babylonia, Assyria, Elymais, Persis, and parts of Tapuria and Traxiana. It was during Mithradates' reign that Media was conquered, opening Mesopotamia to Parthian conquest.

Mithradates' armies also conquered the royal city of Seleucia in 141 BC and expanded as far south as Uruk. These conquests and the establishment of the Parthians as rulers over a vast territory in the Middle East effectively separated the Greeks of Bactria and India from their compatriots in Greece.

This separation was not complete however. The Parthians permitted a great deal of autonomy to the Greek cities they conquered. Among them, Seleucia on the Tigris governed almost autonomously throughout Mithradates' reign, no doubt paying tribute but otherwise ruling itself with an independent senate and municipal council. Only in extraordinary circumstances did this great city invite the Parthian military into its walls to resolve disputes. Similar though less autonomous privileges were granted to most cities under Parthian control.

Mithradates' conquests made the Parthians wealthy and gave them control of the major trade routes to the east, the Silk Road and the Persian Royal Road. Consistent with his enhanced stature and power, Mithradates adopted the Persian title of King of Kings and abandoned the traditional headdress of the Parthians depicted on the front of this coin for an elaborate tiara, a tall and stiff crown that had been a mark of sovereignty among the Assyrian and Persian monarchy.

Coin details and provenance: Parthian King, Mithradates I. 171-138 BC. AR drachm. Obverse: Beardless bust left, wearing bashlyk; border of dots. Reverse: Beardless archer, seated right on omphalos; in right hand, bow; Greek inscription BASILEWS / MEGALOU / ARSAKOU. Reference: Sellwood 10.1. Acquired from Imperial Coins & Artifacts, New York, New York in July 2005.

MENANDER
160 TO 145 BC

This famous Greek king is mentioned in the accounts of ancient historians Strabo, Plutarch and Justin. He ruled in the second century BC over the Gandhara, Punjab and Afghan territories that were conquered by Alexander the Great almost 200 years earlier. During his reign, the eastern Greeks expanded deeper into Indian Territory.

His coin was minted in Pushkalavati, the Lotus City, in what is now northern Pakistan. It shows the head of the Greek god Pallas wearing a plumed helmet surrounded by a Greek legend that declares Menander king. The god Nike appears on the back holding a wreath and a palm within a Karosthi legend that also declares Menander king.

Menander was born a commoner in a village near Kandahar but came to belong to a royal family and later married Agathocleia, the daughter of Greek King Demetrius. Menander was an effective ruler and one of few mentioned by western Greek authors. He was also renowned as a scholar and seeker of truth.

The Buddhist saint Nagasena is believed to have converted Menander to Buddhism. In fact, Menander died a Buddhist monk after turning his kingdom over to his son. He attained Arhatship, the last stage of sanctification under Theravada Buddhism.

Perhaps because of the Parthian conquests during Menander's reign that separated the empires of the western Greeks from the Indo-Greeks, Menander is the last eastern Greek monarch mentioned by ancient western historians.

Interestingly, speculation about his successor revolves in large part over the inscriptions that appear on Indo-Greek coins issued after his death. The traditional view is that he was succeeded by queen Agathokleia who ruled as regent for their son Strato I until he became an adult.

Under this view, the queen and son were only able to hold onto the eastern Punjab and Gandhara parts of the kingdom. A minority view, based on the finding of a single coin, holds that Menander was briefly succeeded by his son Thrason who was murdered before the kingdom came to be ruled by Agathokleia and Strato I.

Coin details and provenance: Menander, Indo-Greek King of Bactria. 160 to 145 BC. Bactria. Pushkalavati. Square AE 18. Obverse: Head of Pallas right, wearing plumed helmet, Greek legend ΒΑΣΙΛΕΩΣ ΣΩΤΕΡΟΣ ΜΕΝΑΝΔΡΟΥ . Reverse: Karosthi legend Maharajas tuataras Menadrasa, Nike holding wreath and palm; Pushkalavati monogram below. 5.66 grams. References: Cf. MA 1821-1823v (monogram). Acquired from David L. Tranbarger Rare Coins, Anderson, Indiana in November 2004.

Mt. Vesuvius before eruption with Bacchus and Agathodaemon
From an ancient fresco excavated from Pompeii

[3]

Republican Rome

THE SLAVE SPARTACUS broke out of the gladiatorial school of Lentulus Batiatus in Capua in 73 BC to lead a massive slave rebellion against Republican Rome. His army of slaves and gladiators defeated Rome's legions and roamed free across the Italian peninsula making camp at the base of Mt. Vesuvius. His success against Rome's legions and the size of the slave army struck fear into the hearts of Rome's citizens. Many feared for the very survival of the Republic.[3]

But in 71 BC, Spartacus and his army were defeated by Rome's legions under the command of Marcus Crassus. Following the defeat, thousands of Spartacus' compatriots were hung out to die on crosses along the Appian Way by Marcus Crassus to mark his conquest and strike fear into the slave population of Rome.

The coin above was issued in that same year by a Roman moneyer to celebrate the role played by the issuer's

---

[3] Silver denarius issued by Manius Aquilius in 71 BC. The front shows Virtus, a Roman god of military power. The back shows a Roman warrior holding a prostrate slave. Acquired from Freeman & Sear, Los Angeles, California in March 2006.

grandfather in putting down Rome's second great slave revolt thirty years earlier. To the freemen and slaves in Rome, the coin's image of a conquered slave and triumphant legionnaire would also serve as a reminder of the more recently conquered slave army of Spartacus and the horrible fate of the defeated slaves left to die and rot along the Appian Way.[4]

Ancient Gladiator Mosaic at the Borghese Gallery in Rome

But, while Spartacus and his army of slaves did not win freedom from Rome, their story would help two thousand years later to bring an end to an era of persecution in America. In 1951, at the height of the Communist witch hunts led by U.S. Senator Joseph McCarthy, one bestselling American author would self-publish a novel about Spartacus and a Hollywood leading man would make his book into a movie in a series of events that would help end the McCarthy era.

---

[4] Approximately 6,000 slaves were crucified and left to die along the 350 miles from the battlefield to the gates of Rome. This equates to about 17 crucifixions per mile.

Howard Fast, the author of *Spartacus*, had been a bestselling author for years when he found himself needing to self-publish his work after his name appeared on Senator McCarthy's black list of communist sympathizers. Notwithstanding the difficulties of promoting, publishing and distributing his work, Fast's *Spartacus* became an instant success. Not only did it reach number one on the New York Times Bestseller List, it also spawned the blockbuster movie by the same name. The book was controversial because of its author and content. McCarthy's followers claimed it was popular reading among Communists.

The actor Kirk Douglas, upset at losing the role of Ben Hur to Charlton Heston in the movie of the same name, bought the screen rights to the book from Howard Fast. Douglas, who had declined the role of Ben Hur's enemy rather than to play second banana to his rival Heston, admitted that his disappointment in losing the role of Ben Hur led him to purchase the rights to *Spartacus*.

Douglas also took the controversial step of hiring Dalton Trumbo, one of the members of the Hollywood Ten, to write the screenplay. Trumbo had been jailed for refusing to cooperate with the House Un-American Activities Committee and had been forced to write scripts under a pseudonym for a decade. Douglas not only hired Trumbo to write the screenplay but also included his name in the movie's credits.

Influential columnist Hedda Hopper denounced Douglas for hiring Trumbo and the American Legion picketed the movie's Los Angeles premiere. Douglas responded by hiring Trumbo to write two more screenplays.

The event marked a turning point in the power of McCarthy's blacklists in Hollywood. And so, in this way, the very real Spartacus from two centuries earlier, helped inspire a bestselling author and a feisty Hollywood actor to collaborate in a way that would help end persecution in twentieth century America.

Jupiter Empowers Aeneas to Start a Roman Nation
From the Borghese Gallery in Rome

This chapter covers the rise of Rome through the Republican period, with coins commemorating great events in Roman and Greek history, ancient gods and the public figures who impacted the events of this period. The coins on these pages include one from an unfortunate senator, Lentulus Clodianus, who was given command of the Senate's legions in 72 BC and was defeated more than once by the slave army of Spartacus. They also include the coin of the Parthian King Orodes II whose general Surenas brought the career and life of the mighty Crassus to an end in 53 BC. Crassus was captured 18 years after his victory over Spartacus by the Parthians at

Carrhae. He was killed by having molten gold poured down his throat. His head was sent to King Orodes as a trophy.

Each year, the Roman Senate would delegate the power to make money to three men, called the *Tirumviri Monetales*, who were given control of the design and production of money during their one year terms. The custom prohibited living individuals from being portrayed but otherwise left the moneyers free to design coins to their liking. The result is a broad and diverse array of coins.

One pair of Roman coins show how subtle the visual messages could be. In 83 BC, a coin was issued by a moneyer appointed by a Senate controlled by seven time consul Gaius Marius to rally Rome against an expected attack by Roman general Lucius Cornelius Sulla. It bears the image of the most powerful of Rome's gods, Jupiter, on one side and the image of a charging chariot on the other. In following year, Sulla issued coins for his marching army that depict Roma on the front and Sulla on a charging chariot being crowned by a winged victory. Sulla won out, defeated the forces of Marius, and purged the Senate.

Sulla's son, Faustus Cornelius Sulla, would later serve the great Magnus Pompey as a general just as Pompey had served Lucius Sulla. To honor his commander, Faustus Sulla issued a coin in 56 BC that displays a replica of the ring Pompey wore to commemorate his three great military victories.

Another Republican coin depicts the sealing of a treaty between the Campanians and Romans who fought together and secured Rome's dominion over the Italian peninsula in the fourth century BC. Another, commemorates the first the vote by ballot in 139 BC with the image of a voter reaching to receive a ballot from an election officer. And one from moneyer Aemilius Paullus remembers the victory of his ancestor Lucius Paullus over the last king of the Macedonia with the image of his predecessor standing proudly next to a military trophy in front of the defeated Macedonian king.

Lictors Bring to Brutus the Bodies of His Sons by Jacques-Louis David 1789

Ten years before he would lead a conspiracy and assassinate Julius Caesar, Marcus Brutus served as a moneyer and issued a coin to honor his famous ancestor Lucius Brutus. In 509 BC, the earlier Brutus drove the ruling Roman King Tarquinius Superbus into exile and then led Rome to self-rule. Lucius Brutus was revered as the father of Republican Rome. So devoted was he to the Republican cause that he ordered the death of his own two sons when they later attempted to restore the monarchy to Rome. Brutus' coin shows his ancestor walking, in Republican fashion, between his protectors, two lictors and an accensus.

Other events critical to the success of Rome are displayed on other coins. One, from Titurius Sabinus, recreates the event that joined the Sabines with the Romans in the eight century BC to form a single Roman community. While under attack from the Sabines, the daughter of the Roman commander offered to betray her people in exchange for what the attacking Sabine warriors wore on their arms, meaning their gold bracelets. The Sabine warriors, instead, threw their shields at her and crushed her to death.

Tradition tells that the Sabines captured the Roman capital but that the Sabine women reconciled the two kings, Tarpeia and Romulus, to ruling together as joint kings. The combination resulted in a single community of Sabines and Romans whose citizens came to be known as Romans. The coin commemorating this seminal event shows the hapless commander's daughter, Tarpeia, being crushed under Roman shields.

The Roman gods appear on many of the coins of this period. Mars and Venus are juxtaposed on one coin from 103 BC just as they are in myth. Mars appears on one side with the goddess Venus, his lover, driving a chariot led by two flying cupids on the other. Greek legends appear on another coin from a moneyer who claimed descent from the god Mercury and the granddaughter of Odysseus. The coin features Mercury and shows the dog Argus recognizing his master Odysseus as he returns home after years of being lost at sea.

Also from this period are coins from the rulers of civilizations outside Rome's boundaries, such as the Remi who served as Julius Caesar's most loyal allies during the Gallic wars and the Virodovix, one of Caesar's aggressive Gallic adversaries. The Remi coin shows three profiles on its front. Many believe one of the profiles depicts their ally Julius Caesar.

From *Intervention of the Sabine Women* by Jacques-Louis David 1799

The great Parthians are represented here too. Their leader Orodes II captured Rome's legionary standards when his army defeated the great Crassus. Orodes portrait appears on his coin bearing the signature forehead wart of the Parthian rulers. So deeply affected were the Roman's by the loss of their standards, that decades later when their return was secured though negotiation, Emperor Augustus issued a coin to commemorate the event.

King Mithradates VI of Pontus thwarted Roman ambitions for decades and is represented on several coins. He saw opportunity in the discord resulting from the great rivalry between Marius and Sulla and rallied Greek opposition to Roman occupation throughout Rome's Greek territories. For decades he was Rome's great adversary, foiling all of Rome's attempts to stop his plans to recreate a Greek empire from Rome's eastern territories. His eventual defeat by Pompey catapulted Pompey to prominence and earned Pompey the name Magnus.

Join Rome's Republican leaders as you follow the narrative on the following pages. Revel with them as they celebrate their accomplishments and history and watch as they struggle to retain a failing Republican system. And see all of this as the Romans did, through the carefully crafted images stamped onto their coins and the coins of their adversaries.

Partial Timeline.

~700 BC Sabines and Romans join together.
509 BC Lucius Brutus overthrows Tarquinius Superbus.
509 BC Roman Republic begins.
290 BC Rome dominates Italy after Third Samnite War.
204 BC Cornelius Scipio leads Roman invasion of Africa.
202 BC Scipio defeats Hannibal at Zama.
200 BC Second Macedonian War begins.
196 BC Rosetta Stone created in Memphis, Egypt.
192 BC Selucid Emperor Antiochus III invades Greece.
191 BC Rome defeats Antiochus at Thermopylae.
171 BC Third Macedonian War begins.
168 BC Paulus defeats Perseus, ends Macedonian War.
167 BC Jewish Maccabes revolt against Seleucids.
146 BC Rome destroys Carthage.
146 BC Rome at war with Numidian Prince Jugurtha.
141 BC Parthians conquer Mesopotamia.
141 BC Independent Jewish kingdom established in Judea.
139 BC First vote by ballot.
135 BC Slave revolt in Sicily begins.
133 BC Rome controls Ephesus, a slave trade center.
133 BC Attalus bequeaths Pergamon to Rome.
111 BC Jugurthine War begins against Numidian ruler.

104 BC Second slave revolt in Sicily begins.
105 BC Jugurtha surrenders to Sulla.
105 BC Germanic forces defeat Rome's legions.
101 BC Second slave revolt ends.
100 BC Gaius Marius assumes control of Rome's legions.
100 BC Julius Caesar is born. Chinese invent paper.
89 BC   Rome's Social War ends.
89 BC   Mithradates invades Roman provinces in Asia.
88 BC   First Mithradatic Wars begins.
88 BC   Sulla becomes consul, then marches on Rome.
87 BC   Marius takes control of Rome.
82 BC   Sulla marches on Rome, becomes dictator.
79 BC   Sulla abdicates and returns to private life.
73 BC   Spartacus leads slave uprising.
72 BC   Spartacus defeats Clodianus' legions.
71 BC   Crassus defeats Spartacus and crucifies survivors.
70 BC   Crassus and Pompey elected consuls.
63 BC   Third Mithradatic War ends.
60 BC   First Triumvirate of Caesar, Pompey and Crassus.
58 BC   Caesar begins conquest of Gaul.
55 BC   Roman war with Parthia begins.
55 BC   Caesar invades Britain.
53 BC   Parthians defeat Crassus at Carrhae.
52 BC   Caesar conquers Gaul, defeats Vercingetorix.
51 BC   Cleopatra and Ptolemy ascend to Egyptian throne.

COINS FEATURED IN THIS CHAPTER.

Slave Rebellion Extinguished, 71 BC
Pinarius Natta, 149 BC

Destruction of Carthage, 3rd to 2nd century BC
Aburius Geminus, 132 BC
Veturius' Oath Scene, 129 BC
Philus & Janus, 119 BC
Vote by Ballot, 113 BC
Blasio & Africanus, 112 BC
Quinctius & Delsutor, 112 to 111 BC
Thorius Balbus, 105 BC
L. Julius Caesar, 103 BC
Cloelius: Marian Victories, 98 BC
The Sabine War, 89 BC
Pergamon, 1st to 2nd century AD
Mithradates of Pontus, 101 to 87 BC
Mithradates & Dionysus, 85 to 65 BC
Gorgon & Nike, Late 2nd to 1st Century BC
Athena, Perseus & Medusa, 85 to 65 BC BC
Ariarathes, 101 to 87 BC
Clodianus, 88 BC
Norbanus, 83 BC
Opposition to Sulla, 83 BC
Sulla's Triumph, 82 BC
Censorinus & Marsysas, 82 BC
Limetanus & Odysseus, 82 BC
Cicero's Rome, 79 BC
Cupid & the Venus Gens, 75 BC
Vestal Virgins, 63 BC
Paullus & Perseus, 62 BC
Juba I, 60 to 46 BC
Amelia Scarus, 58 BC
The Remi, 1st century BC

Virodovix, 57 to 56 BC
Crassus, 54 to 53 BC
Orodes II, 57 to 38 BC
Pompey's Triumph, 56 BC
Q. Cassius Longinus, 55 BC
Marcus Brutus, 54 BC
Rufus & Sulla, 54 BC

Roman, remember by your strength to rule Earth's peoples —
for your arts are to be these: to pacify, to impose the rule of law,
to spare the conquered, and to battle down the proud.

The Aeneid by Virgil
Book VI; 1151–1154

Pinarius Natta
149 BC

The Roman Senate delegated money making to three men, each elected to one-year terms. This "Triumviri Monetales" controlled the design and production of coins for Rome during their term.

In 149 BC, one of those assigned to produce coins was Pinarius Natta who issued this coin with an image of a helmeted Roma on the front and the god Victory on the back riding a biga, or two horse chariot. This was a confident and victorious numismatic statement.

The Romans were fighting their third Punic War with the Carthaginians, who had been the predominant power in the western Mediterranean when the first war began in 264 BC. After suffering momentous defeats and nearly succumbing to the military might of Carthage, the Romans were now, 110 years after the first battles began, near the point of vanquishing their once powerful adversary.

This was a time of war and stress for the Romans. But the Romans had reason for confidence. Their forces had succeeded in subduing their rival eastern Mediterranean adversary in 168, when they defeated the forces of the Macedonian leader Perseus at the Battle of Pydna in Greece. The Roman victory marked the final destruction of Alexander the Great's empire and put the Romans in charge of the Near East.

Now, 19 years later, the Romans initiated a third war with the Carthaginians by sending legions to northern Africa to lay siege to the city of Carthage. The Romans had suffered much in their struggles to replace Carthage as the region's predominate power. Hannibal had succeeded in destroying large Roman armies and occupied the Italian peninsula for years after surprising the Romans with a forced march across the Alps in 218 BC.

Now Rome hoped to exact revenge and subdue their remaining rival for control of the Mediterranean basin. When their legions surrounded Carthage in 149 BC, they prepared for a protracted battle.

Coin details and provenance: Roman Republic. Pinarius Natta, Moneyer. 149 BC. Silver denarius. Rome mint. Obverse: Head of Roma facing right in winged helmet, X behind. Reverse: Victory in a biga moving right, NATTA (TA in monogram) below, ROMA in a linear frame in exurge. 3.556 grams. 18.3mm. References: SRCV I 89, Crawford 208/1, Sydenham 390, RSC I Pinaria 1. Acquired from Forum Ancient Coins, Morehead City, North Carolina in January 2011.

Destruction of Carthage
3ʳᴰ TO 2ᴺᴰ CENTURY BC

The goddess Tanit, who graces this coin, was the patron goddess of Carthage and Phoenician goddess of the Moon. Throughout the ancient world, she was recognized as a symbol of love and fertility.

In 149 BC, one of the last years this coin was last issued, Rome ignited a third and last Punic War with the Carthaginians by sending its legions to lay siege to the city of Carthage. Peace had prevailed for more than 50 years since the Romans defeated their nemesis Hannibal at the Battle of Zama in 201 BC.

After that defeat, Carthage had sued Rome for peace and accepted punishing terms that rendered the once powerful Carthaginians a second-rate military power unable to wage war without Roman consent. Despite this and crushing economic terms, the Carthaginians and Carthage recovered their economic might to become a powerful commercial force in the region.

Using Carthage's defense of its territory against Numidian encroachments as an excuse, Rome declared war. When Rome's legions reached Carthage, they quickly ordered its citizens to abandon their city. When they refused, Rome's legions began a protracted siege.

For three years, the Carthaginians held out against superior forces. Then, in 146 BC, the Romans stormed the city and destroyed it. The city's treasures were looted and its citizens sold into slavery. To complete the destruction, the conquering legions torched the city and watched it burn for 17 days.

The Romans declared that no one would be permitted to build upon the city site again. A thousand years of history, beginning with the city's settlement by the Phoenicians in the first millennium BC, were destroyed in this one catastrophic act of conquest.

In the same year, Rome committed a similar atrocity in Greece, destroying the city of Corinth. The destruction of two great cities sent shock waves through the ancient world and even gave pause to one of the perpetrators of Carthage's destruction. Scipio Aemilianus, the Roman commander at Carthage, wept while he watched the city burn. He worried that Rome was someday destined for a similar fate.

Coin details and provenance: Zeugitania, Carthage. 3rd to 2nd centuries BC. Obverse: Wreathed head of Tanit left, wearing single-pendant earring and necklace. Reverse: Horse standing right, raising foreleg; long caduceus behind. 10.46 grams. 23 mm. References: SNG Copenhagen 327; Müller 254. Acquired from Atlantis Quality Ancient Coins in January 2004.

ABURIUS GEMINUS
132 BC

One of the few restrictions imposed on the Triumviri Monetales who were appointed by the Roman Senate each year to mint coins was the prohibition against portraying a living person on a coin, which was considered a monarchial practice. This coin issued by M. Aburius Geminus contains no human image but still conveyed a message of pride and military strength to Rome's citizens.

Like the earlier coin from moneyer Piniarus Natta, this coin displays the helmeted god Roma portrayed on the front. The back shows the god Sol driving a chariot drawn by four horses to the East. The intended purpose was to commemorate the establishment of Roman rule in Asia Minor the year before when Pergamon's King Attalus III died and bequeathed his kingdom to Rome.

While the legitimacy of the bequest was questioned by would-be heirs to the throne and some members of the Senate questioned the wisdom of accepting the bequest, Rome eventually secured the territory with troops and took control of the region. The kingdom included all of the Seleucid territories in Asia Minor that had earlier been rewarded to the Attalids for their support of Rome during the Third Macedonian War.

The year when this coin was issued, 132 BC, was also eventful in its own right. It saw the end of the first major slave uprising on the Italian peninsula - the First Servile War.

A Syrian slave named Eunus led the revolt in Sicily, which was full with slaves brought in to harvest grain. Eunus rose to prominence in the rebellion through his reputation as a prophet and wonder-worker. He was said to receive visions from a goddess and to blow fire from his mouth. The slaves he led stormed and took the Sicilian city of Enna and crowned Eunus their king. He took the Seleucid name of Antiochus.

His kingdom was short lived, however. In same year, Roman legions defeated the slave uprising and Eunus fled to a cavern where he was later captured.

The year also saw the assassination of the tribune Tiberius Gracchus, who the year before had unsuccessfully attempted to pass a law to redistribute public land to benefit small landowners. Many historians mark the beginning of the decline of the Roman Republic to the year 132 BC and the assassination of Tiberius Gracchus.

Coin details and provenance: M. Aburius Geminus. 132 BC. AR denarius. Obverse: Helmeted head of Roma right; GEM behind; star below chin. Reverse: Sol in quadriga right, holding reins and whip; below, M.A_BV_RI; in exergue, ROMA. 3.88 grams. Acquired from Twelve Caesars Coins in April of 2001.

Veturius' Oath Scene
129 BC

This coin from Tiberius Veturius in 129 BC depicts the sealing of an oath between a Campanian and a Roman soldier. In the fashion of the time, the soldiers stand on either side of a kneeling priest who prepares a pig for sacrifice. The helmeted head of Mars, Roman god of war, appears on the other side of the coin.

The reference is to a fourth century BC alliance between Romans and Campanians that helped the Romans achieve dominance over the Italian peninsula. The Greek Campanians, who made their capital at Capua, joined the Romans to stave off a Samnite invasion. The Macedonians of King Philip II were probably more likely allies for the Campanians but were preoccupied with the Persians at the time.

The first of three Samnite Wars began in 325 BC and continued off and on for three decades. The last Samnite War, which began in 289 BC, saw a confederation of Samnites, Etruscans, Umbrians and Gauls united against the Romans and Campanians.

Rome and its allies prevailed in the end, winning a critical battle at Sanrinum in 295 BC and forcing a full surrender in 290 BC. With the war concluded, Rome consolidated its control over the Italian peninsula, making it a force to be reckoned with on the world stage.

In 129 BC, when this coin was issued, Rome finally secured its Asian province by defeating the pretender to the Pergamon throne who had taken control the year Attalus III died. The pretender, Eumenes III, did everything in his power to thwart Roman plans for annexation until he was defeated in battle by Marcus Perperna, Rome's consul the preceding year.

Eumenes desperate attempts to retain Pergamon included promises of freedom to occupied Greek city-states who would support his claims. When this failed he expanded his promises to include freedom to slaves who joined his cause. The philospher Gaius Blossius, who had supported Roman Tiberius Gracchus in his failed attempts at land reform, joined Eumenes in his lost cause.

Coin details and provenance: Roman Republic. Gens Veturia, Tiberius Veturius, Moneyer. 129 BC. Silver denarius. Obverse: TLVET and X behind the crested helmeted head of Mars left, with aigrette. Reverse: Oath scene. (ROMA) above a Campanian and a Roman soldier either side of a priest (sacerdos facialis) kneeling and holding a pig to be sacrificed. 3.93 grams. 18.79 mm. Reference: Bab 1, Syd 527. References: F.S. Knobloch, Special list, 3-22-1967, Lot 102. Acquired from WCNC in January 2005.

Philus & Janus
119 BC

This coin from the moneyer Furius Philus in 119 BC honors the great Roman god Janus and reflects on a constant in the life of Republican Rome, war. The front of the coin bears the image of Janus facing the past and the future. On the back is the goddess Roma standing with a spear and placing a wreath on a trophy of Gallic arms.

Janus was the Roman god of gateways, doors, beginnings, endings and time. His two heads gave him the unique ability to see the past and the future at the same time. According to tradition, he received this ability as a gift from Saturn in return for hospitality he had shown the god. Saturn was an important god in Rome's pantheon, frequently associated with Jupiter.

Janus was the god of home entrances, gates, bridges and passages. He was the Roman patron of beginnings, both concrete and abstract. In this role, he symbolized change and transitions in religious matters, human life, historical ages and business enterprises. As a symbol of change and transition, Janus represented the progression of the past to the future, the maturing of young people, and the change from one condition to another. As such, he was worshiped at plantings, at harvests, at marriages, deaths and times of change.

Because he could see both the past and the future, he also represented time itself and the inevitability of change. The Romans named the first month of their year after Janus - January. A "Janus Quirinus" stood in the Roman Forum and consisted of walled enclosure with gates of Janus on each end believed to have been consecrated by Rome's second king.

When Rome was at war the two doors were left open. They were closed only in times of peace, which were infrequent in ancient Rome. Livy reported the doors being closed only twice between the sixth century BC and the beginning of the first century AD, in 235 BC following the conclusion of the First Punic War and in 31 BC following Octavian's victory over Marc Antony and Cleopatra at the Battle of Actium.

Coin details and provenance: Roman Republic. M. Furius L.f. Philus. 119 BC. Silver denarius. Obverse: Laureate head of Janus, M. FOVRI. L. F around. Reverse: Roma standing left, holding spear and wreath; to left, trophy of Gallic arms and a carnyx; star above, ROMA to right, PHIL in exergue. 3.78 grams. 20mm. References: Crawford 281/1; Furia 18. Ex-Joseph C. Blazick collection. Acquired from Imperial Coins and Artifacts, New York, New York in March 2011.

Vote by Ballot
113 BC

This coin, issued by moneyer Publius Nerva in 113 BC, commemorates the introduction of ballot voting to Republican Rome three decades earlier when C. Licinius Crassus brought together the 35 tribes of Rome into separate enclosures to vote in the comitia tributa for the election of magistrates. This was a major change from the practice of voting by open declaration.

The front of this coin bears a profile of a helmeted Roma holding a spear and shield. A crescent and a star appear in the background. The reverse depicts the historic first vote by ballot. In the scene, the voter on the left reaches to receive his ballot from an election officer. From there, he walks across a raised platform to the ballot box so that, as depicted on the right side of the coin, he is visible to everyone as he votes. The horizontal lines depict barriers that separate the voting stations.

This voting innovation made it easier for citizens to vote their preferences by making their votes more confidential. But it did not make all voters equal. By tradition, elections were held in the city of Rome and citizens from outside the city, the 31 rural tribes, had to travel to Rome to vote. The wealthy and powerful also voted first, meaning that lesser citizens often had to wait long hours for the opportunity to cast their vote, discouraging many from exercising their right.

In 113 BC, when this coin was issued, Gnaeus Papirius Carbo and Caecilius Metellus Caprarius served as Rome's consul. During the year, the Cimbrians advanced from Gaul into northern Italy and Carbo was sent with an army to confront them. He and his legions, however, were soundly defeated and put to flight. Accusations followed, including some from Marcus Antonius Orator, the grandfather of Marc Antony. Disgraced, Carbo took his life by swallowing poison.

Caprarius had served with Scipio Aemilianus, the Roman general who commanded the siege of Carthage, in his 133 BC campaign to take Numantia in northern Spain. An eight-month blockade reduced the city to starvation and secured Roman control. Caprarius also saw military success in Thrace in 111 BC and in 102 BC would serve as a Senatorial censor with his cousin Quintus Caecilius Metellus Numidicus.

Coin details and provenance: Republican Rome. Publius Nerva moneyer. Vote by Ballot. 113 BC. Silver denarius. Obverse: Bust of Roma left holding a spear and shield, crescent above, "ROMA" behind and star in front. Reverse: "[P] NERVA" above three citizens voting in the comitium. 3.78 grams. References: Licinia 7. Acquired from Aegean Numismatics, Mentor, Ohio in June 2005.

BLASIO & AFRICANUS
112 TO 111 BC

Issued in 112 BC or 111 BC by moneyer Cornelius Blasio, this coin depicts a helmeted Scipio Africanus or Gnaeus Cornelius Blasio. The youthful features suggest the profile of Africanus, a leading contributor to Rome's success during the Punic wars. But the portrait may have been intended to refer to the moneyer's ancestor, Blasio the Elder, who helped to prosecute the First Punic War.

On the back is a depiction of the Capitoline Triad, the three supreme gods of Rome who were worshiped in an elaborate temple on Rome's Capitoline Hill that stood between the Forum and the Campus Martius. Jupiter, the patron deity of Rome, stands between his sister Juno to the right and daughter Minerva to the left. In the temple, each god had a separate chamber, with Jupiter in the center and Juno and Minerva to his sides as depicted on the coin.

Publius Cornelius Scipio, later called Africanus in honor of his great victory over Hannibal at the Battle of Zama, was the great Roman hero of the Second Punic War. Born to a patrician family with a distinguished history dating from the founding days of

Rome's Republic, Scipio was born by Caesarian section into a world where Rome's very existence was challenged by the armies of Carthage. At age 17 in 218 BC, he saved his father's life at the Battle of Ticinus, the first of three disastrous battles survived by the young Scipio. According to the Greek historian Polybius, Scipio charged the force encircling his father "with reckless daring" to secure his rescue.

He is said to have stormed into a meeting with friends and held Roman leaders at sword-point to prevent a surrender of Rome to the Carthagenians. In 211 BC, at the age of 24, he alone volunteered to lead an army to confront the Carthagenians in Spain. Both his father and uncle had died there just the year before while battling the forces of Hasdrubal Barca. Africanus succeeded against great odds, defeating Hasdrubal and eventually driving the Carthagenian commanders out of Spain.

From there he traveled to northern Africa in 206 BC and then to Rome where he was elected as a consul, Rome's highest office. In 202 BC, after raising his own army in Sicily, Scipio met and defeated the army of Hannibal at the Battle of Zama. When he returned to Rome, he was given the name Africanus in recognition of his great victory.

Coin details and provenance: Republican Rome. Cn. Cornelius Blasio moneyer. 112-111 BC. AR denarius. Obverse: Helmeted head of Scipio Africanus or Blasio the Elder facing right; star above and branch behind; missing legend N BLASIO CN F around. Reverse: Jupiter standing between Juno and Minerva; BAL monogram between Jupiter and Minerva; ROMA below. 3.78 grams. References: Crawford 296/1h; Albert 1084. Ex. Künker 153. Acquired from Moneta Nova, Bremen, Germany in February 2011.

QUINCTIUS & DELSUTOR
112 TO 111 BC

Also from the years 112 to 111 BC comes this coin from moneyer and patrician Titus Quincitius. The coin bears the image of Hercules facing right and holding a club. On the back is a desultor riding two prancing horses above a rat with the moneyer's initials to each side - TI and Q.

In ancient times a desultor, or "one who leaps down," was a person skilled at jumping from one moving horse to another or from a moving chariot to a horse. Roman desultors rode bareback and vaulted between two or more moving horses. They were so popular in the Roman circus and in Roman games that Roman men of the highest classes often exhibited these skills at Roman celebrations.

The desultors performed at the great Ludi Romani, a religious festival held in Rome to honor Jupiter in September from as early as 509 BC. By 366 BC, the games had expanded from a single day festival and were held annually. By the time this coin was issued, the festival lasted between 10 and 14 days, beginning on September 5. The games were generally timed to begin after Rome's legions returned from the field in the early fall.

A solemn procession was followed by a great chariot race to kick off each festival. In the Homeric tradition each chariot carried a driver and warrior, with the warrior jumping from the chariot at the end to continue a foot race. The festival included drama and many other celebrations.

On the Ides of September (September 13), a great ritual feast called the Epulum Jovis was held. The gods were formally invited to the feast and attended through their statues, which were arranged at the most honorable spots of the tables. Food was served to both the human and deified guests. Priests, called epulones, conducted the feast and acted as proxies for the gods by eating the food served to them.

When this coin was issued, Roman forces contended against adversaries on multiple fronts. Germanic tribes, the Numidians and the Celtiberians all challenged Roman interests.

Coin details and provenance: Roman Republic, T. Quinctius. 112-111 BC. AR denarius. Obverse: Bust of Hercules seem from behind, head to left club above right shoulder. Reverse: Desultor to left; behind, ·S. Below horses, TI – Q on sides of rat right; in exergue, D·S·S incuse on tablet. 3.64 grams. 20 mm. Reference: Crawford 297/1b. Ex-Joseph C. Blazick collection. Acquired from Imperial Coins & Artifiacts, New York, New York in March 2011.

Thorius Balbus
105 BC

This coin, from moneyer Thorius Balbus in 105 BC, features the goddess Juno wearing a goat skin headdress. Juno was the wife of Jupiter and protector of Rome. Her appearance pays homage to Rome's legions, who frequently wore goat skin while on campaign. On the back is a charging bull and the name of the moneyer.

The depiction of Juno in a goat skin headdress reflects how active Rome's legions were at the time. For almost a decade, Rome's legions had been engaged in defending the German borders. At the same time, Roman legions were fighting Jugurtha, the Numidian ruler of North Africa.

The Roman Senate had declared war on Jugurtha in 112 BC and sent consul Lucius Bestia with an army to Numidia. Jugurtha surrendered, but on such favorable terms that the Roman Senate suspected bribery. When Jugurtha was called to Rome to account for himself he bribed two tribunes to avoid testifying. He later defeated legions led by Roman praetor

Aulus Albinus in 10 BC and 109 BC, apparently again using bribery to achieve his ends.

The ambitious Gaius Marius secured command of Rome's African troops in 107 BC, hoping to win glory and increase his power by defeating Jugurtha. Before he could succeed, however, his cavalry commander Lucius Sulla captured Jugurtha. This earned Sulla the acclaim of Rome and the lifelong enmity of his commander. The two ambitious men would later bring Rome its first civil wars.

The year 105 BC also saw Rome's legions suffer a significant defeat in its northern campaigns. In October, two Roman armies under command of consul Gnaeus Maximus and proconsul Quintus Caepio came upon a force of the Cimbri and Tuetone near the Rhône River.

An advance Roman force was intercepted and destroyed by the Cimbri. The two Roman commanders then quarreled over command and kept their two camps separate. When Maximus dispatched an envoy to the Cimbri commander, Caepio feared a double cross and attacked the Cimbri. His army was destroyed and his camp overrun. The Cimbri then destroyed the legions of Maximus. Very few Romans escaped.

Coin details and provenance: Roman Republic. L. Thorius Balbus. 105 BC. Denarius. Obverse: Juno wearing goat's skin. Reverse: Bull charging right. 3.85 grams. Reference: RSC Thoria 1. Juno was the wife of Jupiter and protector of Rome. Acquired from Nilus Coins, Austin, Texas in August 2009.

L. JULIUS CAESAR
103 BC

This coin was issued by moneyer Lucius Julius Caesar in 103 BC, 50 years before a more famous Julius Caesar crossed the Rubicon and brought the Roman Republic to an end.

The coin celebrates the gens, or family, of the Caesars by honoring their chosen ancestor, the goddess Venus. Mars, the lover of Venus and god of young men and war, adorns the front of the coin. Venus, the goddess of love and sexual desire, appears on the back in a chariot being drawn by two cupids. In Roman mythology, Venus was married to Vulcan, romantically involved with Mars, and the mother of Cupid.

When this coin was issued, Rome and the Republic were under considerable threat. Germanic tribes had invaded the Italian peninsula and threatened the city of Rome itself. And a second slave war, led by a flute player named Salvius, was raging in Sicily.

To counter the threats, Gaius Marius reorganized Rome's citizen army into a full-time professional force. This strengthened

Rome's defenses and enabled Rome to defeat the Germanic invaders and subdue the slave crisis in Sicily.

Roman consul Manius Aquilius, who is honored by his grandson on a coin featured on page 145 at the beginning of this chapter, led the legions who defeated the slave army in Sicily. The slave army numbered 20,000 foot soldiers and 2,000 cavalry.

The standing army that made these successes possible, however, created a new power base in Roman politics. It made the military a potent force in civil life and made the command of an army a route to political power in Rome. Within 20 years, Rome's Republican rule would falter and Gaius Marius and Lucius Sulla would be locked in a power struggle. Their supporters would clash and Sulla would eventually march his legions on Rome and take dictatorial control of the Republic.

Coin details and provenance: Republican Rome. L. Julius L.f Caesar. 103 BC. Denarius. Rome mint. Obverse: Head of Mars, CAESAR behind. Reverse: Venus Genetrix in biga drawn by two cupids, before them lyre, with L IVLI L F in exergue. Cut in obverse. 3.91 grams. References: Cr-320/1, Syd-593a, Julia 4. Acquired from Harlan J. Berk, Ltd., Chicago, Illinois in October 2005.

CLOELIUS: MARIAN VICTORIES
98 BC

This silver quinarius struck in 98 BC by moneyer Titus Cloelius was issued to commemorate the military victories of Gaius Marius. Its issuer was a member of the Marian faction and is remembered for being later tried and acquitted of his father's murder.

On the front of his coin he portrays the laureate head of Jupiter, Rome's greatest god. On the back he shows Victory holding a crown up to a war trophy with a seated captive below. A carynx, or bronze trumpet common to Rome's Celtic adversaries, also appears in the field.

Gaius Marius was a Roman statesman and general who served an unprecedented seven terms in Rome's highest office of consul. His military reforms, undertaken to strengthen the Republic's military at a time when there were great external threats to Rome, changed forever the balance of power within the Republic.

Shortly after being elected consul in 107 BC and fearing a barbarian invasion, Marius set about reducing the status and wealth requirements for service in the military. At the time, only citizens of the fifth census class and above who had property worth at least 3,000 sesterces could qualify to serve. Soldiers were required to provide their own uniforms and weapons. Marius removed the property requirement and relaxed the recruitment standards to admit all citizens, regardless of census class.

This created a larger military to protect Rome from external threats. It also attracted the poor to the army who served alongside their wealthier comrades. The poorer recruits were motivated by the prospect of conquest and the opportunities it afforded them to settle in conquered lands. Loyalties to commanders became strong among these dependent citizen legionnaires.

About a decade after this celebratory coin was issued, and after Marius successfully defended Rome with Sulla in the Social Wars that engulfed the Italian peninsula, Marius attempted to overrule Sulla's appointment to lead Rome's forces against Mithradates in the East. Although he succeeded, Sulla's armies refused to accept a new commander and marched on Rome itself. Marius tried to mount a meaningful defense with an army of gladiators but was easily defeated and fled the city.

Coin details and provenance: Roman Republic. Titus Cloelius. AR silver quinarius. 98 BC. Obverse: Laureate head of Jupiter right, dot H before head. Reverse: Victory crowning trophy, carnyx and captive below, T CLOVELI (EL in monogram), Q in exergue. Reference: RCV 212. Struck to commemorate Gaius Marius' victories. 1.7 grams. 15mm. Acquired from Incitatus Coins and Antiquities, St. Johns NL, Canada in March 2011.

THE SABINE WAR
89 BC

With this coin, Roman moneyer Titurius Sabinus reminds Romans in 89 BC of the historic part his ancestors played in the formation of Rome. It recounts an event from the founding of Rome that Romans considered part of their heritage.

The front of the coin depicts the profile of Tatius, an early king of the Sabines and member of the moneyer's family, whose exploits during the 8th century BC led to the conquest of Rome and combination of the Sabines and the Romans into one people. On the back, the murder of Roman traitor Tarpeia is depicted as she is crushed by Sabine shields.

According to the legend, the early Romans and their King Romulus were attacked by neighboring Sabine King Tatius. During the battles that ensued, Tarpeia, the daughter of the commander of Rome's defensive citadel, approached the Sabine camp and offered to betray her people in exchange for the gold bracelets worn by the attacking Sabine warriors.

Tarpeia reportedly offered to lead them safely into Rome in exchange for what they wore on their left arms. In response, the

Sabine troops threw the heavy shields they also wore on their left arms onto Tarpia and crushed her to death. Her body was then tossed off the Tarpeian Rock, which thereafter became the traditional place where Rome's traitors were executed.

Tradition tells that Tatius succeeded in capturing Rome but was convinced by the Sabine women to rule the combined people jointly with the defeated Roman King Romulus. The combined people became a single Roman community. As reported by Roman historian Livy, Tatius died five years after his conquest, leaving Romulus the sole ruler of an expanded Roman people.

Coin details and provenance: Roman Republic. L. Titurius L.f. Sabinus. 89 BC. Denarius. Obverse: Tatius head right, SABIN in left field. Reverse: Tarpeia buried to waist in shields by two warriors, LTITVR below. 4.04 grams. References: RSC Tituria 4. Acquired from Nilus Coins, Austin, Texas in July 2009.

PERGAMON
1ST TO 2ND CENTURY AD

This coin from Rome's Eastern province of Pergamon was issued in the first or second century AD after the fall of the Roman Republic. It is displayed here because of its depiction of a Roman senator on the left and because, in 88 BC, Pergamon became the site of the first major offensive against Rome from a Roman province.

At the time, Pergamon was fully absorbed into the Roman Empire following its transfer to Rome 50 years earlier by Attalus III. And since its conquest, a large population of Roman settlers had moved to the territory to make their fortunes.

The locals suffered under the occupation. Here and throughout conquered Greece, Roman merchants, slave traders, tax collectors and government officials lived among the natives without blending in. Many lived on land acquired from natives who had been impoverished by excessive Roman taxes. Resentment ran high.

When Mithradates, the eastern prince from Pontus, organized a plot to revenge Roman atrocities, native citizens of Pergamon and many Greco-Asian cities participated. In the spring of 88 BC, on command from Mithradates, citizens throughout the region rose up and slaughtered the Italians living amongst them.

In city after city, Romans were gathered up and murdered - men, women and children alike. More than 80,000 Romans were reported killed. Rome lost its Asian revenues and plunged into recession. And Mithradates expanded his rule from Pontus on the Black Sea to include Greece and Pergamon.

The city of Pergamon had also been home to a great library that was constructed during the reign of Eumenes II, who ruled Pergamon from 197 to 159 BC. His library was said by Plutarch to have included as many as 200,000 volumes, making it second in the ancient world only to the Library of Alexandria.

Legend has it that Marc Antony absconded with the contents of Pergamon's library and gave all 200,000 volumes to Cleopatra to make amends for the great fire that destroyed the Library of Alexandria during Caesar's battles with her brother's legions. Pergamon is also credited with being the city where parchment was developed as an alternative to papyrus.

Coin details and provenance: Quasi-autonomous. First to second Century AD. Head of Senate / head of Roma, Pergamon. Pergamon, Mysia. Obverse: ΘEON CYNKΛHTON, draped bust of Roman Senate right. Reverse: ΘEAN POMHN, draped and turreted bust of Roma right. 3.65 grams. 16 to 17 mm. References: SNG Aulock 1385. Acquired from Rutten & Wieland, Worblaufen, Switzerland in February 2010.

MITHRADATES OF PONTUS
120 TO 63 BC

Mithradates VI Eupator rallied the Greeks of Asia and Greece from his home city of Pontus on the Black Sea to oppose the Romans and contest their occupation of historically Greek territories.

An astute and charismatic leader, Mithradates took advantage of Roman preoccupation with civil war and the deep dislike of Romans in the occupied territories to rally Greeks to armed resistance. He fancied himself a latter-day Alexander the Great who would reunite the Greeks to greater glory. He even dressed like Alexander at official functions.

Mithradates made extensive use of coins to ignite Greek pride and cement his claim as the Greek leader. Here, he reissues the classic Alexander coin, portraying himself in the position of Alexander as Herakles wearing a lion skin headdress. On the back, the Greek god Zeus appears just as he did on Alexanders' coins, sitting on a throne and holding an eagle.

Mithradates issued a wide variety of coins to influence public opinion. His coins conveyed messages of Greek pride and solidarity. Many of them used the gods to remind Greeks of their common heritage, their right to independence, and their ability to resist Rome through cooperation.

On one, the god Dionysus who was outlawed by Romans because of her association with rebellion is prominently displayed. Another shows the terrifying Gorgon on a shield and the Greek personification of victory in the goddess Nike. And still another depicts a story of cooperation among Greek gods and heroes to accomplish a great victory when the hero Perseus slayed Medusa and released the Pegasus from her dying body.

This extensive use of coins as a means of political persuasion reflects the power of coins to communicate. Abundant in number and widely distributed, coins were the first widely distributed media capable of shaping public opinion. As you will see, Mithradates was a master in harnessing the power of coins to persuade and unify the Greeks.

Coin details and provenance: Kings of Pontus, Mithradates VI Eupator. 120 to 63 BC. AR tetradrachm, Odessos mint. Struck in the name of Alexander III of Macedonia, circa 80 to 70 BC. Obverse: Head of Herakles right, with the features of Mithradates VI of Pontus, wearing lion skin. Reverse: Zeus Aëtophoros seated left; ΛAK to inner left, OΔH in exergue. 16.08 grams. 28 mm. References: Price 1192. Acquired from Ancient Numismatic Enterprise, Toronto, Ontario, Canada in June 2010.

MITHRADATES & DIONYSUS
85 TO 65 BC

The most dangerous adversary of Rome and mastermind of the slaughter of tens of thousands of Roman's living in Greece and Ionia in 88 BC, Mithradates adorned this coin with the provocative image of Dionysus, the Greek god banned by the Roman Senate because of its association with slave revolts and rebellion. On the back is a cista mystica, or ceremonial basket used to house snakes used in initiation ceremonies of the Dionysian cult.

Mithradates ruled an empire that included Pontus, Cappadocia, Paphlagonia, and much of the Black Sea coast. Claiming descent from both Alexander the Great and Persian King Darius I, Mithradates was a formidable man with, according to Pliny the Elder, a prodigious memory and the ability to speak 22 languages.

For a quarter of a century, he conquered Roman provinces and frustrated Rome's quest for expansion. In the first of three extended wars, Mithradates acquired most of Asia Minor before eventually conceding Greece to the Romans.

In the second war, instituted by Sulla's lieutenant Lucius Murena in 83 BC, Mithradates repelled the invading Romans to bring an uneasy peace to the region. Roman aggression resurfaced in 74 BC with another attack against Mithradates. Finally, after nine long years of conflict in this third war, Roman general Pompey drove Mithradates east until he fled, defeated, to the last of his provinces in the Crimea.

The victory did much to advance Pompey's career. He had done what others could not by vanquishing Rome's great enemy. When he returned to Rome, his reputation was so enhanced that his commander Sulla was compelled to permit him to enter the city in Triumph. It was this great victory that earned Pompey the title of Magnus.

Coin details and provenance: Mithradiates VI, The Great. Pontos-Amisos. 85 to 65 BC. AE21. Obverse: Head of Mithradates VI as Dionysos, wearing ivy wreath. Reverse: ΑΜΙΟΣΥ Cista mystica on which rests panther skin and thyrsos. Monogram in left field. References: SNG BMC Black Sea 1208; Waddington pg. 66, 24. Acquired from Beast Coins, New Berlin, Wisconsin in March 2004.

Gorgon & Nike
Late 2ⁿᵈ to early 1ˢᵗ century BC

The Hellenized king from Pontus, Mithradates, used images on his coins that his Greek subjects could understand. Here he deploys the image of the terrifying Greek god Gorgon on a shield of Zeus to convey Greek might and power. On the back is Nike, the Greek personification of victory and triumph holding a palm branch. As Mithradates extended his influence throughout Greece, these twin images would convey his power to confront Rome and his allegiance to Greek traditions.

The Gorgon was a vicious female monster with living venomous snakes for hair and fangs for teeth. Homer describes her in the *Iliad* as a dread and awful monster encased in a tasseled aegis. The aegis was the mythological shield of Zeus that was fashioned by the Greek equivalent of Vulcan, Hephaestus. When Zeus shook the aegis, dark clouds would envelop Mount Ida, thunder would roll, and men would be stricken with fear.

Nike, who is depicted on the reverse, was a goddess and companion of Zeus who could fly and run at great speed. She personified victory and triumph and was worshiped in conjunction with Athena, particularly after the Greeks defeated the Persians at the Battle of Marathon. She was also known for presiding over military and athletic contests.

Coin details and provenance: Time of Mithradates. Late 2nd to early 1st Century BC. Pontos-Amisos. Obverse: (No legend) Aegis with gorgon's head at center. Reverse: AMI | SOU with Nike advancing right, long palm branch in both hands over shoulder, monograms in left and right fields. 8.18 grams. 21mm. References: Sear GCV, Vol II, 3642. Acquired from Beast Coins, New Berlin, Wisconsin in May 2006.

ATHENA, PERSEUS & MEDUSA
85 TO 65 BC

This is another coin with a message: Greek cooperation with a Greek hero can work wonders. Here, Mithradates repeats a story of cooperation among Greek gods and heroes as he portrays the helmeted head of Athena with the hero Perseus who stands victorious over the Gorgon Medusa.

The story, known to all Greeks, has the goddess Athena instructing Perseus on how to find the three sisters of the three Gorgons. These three sisters, the Graeae, were ancient women who shared one eye and one tooth that they passed among themselves. Perseus snatched the eye and held it ransom until the blinded Graeae told him how to kill Medusa and where to find the Hesperides.

The Hesperides gave him a knapsack to contain Medusa's head while Zeus contributed a sword and Hade's invisibility helmet. Perseus borrowed winged sandals from Hermes and a polished shield from Athena.

When he entered the Gorgons' cave, he used the shield to safely view Medusa's reflection and cut off her head. When he struck the blow, Pegasus the flying horse and a golden bow sprang from Medusa's neck. The other two Gorgon's chased Perseus but were unable to do him harm because of his helmet of invisibility.

The coin shows Athena wearing a helmet with a Pegasus ornament and Perseus holding the head of Medusa above her decapitated corpse. The message is of Greek pride and the power of Greeks to dispel the Romans through cooperation.

Coin details and provenance: Paphlagonia, Sinope. Athena/Perseus with the Head of Medusa. 85 to 65 B.C. Obverse: Head of Athena facing right, wearing triple-crested helmet, ornamented with Pegasos. Reverse: Perseus standing, facing, holding harpa and the head of Medusa, whose decapitated body lies at his feet; ΣΙΝΩ-ΠΗΣ across field; ME monogram to left. 17.87 grams. 31 mm. References: SNG Von Aulock 228. Adjustment marks. Acquired from Herakles Numismatics, Charlotte, North Carolina in June 2010.

ARIARATHES
101 TO 87 BC

This coin was issued by the son of Mithradates who intermittently ruled ancient Cappadocia, an area roughly corresponding to the territory of modern-day Turkey. The profile on the coin bears a striking resemblance to Mithradates, the power behind the Cappadocian throne.

Ariarathes' story illustrates the unsettled state of Rome's eastern border and Mithradate's frustration with Rome. Mithradates first installed his son on the Cappadocian throne in 101 BC to extend his own rule over the territory. Ariarathes was eight years old at the time. The assassination of the existing Cappadoican, King Ariarathes VII, had given Mithradates the opportunity to install his son.

After a brief rule, the Cappadocian nobles revolted and replaced Ariarathes with a Cappadocian. Mithradates quickly expelled the Cappadocian and restored his son to the throne.

The Roman Senate intervened in 95 BC and ordered Mithradates son to be deposed. After a short rule by Rome's candidate and then a Cappadocian favorite, Mithradates' ally Tigranes expelled the Cappadocian ruler. Mithradates son was again reinstated. He was later deposed for a fourth time by the Romans in 89 BC.

Mithradates' frustration with Roman meddling found other vehicles for expression after his son's last expulsion from Cappadocia. It was the very next year that Mithradates orchestrated the mass murder of Roman citizens throughout their Eastern provinces. Through a remarkably coordinated effort in several Greek city-states, as many as 80,000 Romans were rounded up and murdered in an act that shocked Rome and changed the region's balance of power for decades.

Ariarathes died the following year, in 87 BC, fighting for his father.

Coin details and provenance: Ariarathes IX Eusebos Philopator of Cappadocia. 101 to 87 BC. AR drachm. Obverse: Diademed head of king right, with features resembling his father Mithradates VI of Pontos. Reverse: Athena standing left, holding Nike right, spear and shield on right, surrounded by the kings name and titles in Greek. In exergue the date IΓ (= 13 = 88 BC). 3.97 grams. 22 mm. References: Sear 7299; SNG Cop. 144. Acquired from Gault Coins, Halden, Norway in August 2007.

CLODIANUS
88 BC

This coin bearing the likeness of Mars on one side and Victory leading a chariot on the other was minted in 88 BC, the same year that Mithradates orchestrated the mass murder of Romans throughout Greece and Pergamon.

Sixteen years later, in 72 BC, the Roman who minted this coin, Lentulus Clodianus, was appointed consul and given command of four of Rome's legions to defeat an army of gladiators and slaves that were rampaging through the Italian peninsula in what would come to be called the Third Servile War. Clodianus marched his legions south from Rome to confront a growing slave army that was commanded by Spartacus, Crixus, and Oenomaus, gladiators who had escaped from the gladiatorial school of Lentulus Batiatus in Capua.

At the same time, consular general Gellius Publicola attempted to close on Spartacus from the south. Spartacus attacked and defeated Clodianus and then turned and dispatched the legions of Publicola.

After learning the news, the Senate removed Clodianus and Publicola from command. Their replacement, the wealthy and ambitious Marcus Licinius Crassus, marched south the next year with eight legions to confront the slave army. Boxed in by the legions of Magnus Pompey and Marcus Lucullus who approached from the south, Spartacus threw his slave army at the superior forces of Crassus and was destroyed.

To mark his conquest and strike fear into the slave population of the Italian peninsula, Crassus marched the defeated slave army from the battlefield 350 miles along the Appian Way toward Rome. As they force marched the slaves to Rome, Crassus crucified 6,000 slaves by the side of the road, leaving their bodies to rot on their crosses.

Crassus left this grizzly reminder for all Roman citizens and slaves to see along one of Rome's most active and famous thoroughfares. To avoid inciting the captives under this command during the forced march to Rome, Crassus carefully spaced the crucifixions far enough apart so that the screams of the prisoners left behind to be crucified could not be heard by their marching compatriots.

Lentulus Clodianus survived the humiliation of his defeat by Spartacus' army to serve Pompey years later in 67 BC as a commander in his navy. Pompey had been charged with clearing the Mediterranean Sea from pirates. Clodianus patrolled the Adriatic Sea east of the Italian peninsula.

Coin details and provenance: Gnaeus Corneluis Lentulus Clodianus. 88 BC. Silver denarius. Obverse: Helmeted, crested head of Mars facing right. Reverse: CN LENTVL in exergue. Victory in biga galloping right. 15 mm. References: C. 354/1; S. 702 B. Cornelia 50. Acquired from Hixenbavgh Ancient Art, New York, New York in December 2006.

NORBANUS
83 BC

Gaius Norbanus was a notable Roman whose life illustrates the uncertainty and violence that characterized the Republic as its institutions began to decline. His coin from 83 BC features the profile of Venus, goddess of love and beauty, with his name beneath. The back shows an ear of grain, a fasces and caduecus, the latter two being symbols of power and jurisdiction.

Early in his career, Gaius Norbanus avoided conviction for treason through the eloquence of Marcus Antonius Orator, the grandfather of Marc Antony. Norbanus had been charged with creating disturbances that caused the conviction and exile of Caepio the Elder, great grandfather to Marcus Brutus.

Later, while serving as praetor in 89 BC, Norbanus was responsible for defending Sicily against the aggressions of twelve Italian tribes determined to create an independent state. Assisting in the defense were legions commanded by L. Julius Caesar, Lucius Sulla, Gaius Marius and Pompeius Strabo, the father of Magnus Pompey.

Sulla's successes in these actions helped him gain the notoriety that led to his first election as consul in 88 BC. When Sulla later attempted to return to the Eastern front, he was thwarted by intrigue and violence in the Senate, engineered by his rival Gaius Marius. This caused Sulla to flee to his legions outside Rome. When Sulla returned to Rome with his army in 87 BC, Norbanus sided with Marius.

During the second war with Sulla in 83 BC, Norbanus met Sulla's troops at the Battle of Mount Tifata and was defeated. After a second battle and a second defeat, Norbanus fled to Rhodes, where he committed suicide.

Coin details and provenance: C Norbanus. 83 BC. Denarius. Obverse: Diademed head of Venus, NORBNVS. Reverse: Grain ear, fasces, and caduceus. References: Cr. 357/1b. Acquired from Wayne C. Phillips Rare Coins, Diamond Bar, California in January 2009.

Opposition to Sulla

83 BC

This coin was issued while the Roman Senate was controlled by the Marian party of Gaius Marius and Cornelius Cinna. It was issued as Sulla's army threatened to march on Rome.

The moneyer, also a member of the Marian party, chose Jupiter for the coin's front. On the back he depicts a triumphant charioteer carrying a palm frond, a symbol of triumph and victory.

Sulla had marched on Rome before, an unprecedented act, after the powerful Marius had ignited Rome by reducing the Senate to a body that could not convene a quorum. Sulla's son-in-law was killed in the riots that followed these actions.

After Sulla took the city the first time in 87 BC, he ordered the death of Marius, restructured the city's politics, and returned to his camp to proceed with his planned campaign against Mithradates of Pontus.

Marius, however, escaped assassination and returned to Rome after Sulla's departure. By late 87 BC, Marius was again in control of the city. Sulla's reforms were invalidated and Sulla was exiled. Many of his supporters were murdered.

Marius died the following year, leaving consul Cinna in command of the city. Two years later in 84 BC, Cinna raised an army to confront Sulla and marched it to the Balkan coast east of Italy ostensibly to attack the Illyrians. The Illyrians conveniently stood between Cinna and the returning army of Sulla, fresh off its victories over Mithradates. Before he could engage in battle, however, Cinna was stoned to death by his troops.

The power vacuum this left in Rome encouraged Sulla to advance toward the city. He entered the Italian peninsula at Brundisium unopposed. Newly elected consuls Norbanus and Cornelius Asiagenus quickly prepared legions to meet Sulla's advances. Norbanus confronted Sulla first and was soundly defeated. Asiagenus surrendered without a fight. Others, notably Crassus and a young Pompey joined the Sullan cause.

By 82 BC, the year after this coin was issued, Sulla had prevailed and taken the city. Antonius Balbus, who issued this coin, was slain in the conflict.

Coin details and provenance: Republican Opposition to Sulla. Q. Antonius Balbus. 83 BC. Silver denarius serratus. Rome mint. Obverse: Laureate head of Jupiter right, S C behind. Reverse: Victory in a quadriga right, wreath in right and reigns and palm frond in left, letter below horses, Q ANTO BALB / PR in ex (ANT and AL in monogram). 3.1 grams. 19.5mm. 135°. References: S 279, Syd 742b, Craw 364/1a, RSC Antonia 1. Acquired from Forum Ancient Coins, Morehead City, North Carolina in November 2006.

Sulla's Triumph
82 BC

As General Sulla marched his troops toward Rome in 82 BC, he commissioned his military mint to issue this coin. It is similar to the one issued by the Senate but depicts Roma instead of Jupiter on the front. The back shows a flying victory delivering a crown to the charioteer, intended to symbolize Sulla.

Sulla's commanders included Marcus Crassus and the young Magnus Pompey. After taking the city, Sulla was declared dictator without term by the Senate and instituted a reign of terror unlike any seen before in Rome. Some 1,500 Roman nobles were executed.

Among those targeted was a young Julius Caesar, whose father-in-law Cinna led the Marian party after the death of Marius. Caesar somehow managed to escape the city unharmed. Many believe his escape was made possible only through the intervention of the Vestal Virgins.

After the purge, Sulla enacted a series of reforms that returned control of Rome to the Senate. Two years later, he unexpectedly disbanded his legions, re-established consular government and voluntarily resigned the dictatorship. He lived out his life withdrawn from public life in a villa near Puteoli.

Sulla completed his memoirs while in retirement but only portions remain and those are quoted in other sources. He died in 78 BC. Historians believe he died from liver disease or a gastric ulcer caused by chronic alcohol consumption. He was given a lavish public funeral in the Roman Forum, grander in scale than any previous funeral. His epitaph read - "no greater friend, no worse enemy."

Coin details and provenance: Sulla's Triumph. Roman Republic. L. Cornelius Sulla and L. Manlius Torquatus. 82 BC. Ancient counterfeit denarius. Sulla's military mint. Obverse: L MANLI (T) PRO Q, helmeted head of Roma right, banker's mark on cheek. Reverse: Sulla in quadriga advancing to the right, holding caduceus, crowned by Victory flying above, L SULLA IMP or similar in exergue. 3.618 grams. 15.9mm. References: S 286-7, Cr. 367, RSC Manlia 4 ff. Acquired from Forum Ancient Coins, Morehead City, North Carolina in November 2006.

Censorinus & Marsysas
82 BC

Did this act of hubris cost Censorinus his head? This coin, which he issued in 82 BC as one of the Senate's moneyers, bears the portrait of the god Apollo on its front and the image of a standing satyr named Marsysas on its back. The satyr is naked except for a pilleus, or cap, on his head that symbolizes liberty. He carries a wine skin over his shoulder.

In Republican Rome, Marsysas was renowned as the inventor of augury and a proponent of free speech, particularly speech that voiced the truth to the powerful. For more than 300 years, his statue stood in the Roman Forum near a space reserved for political activity associated with the common people. Invective political verse was frequently posted on the statue, that looked like the image on this coin with a standing Marsysas carrying a wine skin on his left shoulder while holding his right arm aloft.

The story of Apollo and Marsysas was known to all Romans and explains how a satyr came to represent free speech and the continuing struggle between the common people and the elite of Rome. According to the legend, Marsyas picked up a double flute that Athena had discarded and played it with great skill. He entered into a music contest with Apollo that was judged by the Muses. When he lost, Apollo flayed him alive for his hubris in challenging a god.

One version of the story has Apollo nailing the shaggy hide to a tree. Herodotus reported that the skin could be seen where the river Marsyas joined the Celaenae in Phrygia. The Greek philosopher Plato believed that a wine skin was made from the hide of Marsysas, like that carried by Marsyas on the coin.

The Republican sentiments conveyed on the coin in the same year that Sulla attacked and conquered the city of Rome could not have impressed Rome's new dictator. The courage senator Censorinus exhibited by issuing this coin at this time spoke volumes about the passion some Roman patricians had for their democratic ideals. It also likely cost him his life. He was murdered on Sulla's order and his severed head was displayed publicly for all Romans to see.

Coin details and provenance: L. Marcius Censorinus. Denarius. Apollo/Marsyas. 82 BC. Denarius. Rome mint. Obverse: Laureate head of Apollo; banker's marks above and below eye. Reverse: L. CENSOR. Marsyas, bald-headed, walking to the left, with arm raised and holding wine skin over his left shoulder; behind, column bearing statue of Victory; small flan chip. 3.63 grams. 18 mm. References: Crawford 363/1d; Sydenham 737f. Acquired from Herakles Numismatics, Charlotte, North Carolina in December 2010.

LIMETANUS & ODYSSEUS
82 BC

This coin from 82 BC pays homage to the family lineage of the issuer, Mamilius Limetanus. It was typical among the elite patrician families of the day, that family lineage included connections to the gods themselves.

As reflected on his coin, Limetanus claimed descent from the god Mercury and the legendary Odysseus who helped end the Trojan War and then, as chronicled in Homer's *Odyssey*, got lost on his return. Linetanus' family believed themselves to be descended from Mamilia, the daughter of Telegonus, who was the son Odysseus. Common belief held that Odysseus was descended from Mercury.

The front of the coin depicts Mercury in a winged helmet. The back depicts Odysseus being greeted by his dog Argus. The image refers to a scene late in Homer's *Odyssey* when Odysseus finally returns to his kingdom of Ithaca after a long absence.

The Greeks defeated the Trojans after an extended seige of their city through the ruse, concocted by Odysseus, of their departing from the battlefield while leaving a giant wooden horse outside Troy's gates. The horse contained Greek soldiers who slipped out at night after the Trojans brought the horse inside their gate. The surprised Trojans were slaughtered.

Odysseus' adventure, however, had just begun. His ship was thrown off course by a storm when he and the other Greeks left Troy to return to Greece. Lost for the 20 years, Odysseus wandered from adventure to adventure unable to return home.

When he finally made his way home to his beloved wife Penelope and his son Telegonus, much had changed. He was presumed dead and his home was overrun with suitors and revelers.

The scene depicted on the coin tells the rest of the story. Odysseus disguised himself as a beggar so as not to alert the revelers to his return. As he enters his home, he sees a very old dog and realizes it is Argus.

Notwithstanding his long separation or his disguise, Argus quickly recognizes his master and lifts his head and cocks his ears. Odysseus, in tears, embraces his old friend Argus who remained devoted to the end. Argus dies peacefully in his master's arms. Odysseus goes on to slay the interlopers and restores order to his home.

Coin details and provenance: C. Mamilius Limetanus. Roman Republic. 82 BC. Silver serrated denarius. Obverse: Draped bust of Mercury right; caduceus and M behind. Reverse: C• MAMIL LIMETAN; Ulysses walking right, his dog Argus before. 3.75 grams. References: Mamilia 6; Sear I 282. Both the obverse and reverse type of this coin refer to the lineage of the Mamilia family.

CICERO'S ROME
79 BC

Freshly minted copies of this Republican coin from moneyer Naevius Balbus were likely included in Cicero's cash reserves when he traveled to Greece in 79 BC to perfect the rhetorical skills that would make him a power in Roman politics.

Depicting Venus in profile and Victory riding a triga behind three horses, the coin reflects both the power of family and the influence of the military in Roman life. Venus refers to the family gens of Sulla, Pompey and Caesar and here, likely, refers to Sulla who that same year renounced his dictatorship and retired from public life.

Cicero, whose equestrian status was a rank below the most influential patricians, did not serve in the military. He nonetheless advanced to prominence in Roman politics and became widely regarded as Rome's most accomplished orator.

The year 79 BC was also important to the young Cicero for his marriage to the wealthy plebian Terrentia. Her family had money and important connections, substantial enough to secure her sister Fabia's selection as a Vestal Virgin. Terrentia's money provided crucial support to Cicero as he took on controversial legal cases that advanced his career.

Cicero became the great advocate of Republican Rome, often taking up unpopular causes or scouring his political opponents in the name of causes he supported. This earned him admiration and respect. It also created enemies.

Cicero was deeply involved in the turbulent politics that followed Caesar's murder and an outspoken critic of Marc Antony. Over time, Cicero became a vocal supporter of Octavian.

Notwithstanding his support, however. Cicero became vul-nerable when Octavian and Antony formed the Second Triumverate in 43 BC with Lepidus. As part of the compromise that brought these three adversaries together in the Triumverate, Octavian agreed to put Cicero's name on a proscription list. His death came on December 7, 43 BC while he was attempting to flee the city.

Coin details and provenance: C Naevius Balbus. Struck 79 BC. Silver serrated denarius. Obverse: Diademed head of Venus right, SC behind. Reverse - Victory in triga right; numeral CCIIII (Ranging from I-CCXXVI, possibly to reflect numbered coin dies) above, C NAE BALB in exergue. RCV 309. 3.5 grams. 19.5 mm. Aparently weight adjusted. Some coins from this period, particularly serrati, bear one or more blunt tool marks on their surfaces. This was evidently done to lower the weight of the coin (by removing a small amount of metal) to the standard level. One of the few issues bearing the 'Triga', the three-horse chariot. Acquired from Incitatus Coins and Antiquities, St. Johns, NL, Canada in May 2010.

Cupid & Venus Gens
75 BC

This coin from 75 BC contains one the few depictions of Cupid alone on a Roman coin. Cupid, the Roman god of love and son of Venus, was also referred to as Amor or, in Greek, Eros. He is depicted here as a winged child with a bow and quiver on his shoulder. On the coin's reverse is the most powerful of Roman gods, Jupiter, standing with Liberty in a temple.

By these two images, the coin associates the Venus cult of the Julian clan of Sulla, Pompey and Julius Caesar with the virtues of strength and liberty. All of these families claimed descent from Venus through Aeneas, the mythological founder of Rome depicted in Virgil's *Aeneid*.

Augustus Caesar, Rome's first emperor and also a member of the Julian clan, commissioned Virgil to create a heroic history of Rome to rival the Greek's *Iliad*. That history focused on the adventures of Aeneas, a Trojan warrior who leaves a smoldering Troy after its defeat by the Greeks to found a new city and empire on the Italian peninsula.

Julius Caesar honored his family gens by building a temple in the Roman Forum dedicated to the mother of Cupid, Venus Genetrix, after he defeated Pompey at Pharsalas in 46 BC. Pompey also featured Venus on his coins.

Religious belief and ancestral clan affiliation were important to influential Romans. Each gens, or clan, had its own rites that were followed within the family. Religious rites were performed daily and family occasions routinely included a religious ceremony.

Offerings to family ancestors were considered crucial to family health and wellbeing. Honoring your family gens publicly not only showed respect for one's ancestors but also strengthened relations with other clan members. Romans believed that the spirits of neglected ancestors could haunt or bring bad fortune to family members.

Coin details and provenance: Cn. Egnatius Cn. f. Cn. n. Maxsumus. 75 BC. Silver denarius. Obverse: Bust of Cupid, r., bow and quiver on shoulder. Reverse: Jupiter and Liberty standing within distyle temple. 3.44 grams. 19mm. References: cf. Craw 391/2. Comes with an old cabinet tag. Cupid, the Roman god of Love, is only rarely depicted alone on Roman coins. He was the son of Venus, the goddess of female love and sexuality. Julius Caesar and Augustus both claimed descent from Venus, through Aeneas. Acquired from Tom Cederlind Numismatics & Antiquities, Portland, Oregon in October 2009.

Vestal Virgins
63 BC

This ancient counterfeit, or fourée, from 63 BC was produced from a copper flan covered with a silver foil that was heated and stamped with a coin die. The result produced a facsimile coin with less precious metal that could pass in normal commerce. Flecks of the silver coating can still be detected on the coin.

This counterfeit copied a coin issued in 63 BC (some sources say 60 BC) by L. Cassius Longinus to honor the role his predecessor Cassius Longinus Ravilla played in 114 BC in prosecuting and convicting two Vestal Virgins, Marcia and Licinia, of unchastity. Ravilla was the special inquisitor appointed in the case. Both women were put to death for their crimes.

The coin features Vesta, virgin goddess of the hearth and protector of Rome, on the front, and Longinus casting a ballot on the back. Longinus was also instrumental in instituting the secret ballot in Rome. The use of this image would have identified him to Romans and made, with the virgin's portrait on the front, the intended association of the coin clear.

The Vestals were selected by the pontifex maximus from upper class families when they were between six and ten years of age. Their position committed them to 30 years of chastity and required them to keep alive the sacred Vestal fire that resided in their temple located in the heart of Rome.

They also protected important documents such as the wills of Julius Caesar and Marc Antony and played important ceremonial roles. Many believe that their connections and influence throughout Roman society are what enabled Julius Caesar to escape the city in 82 BC when his name was added to the proscribed list of Sulla as one who should be executed.

Coin details and provenance: L. Cassius Longinus. 63 BC. AR denarius (fouree), bronze core only. Rome mint. Obverse: Draped and veiled bust of Vesta facing right; kylix behind. Reverse: Togate male standing facing right, dropping tablet inscribed V into a cista, legend reads LON-GIN. III. with V behind. 2.93 grams. 18 mm. Reference: Cr. 413/1. The tablet with V(TI ROGAS) was used to cast a vote on legislation. The Vesta head on the obverse may allude to the 114 BC trial by a special commission of vestal virgins who were charged with breaking their vows of chastity. An ancestor of the coin's issuer served as a special inquisitor in the trial. Acquired from JJencek, San Mataeo, California in June 2010.

PAULLUS & PERSEUS
62 BC

On this coin from 62 BC, Aemilius Paullus celebrates the victory of his ancestor Lucius Paullus in 168 BC over the last king of Macedonia. The back of the coin shows Lucius Paullus standing to the right in Senatorial garb next to his battle trophy. The conquered Macedonian King Perseus stands to the far left with his half-brother Philippus and son Alexander standing in the background. The front of the coin bears the name of Paullus and the image of the goddess Concordia.

The conquered Perseus had become successor to the Macedonian throne after his father, Philip V, died in 179 BC. The Macedonian's were feeling insecure in their relationship with Rome. Accusations from neighboring Pergamon about aggressive intentions of the Macedonians resulted in frequent interference by the Romans in Macedonian's affairs.

Perseus had played on these insecurities to secure his succession to the Macedonian throne. He managed this by convincing his father that his older brother Demetrius, who was ambassador to Rome, planned to take over Macedonia with help from Rome. Suspicions were so high that Philip ordered Demetrius poisoned in 180 BC. When Philip died the next year, Perseus ascended to the throne.

As king, Perseus quickly renewed Macedonia's treaty with Rome but was distrusted for suspicions about his role in his brother's death. His actions raised further concerns. He frequently interfered with his neighbors, ousted Roman ally Abrupolis from his territory, and made an armed visit to Delphi. He also refused to meet with Roman ambassadors.

In 171 BC, a third war broke out between the two nations and lasted for three years until Perseus was decisively defeated at the Battle of Pydna. Perseus was imprisoned with his half-brother and son and the Macedonian kingdom was dissolved. Four republics replaced it until 146 BC when the Roman Senate officially made Macedonia a Roman province.

Coin details and provenance: L. Aemilius Lepidus Paullus. 62 BC. AR denarius. Obverse: PAVLLVS LEPIDVS CONCORDIA, veiled head of Concordia right. Reverse: Trophy, L. Aemilius Lepidus on right, Perseus of Macedonia and his two sons as captives on left; TER above, PAVLLVS below. 3.58 grams. 19 mm. References: Crawford 415/1; Aemilia 10. Acquired from Roma Numismatics Ltd., Farnham, U.K. in March 2009.

JUBA I

60 TO 46 BC

Numidian King Juba I, a partisan of Pompey, succeeded to a throne that his father had secured with the help of Pompey. Here Juba is portrayed with a scepter on his shoulder and a diadem, or crown, on his head. The obscured legend translates to King Juba. The back of the coin shows an octastyle temple.

Juba's personal allegiance to Pompey was well known and reinforced, insofar as it included opposition to Julius Caesar, during a visit to Rome when Caesar insulted him by pulling his beard. His ties to Pompey were further strengthened when a supporter of Caesar openly proposed that Numidia be sold.

When Caesar conquered Rome in early 49 BC, Juba's position became tenuous. Not unexpectedly, he sided with Pompey and his forces in the civil war that followed. When Caesar sent forces to subdue Africa later that year, Juba defeated them. To mark his triumph, Juba took several Roman senators he captured back to Numidia and put them on public display before executing them.

His triumph was short lived however. When Caesar himself arrived in Africa three years later, Juba was also confronted with a separate invasion by Bocchus II, King of Mauretania. While defending against this threat, he received a plea for reinforcements from Metellus Scipio who was battling Caesar at Thapsus in Tunsia. Arriving in time to see Scipio's defeat, Juba withdrew his troops without joining the battle.

While attempting to retreat, Juba and his general Petreius, who had fled to Africa with Cato after Pompey's defeat at the Battle of Pharsalas, found themselves cut off by Caesar's forces. With no escape available, the two made a suicide pact and took up arms against one another. Juba died in the conflict and Petreius took his own life with the help of a slave.

Juba II, the infant son of the Numidian king, was taken captive and later raised in the household of Augustus. When he became an adult, Juba married Cleopatra Selene, the daughter of Antony and Cleopatra.

Coin details and provenance: King of Numidia, Juba I. Circa 60 to 46 BC. AR denarius. Utica mint. Obverse: Diademed and draped bust right, scepter over shoulder. Reverse: Octastyle temple. 3.39 grams. 20 mm. References: MAA 29; SNG Copenhagen 523; Mazard 84. Two small test cuts on cheek. Ex CNG with sales ticket. Acquired from Inclinatiorama Ancient Coins in August 2006.

AEMILIUS SCARUS
58 BC

This Republican coin portrays a defeated Nabataean King Aretas III kneeling beside a camel in submission to his Roman conquerors. His name Rex Aretas appears below. On the back, the coin shows a triumphant Jupiter riding a four-horse chariot called a quadriga. The coin was issued to coincide with the Aedilician games organized by the coin's issuer and long remembered for their extravagance.

While serving as Pompey's appointed military tribune in Judaea in 66 BC, the coin's issuer assisted the Jewish usurper Aristobulus by ordering the Nabataean Ruler Aretas III to stop a siege of Jerusalem. Aretas was acting on behalf of the deposed High Jewish Priest Hyrcanus at the time.

As Aretas retreated to Nabataea in compliance with Scarus' order, his army was intercepted by Aristobulus and defeated. The ungrateful Aristobulus later accused Scarus of requiring a large bribe for his help.

Two years later, Scarus took advantage of the weakened state of Aretas' army and laid siege to the Nabatean capital of Petra.

The besieged Nabatean king ultimately capitulated and paid Scarus a fine of 300 talents. This was the victory Scarus celebrated on his coin.

Scarus organized the Aedilician games in 58 BC and later became praetor of Sardinia. His management of the island was suspect, however, and in 54 BC he was accused of extorting the province. Cicero defended him in court and secured his acquittal.

Within a year, however, Scarus was accused again. This time the charge was ambitio, a form of bribery. Scarus avoided a trial this time by going into exile.

Scarus did not reappear after that but his actions remain a part of our collective past. In addition to the events described above, he is mentioned in the Dead Sea Scrolls for massacres he carried out. Pliny the Elder records his reputation as a major collector of engraved gems.

Coin details and provenance: M. Aemilius Scarus and Pub. Plautius Hypsaeus. 58 BC. AR denarius. Obverse: King Aretas of Nabataea kneeling beside camel; M SCAVR/AED CVR in two lines above, [E]X S C across field; REX ARETAS in exergue. Reverse: Jupiter in quadriga; scorpion to left, P. HVPSAE/AED CVR in two lines above, [CAPTV] to right, C HYPSAE CO[S]/PREIVE in two lines in exergue. 3.99 grams. 18 mm. References: Crawford 422/1b; Sydenham 913; Aemilia 8. Choice old collection toning. Genuine, but struck with slightly misaligned dies creating appearance of partial seam. Acquired from Civitas Galleries, Middleton, Wisconsin in December 2005.

The Remi
60 TO 50 BC

Could this remarkable little coin from a Belgic tribe of northeastern Gaul bear the earliest coin portrait of the great Roman general Julius Caesar? The Remi were one of the most powerful tribes in Gaul during the first century BC and, during Caesar's campaigns there, one of his most reliable allies.

No one knows with certainty the identity of the three figures on the face of this coin minted between 60 and 50 BC. But some historians speculate that the three may be those of two Remi leaders Iccius and Andecombogius with the third profile being that of their ally Julius Caesar. The back of the coin depicts a biga, or chariot drawn by two horses.

The Remi occupied the Champagne-Ardenne region in what is now northwestern France and were renowned for their horses and cavalry. Before Iccius and Andecombogius allied the Remi with Caesar and the Romans, the Remi had allied with Germanic tribes and regularly fought the Gallic Parisii and Senones. Their tribal capital was in Durocortum where the modern city of

Reims not stands and where many kings of France were later crowned.

Coin details and provenance: The Remi. Circa 60 to 50 BC. Celtic, Northern Gaul, Comata [Remiae]. AE potin (an alloy with a high tin content), cast unit. Obverse: Three young male busts jugate facing left, REMO below. Reverse: Victory driving biga left, REMO below. 2.8 grams. 15 mm. References: LT8040, GCV137. Ex: M King Collection. Acquired from Mike R. Vosper Coins, Brandon, United Kingdom in June 2008.

VIRIDOVIX
57 TO 56 BC

The Unelli were a Celtic tribe from the northwest coast of Gaul who fought the Romans during the Gallic Wars. Their chief Viridovix, to whom this coin is attributed, led the Unelli and the neighboring Veneti, Aulerci, Sexovii, Osismii and Curiosolitae tribes against the Romans in 56 BC. The coin bears a profile on its front and a stylized chariot on its reverse.

The Unelli and their confederates were ultimately defeated by Caesars' legate Quintus Titurius Sabinus and the three legions under his command. Julius Caesar, who recorded his Gallic adventures in his *Commentaries*, offers this unflattering description of the Unelli's defeat:

> Sabinus arrived in the territories of the Unelli. Over these people Viridovix ruled, and had collected a large and powerful army. The Aulerci and the Sexovii warriors murdered their Senate because they would not consent to be promoters of the war and united themselves to Viridovix. They attacked the Roman camp with great

speed and arrived quite out of breath. Sabinus ordered a sally to be made suddenly from two gates. It happened that they could not stand one attack of our men, and immediately turned their backs; and our men followed them while disordered, and slew a great number of them." (Condensed from the *Commentaries* 3:17-19).

Few escaped the Roman pursuers. The Unelli's downfall appears to have come from believing the Romans were about to retreat and from their failure to take into account the nearly mile long slope they would have to charge up in order to attack the Roman's in their camp. Their miscalculation left them breathless and vulnerable when they reached the Roman camp.

The triumphant Roman commander Sabinus also fell prey to the vicissitudes of war in Gaul. He returned to northern Gaul in the winter of 54 BC to set up camp for the season. Within two weeks of arriving, he and General Lucius Cotta were attacked by the Ambiorix and Cativolcus. Sabinus accepted a flag of truce from the Ambiorix but was massacred with Cotta and their legions.

Coin details and provenance: Viridovix. The Unelli. Celtic. Northwest Gaul. Late 57 to 56 B.C. Billon stater. Obverse: Head facing right, V-shaped mouth with extra hair behind lower earlobe. Reverse: Stylized chariot right with boar below. 5.28 grams. 21 mm. References: Hooker Z/O, 92; De Jersey II/51; Gruel and Morin 894; SCBC 15. Acquired from John C. Lavender Classical Numismatist, Watkinsville, Georgia in January 2006.

CRASSUS

54 TO 53 BC

Marcus Licinius Crassus was the son of a distinguished Roman general and consul who grew up to be one of Rome's wealthiest and most powerful men. He was a skilled, and some believed unscrupulous, businessman who made his first fortune by taking advantage of the misfortune of others.

When Sulla proscribed thousands following his invasions of Rome, Crassus bought up the properties of the displaced and resold them at handsome profits. He did the same thing with properties destroyed by Rome's many fires, keeping as many as 500 slaves who were skilled at building ready to rebuild the properties he bought on the cheap. Many suspected him of setting fires that brought him profit.

His wealth, and its ability to fund a large army, secured for him the title of praetor and the commission to lead eight of Rome's legions against the great slave army of Spartacus in 72 BC. He prevailed but in the course of his command confirmed his reputation for ruthlessness. When a deputy's legion suffered defeat in a battle against Spartacus, Crassus ordered the 500 most responsible soldiers to be decimated, a gruesome punishment that condemned every tenth man to be killed in front of the troops. After he defeated the slave army he ordered 6,000 of them to be crucified along the Appian Way.

Crassus' wealth also helped build the careers of others, such as Caesar and Cataline, and bought him influence with those dependent on his wealth. He held the consulship with Pompey in 70 BC and again in 55 BC. In between, he served with both Caesar and Pompey in the First Triumvirate that ruled Rome beginning in 59 BC.

This coin comes from the brief period that Crassus served as governor of Syria, an appointment he hoped would secure him further wealth and an opportunity for military glory against the Persians.

The coin is from Antioch and in the Greek style with the god Zeus in profile on the front and sitting on a throne on the back. Once in Syria, Crassus assembled his army and made plans to invade Parthian. By 53 BC, he was on the march into Parthian territory hoping for military victories that would rival those of Rome's other leading men, Julius Caesar and Magnus Pompey. He would not succeed.

Coin details and provenance: Syria, Antioch, Under Roman Rule. Marcus Licinius Crassus, Governor. 54 to 53 BC. AE19. Obverse: Laureate head of Zeus facing right. Reverse: Zeus seated on a throne and facing left, legend ANTIOX and date in field. 7.0 grams. 19 mm. Reference: SG 5853. Acquired from Rusty Romans in June of 2010.

Orodes II

57 to 38 BC

Rome's able adversary on its eastern border, Orodes II, ruled Parthia from 57 to 38 BC. His reign began when he and his brother Mithradates murdered their father Phraates III. Mithradates went on to rule Media but was soon expelled by Orodes.

This coin shows the king regally attired with a star and crescent behind and a prominent wart on his forehead. The back of the coin shows a seated archer with a legend that declares Orodes King of Kings in Greek - ΒΑΣΙΛΕΩΣ ΒΑΣΙΛΕΩΝ.

In 53 BC, Marcus Crassus and his Roman legions invaded Parthian territory hoping to expand Rome's empire. Orodes defeated these ambitions when Parthian troops, commanded by his general Surenas, defeated Crassus' legions at the Battle of Carrhae (now Harran, Turkey) and took Marcus Crassus prisoner. Shortly afterwards, Orodes invaded Armenia and forced their King Artavadses to switch allegiances from the Romans to the Parthians.

The captured Crassus was one of the wealthiest and most powerful men in Rome at the time of his capture. In 71 BC, he had led Rome's legions to victory against Spartacus, crucifying thousands of rebellious slaves afterward along the Appian Way.

Now, after defeat, he was put to death in a manner first employed by Mithradates of Pontus to strike terror in his Roman adversaries. Crassus was brought before Surenas and restrained while molten gold was poured down his throat. His severed head was sent to Orodes.

The Parthian king sided with Pompey after civil war broke out in Rome after Caesar's assassination, switching allegiances to Brutus and Cassius after Pompey's defeat. In 40 BC, Orodes' son Pacorus took advantage of Rome's internal conflict and conquered large parts of Syria and Asia Minor.

After Pacorus was defeated and killed by the Romans two years later, Orodes reign came to an end. His second son, Phraates IV, became heir apparent with the death of Pacorus and quickly arranged the murder of Orodes and all of 30 of Orodes' other sons and their families.

Coin details and provenance: 57 to 38 BC. Parthia. Orodes II. Silver drachm. Obverse: King facing left, crescent and star behind, star in front, with royal wart on forehead. Reverse: archer seated, holding bow, anchor behind, mint mark below bow, Greek legend ΒΑΣΙΛΕΩΣ ΒΑΣΙΛΕΩΝ ΑΡΣΑΚΟΥ ΕΥΕΡΓΕΤΟΥ ΔΙΚΑΙΟ Υ ΕΠΙΦΑΝΟΥΣ ΦΙΛΕΛΛΗΝΟΕ. 3.93 grams. References: Sellwood 48.7. Acquired from Pars Coins, San Jose, California in January 2004.

Pompey's Triumphs
56 BC

This coin was issued by the son of Lucius Sulla to honor Magnus Pompey. It bears the profile of Venus on its front and three military trophies on its back. The same image of three standing trophies was also worn on the signet ring Pompey used to seal his correspondence. They represent Pompey's great military victories on three continents – Asia over Mithradates, Africa over the Marians, and Europe over Quintus Sertorius.

The younger Sulla served Pompey as a general just as Pompey had served his father. He was also Pompey's son-in-law, having married Pompey's daughter Pompeia. He fought with Pompey in Asia and was the first to climb over the walls of the Temple of Jerusalem in 63 BC when it was stormed by Pompey.

The first two victories depicted on the coin earned Pompey the honorary title of Magnus. They also gave Pompey the leverage to demand a formal Triumph through the streets of Rome from his commander Sulla. He received Sulla's acquiescence by refusing to disband his legions when they returned to Rome in 81 BC.

Forced to capitulate to the young commander's demands, Sulla nonetheless diluted the impact of Pompey's Triumph by staging his own lavish Triumph first and then granting a second Triumph, also before Pompey's, to Mettellus Pius.

Pompey, for his own part, tried to steal the show by entering Rome in a chariot drawn by an elephant but was embarrassed and prevented from doing so when the elephant's size prevented it from passing through the ceremonial gate leading into the city. Sulla, no doubt, enjoyed his young general's disappointment.

Sulla's son Faustus, who issued this coin, got caught up like every other Roman in the civil wars following Julius Caesar's assassination. He fought with Pompey at the Battle of Pharsalas. After that, he fled to Northern Africa to again take up the cause, eventually being killed while trying to escape after the Battle of Thapsus.

Coin details and provenance: Faustus Cornelius Sulla. (Pompey's Triumphs). AR silver denarius. Struck 56 BC. Obverse: Laureate and diademed bust of Venus right; scepter on shoulder, SC behind. Reverse: Three military trophies between capis and lituus; FAVSTVS, monogrammed, in exergue. 3.9 grams. 18 mm. References: RCV 384. This coin, struck by Faustus in 56 BC, honors Pompey's victories an all three continents. Pompey had a signet ring with the same three trophies on it, with which he sealed his correspondence. Acquired from Incitatus Coins and Antiquities, St. Johns, NL, Canada in March 2006.

Q. Cassius Longinus
55 BC

Quintus Cassius Longinus, who issued this coin, was a relative of both Julius Caesar and the assassin Gaius Cassius Longinus (known to history as Cassius) who conspired with Brutus to murder Caesar in 44 BC. Longinus was an active supporter of Caesar who served Rome's first citizen as governor of Hispania.

Longinus issued this coin in 55 BC while serving as a moneyer for the Roman Senate. It bears the image of Genius Populi Romani on the front and an eagle standing on a thunderbolt. To the Romans the genius was a spirit or guardian who, in the case of Populi Romani served to protect the Roman people in general. A shrine to this genius appeared in the Roman Forum.

After his year as moneyer, Longinus managed the financial affairs of Hispania Ulterior for Pompey. By the time Caesar crossed the Rubicon in 49 BC and took Rome, Longinus, then a tribune, supported Caesar and was rewarded with the governorship of Hispania. His rule in the region, however, earned him a reputation for cruelty and severity, which did not serve Caesar well.

After just a year as governor, Longinus was directed to take the field against Juba I in Numidia but was delayed by an insurrection at Cordoba. Although he put down the insurrection, the merciless punishments he meted out to its leaders led to a subsequent revolt by his legions. The mutinous troops surrounded Longinus at Ulia.

Caesar's General Marcellus Lepidus (who would later serve with Octavian and Marc Antony on the Second Triumverate) and King Bogud of Mauretania had to intervene to secure Quintus' freedom. After being rescued, Quintus boarded a ship at Malaca in southern Spain. He was lost at sea when his ship ran into a severe storm.

Coin details and provenance: Q. Cassius Longinus. 55 BC. AR denarius. Rome mint. Obverse: Head Genius Populi Romani right; scepter behind. Reverse: Eagle standing right on thunderbolt; lituus to left; capis to right. 3.77 grams. 18 mm. References: Cr. 428/3. Acquired from JJencek Ancient Coins & Antiquities, San Mataeo, California in September 2009.

Marcus Brutus
54 BC

This coin, commissioned by the future assassin of Julius Caesar, features the profile of Libertas on the front and a depiction of Brutus' famous ancestor Lucius Brutus on the back. In that image, Lucius Brutus, the first counsel and founder of the Roman Republic, walks between two lictors and behind an accensus.

In 509 BC, Lucius Brutus drove the Roman King Tarquinius Superbus and his family into exile. Instead of seeking the kingship, Lucius Brutus declared that the ruling power would reside with the Senate and made the Senators swear an oath never to allow any man to be king of Rome. According to the historian Livy, Tarquin had earlier orchestrated the murder of Brutus' brother, a powerful Senator who had opposed his ascension to the throne.

Legend has it, however, that it was the rape of Brutus' kinswoman Lucretia by Tarquinius' son that led Brutus to open revolt. Lucretia committed suicide after confessing her shame to her family. On hearing of her death, Lucius Brutus is said to have grabbed the dagger from Lucretia's chest and shouted for the overthrow of the Targuins.

However accurate or embellished, this was the family history held dear by Marcus Brutus and known to Romans everywhere. The coin Brutus issued in 54 BC expressed his pride in his Republican lineage and foreshadowed his involvement ten years later in the brutal assassination of Rome's dictator, Julius Caesar.

Coin details and provenance: Marcus Junius Brutus (During this period, also known as Quintus Servilius Caepio Brutus). 54 BC. AR silver denarius. Struck as moneyer. Obverse: LIBERTAS, head of Libertas right, hair in bun. Reverse: BRVTVS, the Consul Lucius Junius Brutus walking left, between two lictors, carrying axes over their shoulders, and preceded by an accensus. 3.7 grams. 20 mm. References: RCV 397. A popular issue, clearly showing Brutus' political sentiments a full ten years before Caesar's assassination. The obverse personification of Libertas speaks for itself. The reverse type refers to his celebrated ancestor, Lucius Junius Brutus, the first Consul and founder of the Republic who expelled the Tarquins from Rome while he held the consulship in 509 BC. Acquired from Incitatus Coins, St. Johns, NL, Canada in June of 2008.

RUFUS & SULLA
54 BC

In the same year that Brutus issued his coin honoring his family's Republican bona fides, fellow senator Quintus Pompeius Rufus issued this coin to honor his grandfather Rufus and his father-in-law Lucius Cornelius Sulla, both of whom served as consul in 88 BC. In stark contrast to Brutus' coin, this coin honors the first Romans to attack Rome and abolish its government for short term dictators.

Sulla was one of the orators Cicero remembered listening to as a youth and the first Roman general to march his legions on the city of Rome. As a general, the elder Rufus served in Sulla's legions and fought King Mithradates of Pontus on Rome's eastern front.

After the first civil war broke out between the partisans of Sulla and Marius, the Marians deprived the elder Rufus of his consulship and caused him to flee to Nola, a city in the plain below Mt. Vesuvius. There, Rufus met up with Sulla and his army.

When Sulla returned to the eastern front after the conclusion of the first civil war he left Rufus in charge of Italy and put Pompeius Strabo (father of Magnus Pompey) in charge of the legions fighting the Marsi tribe to the west of Rome in the Social Wars. When Strabo later refused to relinquish his command and Rufus attempted to intervene, Strabo's soldiers murdered Rufus. A lightning strike ended Strabo's life a year or two later.

Sulla prevailed in a second civil war with the Marians to become Rome's absolute dictator in 82 BC. He purged Rome of more than a thousand Roman nobles after taking the city. Two years later he resigned, disbanded his legions and returned consular government to Rome.

The curule chairs shown on both sides of this coin are a traditional symbol of Roman authority. They were the seats used by military commanders while on campaign.

Coin details and provenance: Quintus Pompeius Rufus & Lucius Cornelius Sulla. 54 BC. AR silver denarius. Struck at Rome. Obverse: Q POMPEI Q F RVFVS above, curule chair flanked by arrow & laurel branch; COS on raised tablet below. Reverse: SVLLA COS above, curule chair flanked by lituus & a wreath; Q POMPEI RVF on raised tablet below. 3.7 grams. 17 mm. References: RCV 400. The moneyer Quintus Pompeius Rufus here honors his two grandfathers, Quintus Pompeius Rufus and Lucius Cornelius Sulla (Dictator) who were, coincidentally, both Consul in 88 BC. Acquired from Incitatus Coins and Antiquities in October 2008.

The Eventual Victor: Octavian Wearing Civic Crown
Glyptothek, Munich

[4]

Caesar's Legacy

ROMAN LAW PROHIBITED its legions from crossing the Rubicon River in the northern part of the Italian peninsula. The river marked the border with Cisalpine Gaul, a part of the European continent Julius Caesar and his legions had spent years in conquering.[5]

But on the evening of January 10th in 49 BC, after the Roman Senate had replaced Caesar as commander of Gaul with Domitius Ahenobarbus, Julius Caesar and one legion approached the river from the north headed toward Rome. The historian Suetonius reports that a supernatural apparition urged Caesar on as he approached the river, giving evidence to the doubt Caesar must have felt about the civil war his actions were sure to provoke.

---

[5] Julius Caesar on a coin issued just weeks before his assassination. Called the "coin that killed Caesar" by collectors, this was the first Roman coin to contain an image of Caesar. Its legend declares him perpetual dictator. The image and the legend were both affronts to Republican custom.

Both Suetonius and Plutarch report that Caesar proclaimed "the die is cast" as he crossed the river. Plutarch says he made the statement in Greek before leading his army across the river.

Whatever the truth, the action taken that 10th day of January has become ingrained in the English lexicon. Anyone who "crosses the Rubicon" is said to embark on a risky or controversial course of action.

The action also plunged Rome into a civil war that would pit Caesar against Pompey and result five years later in the assassination of Julius Caesar on the floor of the Roman Senate. This, in turn, lead to a series of civil wars over 18 years that eventually would elevate Caesar's grand-nephew Octavian to the role of Rome's first emperor, known today as Augustus.

Before that could happen, however, Julius Caesar would enter Rome without resistance and secure the silver left in Rome's treasury when Pompey evacuated the city to join his armies in Greece. Caesar would leave Marc Antony in charge of Rome while he headed west to join his Gallic legions and confront Pompey's forces in Spain.

After dispatching his enemies there, Caesar headed east to engage Pompey and his Greek legions. On July 10 of 48 BC, a year and a half after he crossed the Rubicon, Caesar engaged the armies of Magnus Pompey at Dyrrhachium and barely escaped defeat. After regrouping, he went on to decisively defeat Pompey's army at Pharsalus.

Caesar was then appointed dictator and returned to Rome to preside over his election to a second consulate with his colleague Publius Servilius Vatia and resign his appointment as dictator.

Caesar then left Rome to pursue the retreating Pompey in Alexandria, which itself was embroiled in a civil war between Cleopatra VII and her younger brother Ptolemy XIII. When Caesar arrived, he was presented with the severed head of Pompey and openly wept at the sight. Pompey had been murdered by a Roman serving in the court of Ptolemy XIII.

Caesar commanded both Cleopatra and Ptolemy to appear before him in Alexandria and became engaged in the Egyptian civil war after a first meeting that ranks among the most fantastic introductions in history. Unable to meet Caesar's command to appear in Alexandria because the city was controlled by forces loyal to Ptolemy, Cleopatra snuck into the city in a small merchant vessel and had herself carried to Caesar wrapped up in a rug. So disguised, she was taken into the room where Caesar was presiding and emerged from the rug when it was placed on the floor.

The 52-year-old Caesar was reportedly enthralled with the 21-year-old Cleopatra. She would become his mistress and travel to Rome to be by his side, bearing him a son, Caesarion, and complicating Roman politics in the process.

In 47 BC, Caesar defeated Ptolemy's forces at the Battle of the Nile and installed Cleopatra as the sole ruler of Egypt. After celebrating his victory with Cleopatra in a lavish Triumph on the Nile, Caesar headed east to defeat Pharnaces of Pontus. He then went to northern Africa to deal with the remaining Senatorial supporters of Pompey and defeated them at the Battle of Thapsus.

Cleopatra before Caesar by Jean-Léon Gérôme 1866

Following this, Caesar was appointed dictator for ten years but still had to contend with armed opposition. Gnaeus and Sextus Pompey, sons of Magnus Pompey, assembled an army in Spain determined to resist. Caesar made chase and defeated them at the Battle of Munda in March of 45 BC. With no armies left to oppose him, Caesar returned to Rome as victor and first citizen of the empire.

In just one year, however, Julius Caesar would be assassinated in full view of the Roman Senate by a cadre of Senators led by Marcus Brutus and Gaius Cassius. Plutarch reports that when

Caesar entered the Senate on the Ides of March that year, he was surrounded by the conspirators and brutally attacked. He was stabbed 23 times before he died.

With the bloodied body of Caesar lying on the floor, Brutus turned and addressed the stunned Senators who witnessed the attack, many of whom quickly fled, and then left with his conspirators crying out "people of Rome, now we are free!"

La Mort de César by Jean-Léon Gérôme 1867

After the assassination, the Senate granted amnesty to the conspirators to prevent further bloodshed. A 19-year-old Octavian returned from assignment in the East to claim his place as Caesar's heir and, after obtaining the consulship from the Senate in 43 BC, had the assassins declared enemies of Rome. A Triumvirate consisting of Marc Antony, Octavian and Caesar's cavalry commander Lepidus was officially formed in November of 43 BC to rule the empire.

In the following year, the combined legions of Octavian and Antony met the legions of Brutus and Cassius on the plains of Philippi in northeastern Greece. Brutus and the conspirators were defeated on October 19, 42 BC. Brutus, who committed suicide after fleeing the battle, was nonetheless accorded honors by Antony, who had Brutus' body wrapped in his most expensive mantel before having him cremated.

After the victory, the three Triumvirs divided the empire into spheres of influence. Marc Antony moved to Alexandria to live openly with Cleopatra. Frictions grew as Octavian consolidated his hold on the west and Marc Antony increased his influence in the east. A marriage of Marc Antony to Octavian's sister Octavia was arranged in 40 BC to bridge the growing differences. But, after a few years, Marc Antony left Octavia to mount a campaign against the Parthians and reunite with Cleopatra.

Marc Antony and Cleopatra lived together for almost a decade after the arranged marriage to Octavia and ruled an eastern Roman Empire. While they were together, he proclaimed Caesarion, Cleopatra's son, the legitimate heir to Julius Caesar and created an irreconcilable rift with Octavian.

They were eventually defeated by Octavian, whose general Marcus Agrippa orchestrated a brilliant battle plan that destroyed the combined navies of Marc Antony and Cleopatra off the shores of Actium in northeastern Greece in 31 BC.

Cleopatra participated directly in the battle but fled before it ended. Seeing her ship depart, Marc Antony followed suit, demoralizing his troops in the process. The two committed suicide later in Alexandria after being pursued by Octavian's forces. Octavian now reigned supreme in the empire. Eighteen years of civil war had come to an end.

On these pages you will find coins from many of the players in this struggle for dominance in Rome. One shows the great Arverni chieftain Vercingetorix who led the Celtic resistance to

Caesar in southern France. After brutal warfare and Vercingetorix's eventual surrender, Caesar imprisoned him in Rome for five years. After the coin was issued, Vercingetorix was publicly displayed in Caesar's Triumph of 46 BC and put to death.

Julius Caesar's presence dominates from 49 BC to his assassination in 44 BC. His coins use images that conveyed messages to his contemporaries that require some explanation today. One coin shows a trophy of Gallic arms with seated captives to portray his military prowess. Another preempts the images of the gods used earlier by Pompey to proclaim himself Pompey's conqueror. The goddess Venus Genetrix and the Discoursi are used on another to celebrate Caesar's military achievements and his family.

Caesar's adversaries and assassins appear here too. The most famous of the assassins, Marcus Brutus, has a coin that portrays himself as ruler and celebrates his role in Caesar's murder with depictions of the daggers used to stab Caesar to death. Cassius, who struck Caesar in the face as his conspirators drove daggers into his flesh has a coin issued to pay the troops he assembled in Greece. Decimus Brutus, who struck the third dagger into Caesar's body, has a coin here issued four years before the assassination.

Lucius Ahenobarbus, who was appointed by the Senate to replace Caesar in Gaul, led the only legions to resist Caesar's advance on Rome. He appears on a coin issued in 41 BC by his son Gneaus Ahenobarbus. The later Ahenobarbus served as a commander in the army of Brutus and Cassius and later as a general to Marc Antony. Cato, who opposed Caesar from the Senate floor, is here with a coin he issued shortly before his defeat by Caesar in northern Africa.

Sextus Pompey helped his father Magnus resist Caesar and continued as a force to be reckoned with well after the death of Caesar. His coin comes from the island of Sicily where he established a power base that challenged both Octavian and Marc Antony after Caesar's death. Also here from Caesar's battles with Pompey's forces is an artifact that is not a coin. From the battlefield of Munda in Spain, where Caesar scored an important victory against the forces of Gorgon, is a lead sling bullet that bears the inscription of Magnus Pompey - CN MAG.

The great Magnus Pompey ruled Rome as part of the First Triumvirate with Marcus Crassus and Julius Caesar. He was Caesar's ally and husband to Caesar's daughter Julia. After both Crassus and Caesar's only daughter died, however, Pompey's interests diverged from Caesar's and they became rivals. Two coins here reflect Pompey's imposing presence in Roman life, one with his profile depicted as the all-seeing Janus and another (featured in an earlier chapter on page 227) from the son of Sulla bearing the image Pompey wore on his signet ring to seal his correspondence. That image shows three trophies celebrating Pompey's renowned military victories on three continents.

Marc Antony and Cleopatra also issued coins. One from Cleopatra bears her profile and the image of an Egyptian eagle. Another issued when she was in exile and fighting for her survival has a shadowy image of a young Cleopatra looking to the heavens. Another issued in her name from Alexandria while she was in exile appears to depict a young male ruler, perhaps a reference to her brother Ptolemy whose advisors where preparing to attack Cleopatra in Cyprus.

Marc Antony's coins include one issued to celebrate his marriage to Octavia. It has his profile and an image of Octavia separated by two serpents. Another that he issued to pay his troops before the battle of Actium depicts a battleship and his legionary standards. Still another depicts the Queen of the Nile as the Greek goddess Aphrodite. Antony's depiction of the Greek goddess of love, beauty and sexuality on this coin may provide some insight into the respect Antony felt toward Cleopatra.

Octavian is represented here too with coins that celebrate his victories over Brutus and later Marc Antony and honor his friend and general Marcus Agrippa. Three celebrate his victory over the assassins who murdered Julius Caesar and two commemorate his final victory over Marc Antony and Cleopatra. Another shows Octavian and Agrippa with a crocodile, the Roman symbol for Egypt, chained to a palm tree.

Other coins from the era's non-Roman rulers are here too, including a Parthian king who murdered his father and 30 siblings, a Mauritanian king who married Cleopatra's daughter, and a Cappadocian client-king of Rome. Each, like the other coins in this chapter, provide a unique window to the Roman civil war and the players whose passions and actions changed Rome and the Western world forever.

Partial Timeline.

63 BC   Cato confronts Caesar on Senate floor.
60 BC   1st Triumvirate: Caesar, Pompey and Crassus.
58 BC   Caesar begins conquest of Gaul.
55 BC   Caesar invades Britain.
53 BC   Crassus defeated and killed by Parthians.
52 BC   Caesar's victory over Vercingetorix.
51 BC   Cleopatra and Ptolemy rule Egypt.
49 BC   Caesar crosses the Rubicon. Pompey flees.
48 BC   Caesar defeats Pompey at Pharsala.
48 BC   Pompey murdered. Caesar meets Cleopatra.
48 BC   Library of Alexandria destroyed.
47 BC   Caesar places Cleopatra on the Egyptian throne.
47 BC   Caesarion born to Caesar and Cleopatra.
46 BC   Vercingetorix displayed in Caesar's Triumph.
46 BC   Caesar defeats resistance in Africa.
45 BC   Caesar defeats Pompey's sons at Munda.
44 BC   Julius Caesar assassinated on Senate floor.
44 BC   Octavian returns to Rome with Agrippa.
44 BC   Brutus and Cassius flee east.
43 BC   2nd Triumvirate: Octavian, Antony and Lepidus.
42 BC   Brutus and Cassius defeated at Philippi.
39 BC   Marc Antony and Octavia wed.
36 BC   Octavian defeats Sextus Pompey in sea battle.
36 BC   Lepidus is stripped of power.
36 BC   Empire divided between Octavian and Antony.
34 BC   Antony names Cleopatra Queen of the East.
34 BC   Antony declares Caesarion heir to Caesar.
31 BC   Octavian defeats Antony and Cleopatra at Actium.

30 BC   Antony and Cleopatra commit suicide.
30 BC   Octavian becomes first citizen of Rome.

COINS FEATURED IN THIS CHAPTER.

Julius Caesar as Dictator for Life, 44 BC
Decimus Brutus 48 BC
Vercingetorix, 48 BC
Hostilius Saserna, 48 BC
Julius Caesar, Conqueror, 46 to 45 BC
Cato, 47 to 46 BC
Pompey, 43 to 36 BC
Cleopatra in Exile, 51 to 30 BC
Cleopatra, Egyptian Queen, 51 to 30 BC
The Last Pharaohs, 51 to 30 BC
Juno Monetas, 46 BC
Caesar's Triumph, 46 BC
Battle of Munda, May 17, 45 BC
Julius Caesar, Dictator, 45 BC
Dictator for Life, 44 BC
Fulvia, 43 to 42 BC
Ariobarzanes, 52 to 42 BC
Antioch, 43 to 42 BC
Brutus, 42 BC
Cassius, 42 BC
Octavian at Philippi, 27 BC
Victory over Brutus, 27 to 10 BC
Ahenobarbus, 41 BC
Sextus Pompey, 37 to 36 BC
Marc Antony & Octavia, 39 BC
Phraates IV, Parthian King, 38 to 32 BC

Cleopatra as Aphrodite, mid 30s BC
Octavian Cut Coin, 36 BC
Cleopatra as Aphrodite, mid 30s BC
Marc Antony's Legions, 32 to 31 BC
Caesarion, 44 to 30 BC
Octavian, Victory at Actium, 26 AD
Marcus Agrippa, 63 to 12 BC
Augustus & Agrippa, 29 to 10 BC
Juba II, 25 BC to 23 AD

Caesar makes no complaints about you to be sure,
except for a remark which he attributed to you:
"We must praise the young man, reward him, and discard him."
He added that he has no intention of letting himself be
discarded.

Decimus Brutus speaking to Cicero on May 24, 43 BC
The young man referred to is Caesar Octavian

DECIMUS BRUTUS
48 BC

This coin was issued by a partisan, and perhaps child, of Julius Caesar less than a year after Caesar crossed the Rubicon in 49 BC. The moneyer was Decimus Brutus, a distant cousin of Caesar and a general of his legions. Some believe that it was this Brutus, and not his more famous cousin Marcus Brutus, who was the illegitimate son of Julius Caesar that contemporaries of Caesar whispered about.

Decimus earned Caesar's respect and trust as a general in his Gallic campaign. After Caesar subdued the city of Rome in 49 BC and looked to consolidate his control over the empire, he entrusted his navy to Decimus Brutus. When Caesar took his legions to Spain to confront the armies of Pompey, Decimus led the navy against Pompey's son Sextus in Sicily.

In 45 BC, Decimus was serving Caesar as a commander in Gaul. Despite his close professional and family ties to Caesar, Decimus sided with Cassius and his cousin Marcus Brutus when plans were made to murder Julius Caesar on the Ides of March in 44 BC. Decimus was with Caesar at his villa on that fateful day.

When Caesar's foreboding led him to cancel his plans to attend the Senate, it was Decimus who calmed his fears and convinced him to attend.

When the conspirators rushed Caesar in front of the assembled Senate, Decimus was among the first to bury his knife into Caesar's body. More stabbings followed until Caesar was stabbed 23 times.

After the attack, Marcus Brutus shouted that liberty was restored and called out Cicero's name. Fearing more violence, Cicero and other watching Senators fled. The assassins, guarded by a private army of gladiators hired by Decimus, made their way up the Capitoline Hill.

Days later, when Mark Antony addressed the city at Caesar's funeral, he showed the crowd Caesar's cloak, bloodied and torn by knives. He then read Caesar's will which made a bequest to every citizen of Rome. When the crowd learned that Decimus had been named a secondary heir in the will, it became violent and attacked the homes of the conspirators and their sympathizers.

The coin above, issued just four years earlier by Decimus, seems ironic in light of these events. The front features Pietas, the Roman goddess of duty and devotion. The reverse shows two joined hands and a caduceus, a Roman symbol for commerce and negotiation.

Coin details and provenance: Decimus Junius Brutus Postumius Albinus. 48 BC. AR silver denarius. Obverse: Head of Pietas right, PIETAS behind. Reverse: Two joined hands holding a caduceus, ALBINVS BRVTI F below. 4.0 grams. 18 mm. References: RCV 427. Acquired from Incitatus Coins, St. Johns, NL, Canada in July of 2009.

VERCINGETORIX
48 BC

The great Averni chieftain Vercingetorix spent the last five years of his life in a Roman prison at Tullianum. He is depicted here in profile with a chain around his neck. The coin was issued by his captors while Vercingetorix sat imprisoned in a Roman jail. On the back of the coin is a naked Gallic warrior with spear and shield behind a racing chariot.

Vercingetorix, whose name translates to "over-king of warriors," organized the Celtic tribes outside modern-day Provence to resist Julius Caesar's invasion of Gaul. His armies scored several victories against Rome's legions but were eventually defeated by Caesar's troops in 52 BC at the Battle of Alesia. Afterward, Vercingetorix surrendered and lay himself prostrate before Caesar. He was later was taken in chains to Tullianum, a prison in the Forum Romanum in Rome.

Julius Caesar regarded Vercingetorix as a formidable adversary, noting in his *Gallic Wars* how Vercingetorix strategically retreated to natural fortifications and torched towns to prevent Rome's legions from living off the land.

In 48 BC, Roman moneyer Hostilius Saserna issued this coin in praise of Julius Caesar, who had crossed the Rubicon and subdued Rome the year before. The coin's dramatic portrait and battle scene with a Gallic chariot reminded Romans of the Gallic threat Caesar had subdued and the military prowess of their new ruler.

Two years later, in 46 BC, Vercingetorix was paraded through the streets of Rome in chains as part of a great Triumph staged to honor Caesar's victories. He was put to death shortly after the celebration.

Coin details and provenance: Republican Rome. Vercingetorix, Celtic Overlord. L. Hostilius Saserna. 48 BC. Roman Republic. Silver denarius. Obverse: Head of captive Gallic warrior, chain around neck, shield behind. Reverse: Naked Gallic warrior holding spear and shield, in biga driven right by charioteer, legends L · HOSTIL[IVS] above and [SASERN] below. 3.38 grams. References: Hostilia 2; SM.418 Acquired from Walter Holt's Old Money, Sydney, Australia in August of 2005.

Hostilius Saserna
48 BC

The events of this year are among the best known and most fateful in antiquity. Julius Caesar, having seized power after crossing the Rubicon a year earlier, has now confronted Pompey's army of 50,000 at Pharsalus in Thessaly and achieved a decisive victory. Pompey flees to Alexandria hoping to rally his allies and mount a counter attack but is murdered by the Egyptians before he reaches shore.

When Caesar's pursuit brings him to Alexandria later in the year he is greeted with a gift of the severed head of Pompey, which brings Caesar to tears. The men, though rivals, had been brothers-in-law as well, Pompey having been married to Caesar's only child.

Civil war is raging in Egypt when Caesar arrives. The ministers of young Ptolemy XIII control he city and have the army of his sister, Cleopatra VI, surrounded on Cyprus. Caesar commands both Ptolemy and his sister Cleopatra to appear before him. Cleopatra somehow manages to escape the island and sneak into Alexandria on a small skiff traveling up river into the city.

She appears unannounced to Caesar on the shoulder of a Sicilian Greek in a bag or carpet tied with straps. Caesar is immediately taken with the 21-year-old Cleopatra. Her appearance, keen intellect, and forceful personality captivate him.

Cleopatra became Caesar's mistress and they became allies in the Egyptian civil war. With limited forces at his command in Alexandria, Caesar nonetheless manages to prevail and defeat the forces of Ptolemy, placing Cleopatra on the throne. There is a heavy cost to the conflict, however. Flames engulf the great Library of Alexandria and destroy its priceless collection.

When Caesar leaves Alexandria to pursue the remnants of Pompey's forces in North Africa, Cleopatra is pregnant with his child. Within the year, Cleopatra will move to Rome with her child, named Caesaron, to the consternation of many Romans.

Coin details and provenance: L Hostilius Saserna, ally to Julius Caesar, Dictator of Rome. 48 BC. Rome mint. Silver denarius. Roman Republic. Obverse: Female head (Pietas or Clementia) facing right, wearing oak wreath, cruciform earring, necklace, jewel above her ear, hair collected into a knot behind, and falling down her neck. Reverse: Victory running right, winged caduceus in right, Gallic trophy and palm fronds in left, legend L HOSTILIVS SASERNA. 3.362 grams, 19.1mm. VF, toned, grainy, light scratches. References: RR71936, Crawford 448/2, Sydenham 951, BMCRR I Rome 3989, RSC I Hostilia 5, Sear Imperators 17, SRCV I 417. Provenance: from the Andrew McCabe collection, ex Roma Numismatics e-auction 10, lot 589. Acquired from Forum Ancient Coins, Morehead City, NC in 2015.

Julius Caesar, Conqueror
46 to 45 BC

Julius Caesar broke with Rome and its Republican tradition when he crossed the Rubicon River in the northern part of the Italian peninsula on the evening of January 10 in 49 BC. Attended by a solitary legion, he nonetheless signaled an irreconcilable break with the ruling Republicans.

Traveling south toward Rome, Caesar met with little resistance until he arrived at the fortified city of Corfinium, due east of Rome. There he was confronted by an army of thirty cohorts (18,000 men) commanded by his adversary Domitius Ahenobarbus, the man whose appointment to succeed Caesar in Gaul had triggered Caesar's march on Rome.

Caesar quickly surrounded the city. By mid-February and with no reinforcements from Pompey, Ahenobarbus surrendered to Caesar, who offered clemency to the surrendering soldiers.

Caesar next marched to Brundisium, where Pompey had gone after abandoning the city of Rome. He hoped to reach Brundisium before ships could arrive to transport

Pompey and his legions to Greece. He failed. Pompey set sail before Caesar and his army arrived. Pompey's plans were to consolidate his Italian legions with loyal legions in Greece and to make a stand against Caesar there.

After missing Pompey, Caesar entered Rome unopposed. He conferred, unsuccessfully, with those Senators he could convene and then broke into the Temple of Saturn and seized the government's silver reserves. They had been left behind by Pompey in his rush to flee the city.

This coin, which may have used some of the silver seized from the temple, was minted in Spain while Caesar pursued Pompey's forces there. It features the goddess Venus on the front and a trophy of Gallic arms and captives on the reverse.

Coin details and provenance: Julius Caesar. Struck 46 to 45 BC in Spain. Silver denarius. Obverse: Diademed head of Venus facing right with a small Cupid at shoulder behind. Reverse: CAESAR - Trophy of Gallic arms between seated male and female captives. 3.84 grams. 19.3 mm. References: Sear-1404, Cr-468/1, CRI 58, RSC-13. A much larger flan than normal with lots of luster remaining on both surfaces. Just a touch off center, but complete designs are on both sides due to the larger planchet. Lightly toned. Acquired from Glenn W. Woods Numismatics, Dallas, Texas in June of 2005.

CATO
47 TO 46 BC

This coin was issued by Marcus Procius Cato, known to the world as Cato the Younger, while he was stationed in Africa as part of the forces loyal to Magnus Pompey. It was issued shortly before Cato committed suicide in April of 46 BC. A staunch opponent of Caesar, Cato threw in with Pompey to resist Caesar's advances. Shortly after the army he was attached to was defeated in northern Africa, Cato took his own life. He refused to submit to a world ruled by Caesar.

The images on his coin reflects Cato's beliefs and his appearance. On the front is a profile of the god Liber, who the Romans associated with free speech and the coming of age. The portrait has disheveled hair like that of Cato, who was known for his unconventional appearance. On the reverse is a winged Victoria, the Roman personification of victory, sitting on a throne.

A brilliant orator and man of unquestioned integrity, Cato was the voice of the conservative Republicans who wanted to preserve the institutions and privileges of Rome's upper class. He was also a practicing stoic who wore black robes to protest the pretensions of Rome's ruling elite. True to his philosophy, he disdained the trappings of wealth and, unlike many Romans of power, refused to profit personally when given a potentially lucrative foreign assignment.

He was also reputed to be inflexible and humorless. Cato became the adversary of both Julius Caesar and Pompey when they joined forces with Crassus to form the First Triumverate in 61 BC. Before that in 63 BC, he assisted Cicero in quashing the Cataline conspiracy that threatened to overturn the Republic. When Julius Caesar opposed Cicero's proposal to execute the conspirators, it was Cato's impassioned arguments that swayed the Senate to proceed with the executions.

Cato's passionate opposition to Caesar was said to be born during these same Senate arguments. Cato accused Caesar of being involved in the conspiracy and then demanded Caesar read a letter he was looking at during the debate. Caesar read it out loud. It was a love letter from his mistress, Cato's half-sister Servilia Caepionis.

After Caesar crossed the Rubicon, Cato traveled and fought with Pompey. His escape after Pompey's defeat at Pharsalus led him to Africa with the remains of Pompey's legions.

Coin details and provenance: Marcus Porcius Cato. 47 to 46 BC. Quinarius. Mint in Utica, Africa. Obverse: Head Liber facing right with ivy wreath M CATO. Reverse: VITRIX; Victoria enthroned facing right holding patera and palm branch. 13 mm. 1.9 grams. References: Crawford 243/2b. Acquired from Gitbud & Naumann, Munchen, Germany in January of 2013.

POMPEY
43 TO 36 BC

Magnus Pompey, facing right above, was Rome's leading citizen and most decorated general when Julius Caesar crossed the Rubicon. He was Caesar's greatest rival and expected by many to defend Rome and defeat Caesar on Italian soil. Instead, he fled Rome and left the city defenseless.

As Caesar approached Rome, Pompey gathered his Italian legions and headed for the port city of Brundisium to await transport to Greece. His plan was to join up with his eastern armies and allies and prepare for full-scale war. It proved only to delay the inevitable. Pompey's legions were eventually defeated by Caesar's army at Pharsalus in August of 48 BC, after which Pompey fled to Alexandria.

When he arrived in Egypt he was assassinated by agents of the young King Ptolemy, who stabbed him after he stepped onto a small vessel sent by the Egyptians to ferry him to shore. Julius Caesar wept when servants of Ptolemy later brought him Pompey's head and signet ring. Two of Pompey's assassins were executed on Caesar's order.

Pompey first came to fame fighting for Roman general Sulla in Picenum, Sicily, and Africa. His success as a general was so great that he was given the honorary title Magnus and permitted to enter Rome in Triumph.

Pompey also helped end the slave revolt of Spartacus, conquered new territories for Rome, and served on the First Triumvirate with Julius Caesar and Marcus Crassus in 60 BC. After the death in 54 BC of Pompey's wife Julia, who was Caesar's daughter, Pompey became Caesar's open adversary.

This coin was issued by Magnus Pompey's son Sextus after the elder Pompey and Julius Caesar had died. Sextus became a force in Roman politics after Caesar's assassination, operating from a base in Sicily. His navy commanded much of the sea around the Italian peninsula and challenged the ambitions of Rome's Three Triumvirates until Octavian's General Agrippa defeated him in 36 BC off Naulochus cape in northern Sicily. Sextus was summarily executed in the Greek city of Miletus the next year after his capture by Antony's legions.

The coin depicts the Pompeys as the two-faced god Janus on the front and shows the prow of a galley on its reverse. Janus was the Roman god of gateways and time. He was able to see both the past and the future.

Coin details and provenance: Sextus Pompey. 43 to 36 BC. Æ As. Sicilian mint. Obverse: Laureate head of Janus with features of Cn. Pompeius Magnus (Sextus Pompey, son of Magnus Pompey) and his father Magnus Pompey. Reverse: Prow of galley facing right. 14.30 grams. Acquired from Barry P. Murphy, Willow Street, Pennsylvania in September of 2004.

Cleopatra in Exile
51 to 30 BC

This faint image of a young woman on a coin minted for Cleopatra in Cyprus is the perfect introduction to antiquity's most famous queen. While the attribution and mint date of this coin is uncertain, it may well have been minted to pay Cleopatra's troops who, in 48 BC, were pinned down on the Island of Cyprus and preparing for battle with the numerically superior forces of Ptolemy XIII. She was 21 at the time and Ptolemy was just 13.

When their father died in 51 BC, Cleopatra and Ptolemy became joint monarchs. Within six months, relations broke down between Cleopatra and the officials who managed Ptolemy. Cleopatra began ruling alone and issued coins in her image without portraits of her brother. Times were hard and for three years she ruled an empire in crisis faced with inadequate flooding and famine.

Within a year of her ascension, Cleopatra was contending with Roman forces left in Egypt by general Aulus Gabinius who had gone native and aligned with the advisors to Ptolemy for the purpose of restoring the young Ptolemy to the throne.

The war that followed cost Cleopatra her throne. In the end, she had to flee Alexandria to avoid capture by forces commanded by the eunuch Pothinus, who planned to rule Egypt in the name of the young Ptolemy.

Cleopatra's exile took her to Cyprus, where she prepared to fight for her place on the throne. Her odds of succeeding were not good. Then the Roman civil war intervened.

In 48 BC, while Cleopatra was in exile, the great Roman general Pompey fled to Alexandria after a disastrous defeat at the hands of Julius Caesar in Greece. He hoped to garner assistance from his Egyptian allies but, instead, fell prey to their desire to curry favor with Caesar. Before Pompey could set foot on Egyptian soil, a welcoming party sent by Pothinus murdered him on the small vessel sent to bring him to land. Cleopatra's prospects had changed.

Coin details and provenance: Rare small AE12 (dichalkon or eighth unit) of Cleopatra VII. 51 to 30 BC. Minted in Paphos, Cyprus. Ptolemaic Kingdom of Egypt. Obverse: Diademed and draped bust right. Reverse: Double cornucopia. 1.52 grams. 12mm. References: Kreuzer p. 43; Svoronos 1161 (Ptolemy IV); Weiser; SNG Copenhagen 649. Kreuzer, in his book The Coinage System of Cleopatra VII and Augustus in Cyprus, assembles evidence pointing towards a later date for the small Ptolemaic bronzes in circulation on Cyprus, attributing them to Cleopatra VII, rather than the time of Ptolemy IV and Arsinoë III. The evidence includes the discovery of a Ptolemaic mint at Paphos, striking these small coins at the very end of the Ptolemaic period. Acquired from Ancient Coins Canada, Ontario, Canada in December of 2010.

Cleopatra as Queen
51 to 30 BC

In October of 48 BC, Julius Caesar arrived in Alexandria in pursuit of Pompey and was shocked when the royal courtier Pothinus presented him with the severed head of Pompey. Witnesses said Caesar wept upon seeing the disfigured head of his former rival and son-in-law.

He was also surprised to find himself embroiled in an Egyptian civil war, with advisors to Ptolemy XIII ruling and intent upon destroying the remaining forces of the exiled Cleopatra. Notwithstanding the precarious situation and with few troops at his disposal, Caesar nonetheless directed both monarchs to lay down their arms and meet him in Alexandria.

This presented Cleopatra with both an opportunity and a challenge. If she could make her case to Caesar, she might be able to enlist the great Roman's assistance in retaking her throne. But, to plead her case she had to get to Caesar in a royal palace in Alexandria that was controlled by the forces of Pompey.

Unable to safely enter the city through conventional means without giving Pothinus the opportunity to do to her what he had done to Pompey, Cleopatra made arrangements for a quiet entrance into the palace. Avoiding the ocean harbor, the Egyptian queen snuck into Egypt and boarded a small skiff that brought her up-river into Alexandria.

From there she had herself carried to Caesar slung over the back of a Sicilian Greek in a bag tied with straps. She was delivered to Caesar's feet where she exited the bag looking, according to one witness, both majestic and pitiful.

Plutarch reports that the 52-year-old Caesar was utterly captivated by her. He would stay with her for months and help her regain her throne.

After months of intrigue and open warfare that called on all the skill that Caesar could muster, the undermanned Roman contingent prevailed. After defeating Ptolemy's forces at the Battle of the Nile in 47 BC, Caesar installed Cleopatra as sole ruler of Egypt. He remained in Egypt for a few months and then returned to Rome, later to be joined by Cleopatra and their newborn son Caesarion.

The coin above shows the queen in profile on one side but, unlike the one issued from Cyprus, bears the emblematic Egyptian eagle on the other.

Coin details and provenance: Cleopatra VII. 51 to 30 BC. Æ 80 drachma. Obverse: Diademed bust of Cleopatra. Reverse: Eagle standing left, on thunderbolt. 18.32 grams. References: BMC 4. Acquired from Frank L. Kovaks Ancient Coins & Antiquities, Corte Madera, California in April of 2006.

THE LAST PHARAOHS
48 BC

This coin from the fourth year of the reign of Cleopatra, is in the traditional style of the Ptolemy coins. It depicts the founder of the dynasty, Ptolemy I, on the front with the Egyptian eagle on the back. But unlike most Ptolemy coins, this one depicts a surprisingly young looking Ptolemy.

At the time of its issuance, a 13-year-old Ptolemy XIII was at war with his sister Cleopatra. He was, in reality, being used by Pothinus, his prime minister, Archillas, the commander of the royal guard, and Theodotus, his rhetoric master, to advance their ambition to rule Egypt. Was this portrait of a young Ptolemy issued to support the young Ptolemy's claim to the Egyptian throne?

While his older sister was pinned down on Cyprus, Ptolemy stood off the shallow waters off Pelusium with Pothinus, Archillas, and Theodotus while Pompey was being escorted off his ship by Egyptian officials.

Pompey had just lost a major battle to Julius Caesar and had come to Egypt to seek aid from his Egyptian allies. But when those allies learned of his approach, they made a fateful decision. After Pompey stepped aboard the "wretched little boat" sent for him by the Egyptians, he was brutally murdered. Just yards away, Pompey's wife Cornelia cried out in horror as the Egyptians severed Pompey's head from his body. The boy-king Ptolemy stood on shore in his purple robes watching Pompey meet his end.

While debating Pompey's fate, Theodotus had advised that "dead men do not bite." Their rash action, however, doomed Ptolemy and his handlers. When Caesar later arrived he allied with Cleopatra and defeated the forces of Ponthius, Archillas and Theodotus. Ptolemy paid with his life and Cleopatra was re-enthroned as Egypt's queen to begin a fantastic journey.

For the next 18 years, her status as Egypt's queen placed her near the center of the world stage as Caesar consolidated his power, died at the hands of assassins and Rome entered into a bloody and extended civil war. As the mother of Caesar's son, Cleopatra would astutely realign with Marc Antony, bear his children and nearly survive to establish with him an expanded Egyptian empire. When she and her son Caesarion died in 30 BC at the hands of Octavian, the Ptolemy's 300 year reign of Egypt came to an end.

Coin details and provenance: Ptolemaic Kings of Egypt. Era of Cleopatra VII Thea Neotera. 51 to 30 BC (dated Regnal Year 4). AR tetradrachm. Minted in Alexandria. Obverse: Diademed bust of Ptolemy I, wearing aegis. Reverse: Eagle standing left, on thunderbolt; L Δ (date). 12.38 grams. 25 mm. References: Svoronos 1819; SNG Copenhagen 400-1. Acquired from Holyland Numismatics in West Bloomfield, Michigan in July of 2012.

Juno Monetas
46 BC

This coin from moneyer Titus Carisius celebrates the creation and minting of ancient Roman coinage. On the front it bears a likeness of the goddess Juno Monetas. Juno was the daughter of Saturn, the sister to Jupiter and the mother of Mars and Vulcan. More importantly, she was considered a protector and counselor to the state.

As Monetas, she was also the protector of funds. It is in this role that she is venerated on this coin and because of this that the Roman mint was located in or near her temple on the Capitoline Hill. The modern word "money" is derived from the goddess's name.

The back of this coin displays the implements of coin making: an anvil die, a punch die, tongs and a hammer. The process involved the creation of dies by artisans called celators, who engraved the coin's image in reverse, a process called intaglio, into dies that were then hammered onto heated planchets to create coins.

The planchets were metal discs created by pouring molten metal into molds. After cooling they were reheated, retrieved using tongs, and then placed between a die embedded in an anvil and a separate punch die. A hammer was then used to strike the punch die and embed images into the two faces of the planchet. Once the coin had cooled it was ready for circulation.

Because of the many variables involved, such as the temperature, the width and shape of the planchet, the alignment of the dies, and the force and accuracy of the hammered blow, no two coins are exactly alike even when created from the same dies. Most dies were made from bronze and had to be replaced frequently, adding to the variation among coins.

Rome did not begin minting coins until 260 BC, hundreds of years after the Greeks and Lydians began issuing their coins. Even so, from that late beginning until Caesar's assassination 215 years later in 44 BC more than 100 moneyers were authorized by the Roman Senate to create coins and they issued more than 900 different coin varieties. Variation in coin types became even more common in the aftermath of Caesar's death as each would-be successor to Caesar issued their own coins to pay their troops or to celebrate their successes.

Coin details and provenance: Republican Rome. T Carisius, moneyer. Commemorating the Roman mint. AR silver denarius. Struck at Rome, 46 BC. Obverse: Head of Juno Moneta facing right, MONETA behind, lock of hair on neck. Reverse: Coin minting implements, anvil die with garlanded punch die above, between tongs and hammer, all within laurel wreath. Reference: RCV 447. 3.3 grams. 17 mm. Acquired from Incitatus Coins and Antiquities in May 2001, St. John's, NL, Canada.

Caesar's Triumph

46 BC

This coin was issued by moneyer Cordius Rufus when Julius Caesar returned to Rome near the end of his wars with Pompey. It foreshadows Caesars' plan for a Triumph through the city of Rome and construction of a new temple to Venus.

To commemorate his victories in Gaul, Egypt, Pontus, and Africa (his victory over Pompey in Greece being deliberately omitted), Caesar staged a grand celebration that included the dedication of the Forum and the consecration of the temple of Venus Genetrix, the latter being reflected on the reverse of this coin. The temple consecration was intended to commemorate Caesar's victories and honor the goddess most closely affiliated with his family.

Each day included a triumphal procession through the city and display of prominent prisoners such as Vercingetorix, Cleopatra's sister Arsinoe, and the son of King Juba of Numidia. Caesar rode in each triumphal parade wearing a purple toga on a chariot drawn by three white horses. His soldiers followed him and sang satirical songs, as was the tradition.

The parades were followed by gladiatorial games, theatrical performances, musical contests, horse racing, and a grand feast. The troops were honored and paid handsomely.

The scale of the Triumph was unprecedented. So too was the parading of a former queen of Egypt in chains, on whom the crowds took pity.

The celebrations culminated in a war of captives, more than 2,000 with horse and elephants on each side, fighting to the death in the Circus Maximus. Rioting followed that only ended after two rioters were sacrificed by priests on the Field of Mars.

The great Gallic warrior Vercingetorix, who no longer served a purpose after languishing in a Roman prison, was executed after the celebration. Offspring of defeated Roman adversaries were treated better. The young Juba II and Cleopatra Selene were spared and raised by prominent Roman families. They later married and ruled the Roman province of Numidia as client rulers.

Coin details and provenance: Mn. Cordius Rufus moneyer. 46 BC. Denarius minted in Rome to celebrate Julius Caesar's quadruple triumph. Obverse: RVFVS III VIR beside jugate heads of Dioscuri facing right, wearing laureate pilei. Reverse: MN CORDIVS beside Venus Verticordia standing left, holding scales in right hand and scepter in left hand, Cupid hovering behind her left shoulder. 3.9 grams. Ex. Eden Seminary Collection. Acquired from Vaughn Rare Coin Gallery, Alton, Illinois in April of 2006.

Battle of Munda
March 17, 45 BC

This inscribed lead sling bullet was used by the forces of Magnus Pompey under command of Titus Labienus and Pompey's son Gnaeus Pompey in the last great battle between the forces of Pompey and Julius Caesar. The inscription of CN MAG was engraved into the mold used to make the bullet.

The battle helped seal Caesar's dominion over the Republic by removing the Pompeian forces as a viable threat. Unknown to Caesar, however, was how short lived this dominion would be. He would die from multiple stab wounds less than one year later on the floor of the Roman Senate.

The battle took place on the Spanish plains of Munda with Pompey's forces camped in a favorable position on a gentle hill. The fighting lasted for hours with no clear advantage for either side until Julius Caesar personally took command of his tenth legion on the right wing.

Responding, Gnaeus Pompey moved a legion from his right wing to support his left wing now under more vigorous attack from Caesar's tenth. In response, Caesar's cavalry attacked Pompey's depleted right wing while Caesar's ally, King Bogud of Mauritania, attacked Pompey's rear. Labienus' troops panicked and broke their line.

Approximately 30,000 perished in the battle, most of them troops of Pompey. This lead sling bullet with its reference to Magnus Pompey was recovered from the battlefield. It would have been launched at Caesar's legions by Pompey's sling archers. After the battle, which cost both Labienus and Gnaeus Pompey their lives, Caesar returned to Rome to govern as dictator.

Sling bullets like these were a staple of both Greek and Roman battle. And messages were frequently included on the bullets. Bullets found on the battlefield of a later engagement between forces of Caesar's appointed heir Octavian and those of Marc Antony's brother Lucius bore messages mocking Lucius Antony's baldness and making crude remarks about Antony's wife Fuliva. In the same battle, Lucius Antony's legions launched bullets with crude messages referring to Octavian's arse and the depicting Octavian as depraved.

Coin details and provenance: Datable lead slingshot used on March 17th, 45 BC. Inscribed with CN MAG, the abbreviated name of Gnaeus Pompeius, Pompey the Great. Found on Roman Imperatorial battlefield site of Munda (near Seville) in Spain. 3.89 centimeters. Typical white patina for excavated lead which has been lightly waxed to better highlight the inscription. Acquired from Lodge Antiquities, Grantham, United Kingdom in January of 2005.

Julius Caesar, Dictator
45 BC

While Caesar's unruly Triumph in 46 BC raised concerns among some of Rome's elite, this coin and the next one bearing Caesar's profile likely inflamed the opposition more. Issued with images declaring Caesar's victory over other Roman noblemen, it also proclaims Caesar as dictator with the words CAESAR DICTER.

Just the year before, having scored a major victory over the legions of Cato in North Africa, Caesar was proclaimed dictator for ten years by Rome's Senate. In the year the coin was issued, he was elected sole consul, another affront to Rome's republican traditions that called for two consuls to rule jointly.

These were unprecedented acts. But having defeated his adversaries and consolidated his control over Rome, Caesar dared to proclaim his authority by putting his position as dictator and the image of a winged Victory on his coins.

Minerva, who was the virgin goddess of warriors, poetry, medicine, wisdom, and commerce, as well as the inventor of music, graces the reverse side of this coin. Years earlier, Pompey had compared Minerva with the Greek goddess Pallas Athena, bestower of victory, when he built a temple to her using the proceeds from his successful eastern campaign.

With Caesar fresh off his victories in Spain and Pompey's forces largely destroyed, the choice of symbolism is clear. Caesar had surpassed and replaced his former son-in-law Magnus Pompey as Rome's first citizen.

Coin details and provenance: Julius Caesar. 45 BC. Bronze dupondius struck at Rome. Obverse: CAESAR DICTER - Winged and draped bust of Victory facing right. Reverse: C CLOVI PRAEF - Minerva advancing left, holding trophy, spears and shield, snake at lower left. 12.79 grams, 27.3 mm. References: Sear-1417, RPC I-601, Cr-476/1, CRI-62. A choice example of this lifetime issue of Julius Caesar. Acquired from Glenn W. Woods Numismatist, Dallas, Texas in September of 2005.

DICTATOR FOR LIFE
44 BC

If Caesar's earlier coin from 45 BC bothered some among Rome's ruling class, this one surely helped inflame some to conspiracy and murder. Called "the coin that killed Caesar" by collectors, it was minted just months before Brutus, Cassius and the other "liberators" brought Julius Caesar to a bloody death on the floor of the Senate on the Ides of March in 44 BC.

After defeating Pompey's legions and returning to Rome, the now captive Senate bestowed on Caesar the title Dictator Perpetuo, or dictator for life, and granted Caesar the right to place his own image onto Roman coins. Both of these honors were extraordinary in a Republic that for centuries had limited the terms of their consuls to one year and had forbade contemporary images on their coins. This would be the one and only coin issued in Caesar's lifetime to reflect these unprecedented honors.

On the coin, Caesar can be seen wearing a crown and a veil. The crown reflects his triumphs while the veil is a reference to his religious office of Pontifex Maximus. The legend DICT PERPETVO appears behind Caesar with the legend CAESAR, partially obscured in front.

The reverse of the coin shows the goddess Venus next to a military shield with an outstretched arm holding victory. The name of the moneyer who issued the coin, P. Sepullius Macer, appears obscured in the margin. Venus was the goddess Caesar's family claimed as an ancestor. The shield and victory make reference to Caesar's military triumphs.

Many of these coins, which were minted to pay the troops Caesar was amassing to attack the Parthians, are imperfect and appear carelessly struck indicating that the mint may have been working under pressure. Caesar's death and the ensuing civil wars brought an end to plans to attack Parthia, at least until Marc Antony's unsuccessful efforts to subdue the Parthians later after the Second Triumverate had allocated dominion to Antony over the eastern portion of the Roman Empire.

Coin details and provenance: Julius Caesar, Dictator for Life, Assassinated 15 March 44 B.C. Silver denarius. Rome mint. Obverse: CAESAR DICT PERPETVO, veiled and wreathed head of Caesar right. Reverse: P SEPVLLIVS MACER, Venus standing left, Victory in extended right, long scepter vertical in left, shield at feet right. Fine grade, scratches, polished. 3.466 grams, 18.4mm. 135°, References: SH72074. Sydenham 1074, Crawford 480/13, Sear Imperators 107d, RSC I 39, BMCRR 4173, Vagi 56, SRCV I 1414. Ex Andrew McCabe Collection, ex Roma Numismatics e-auction 3 (30 Nov 2013), lot 481. Acquired from Forum Ancient Coins, Morehead City, North Carolina in January of 2015.

FULVIA

43 TO 42 BC

Fulvia, the politically active and ambitious third wife of Marc Antony, was the first living woman to appear on a Roman coin. Here she is depicted as Nike on the front with a lion, the birth sign of Marc Antony, on the back. The coin was minted in the Greek town of Eumeneia, which Marc Antony had renamed Fulvia.

Fulvia and Antony were married around 47 BC, a few years after the death of Fulvia's second husband. She had been active in the political careers of her husbands and provided Antony with needed money, organization and partisan street gangs she had assembled for her last husband.

When Antony became the most powerful man in Rome after Caesar's assassination, Fulvia helped Antony manage his power and grow his wealth. So strong was her influence that Fulvia largely controlled Roman politics in 42 BC while Antony and Octavian were pursuing Brutus and Cassius in Greece. Her influence continued even after her death, when her daughter Claudia was married to Octavian to seal the alliance created when Antony, Octavian and Lepidus formed the Second Triumvirate.

Fulivia's demise came when Octavian returned to Rome in 41 BC after the battle of Philippi to secure lands for his legions and the legions of Antony. Marc Antony's brother Lucius opposed confiscation of the land and with Fulvia's aid raised eight legions and seized Rome. When Octavian and Lepidus combined their legions to respond, Lucius retreated with his army to Perusia (modern day Perugia). The ensuing siege of the city became so personal that Octavian's troops inscribed their sling bullets with insults directed at Fulvia. After Lucius surrendered, Fulvia fled to Greece where a frosty reception from Antony probably contributed to her deep depression and death.

Fulvia is perhaps most famous for her animosity toward Rome's great orator Cicero. He embarrassed her when he prosecuted her husband P. Clodius Pulcher in 62 BC for sneaking into the women-only ritual of Bona Dea dressed as a woman. Cicero later became Antony's most outspoken critic after Julius Caesar's death. Fulvia's hatred became so great that after Cicero's execution in 43 BC, she had his severed head delivered to her so she could drive hairpins into his lifeless tongue.

Coin details and provenance: Fulvia. 43 to 42 BC. Quinarius. Obverse: Winged bust of Fulvia right depicted as Nike. Reverse: Lion advancing right; LVGV DVNI A XL. 1.67 grams. Fulvia was the third wife of Marc Antony. It has been suggested that the XL on the reverse refers to Antony's age and the lion to his birth sign of Leo. Fulvia was the first non-mythological woman portrayed on a Roman coin. Acquired from Loge Antiquities, Grantham, United Kingdom in January of 2010.

Ariobarzanes
52 to 42 BC

The uncertainties that followed Caesar's crossing of the Rubicon and later assassination unleashed 18 years of civil war that would affect the city of Rome and all her territories. Even being a Roman client-king became difficult as power shifted and rivals demanded allegiance and support from client-kings in the territories.

Cappadocian ruler Ariobarzanes III and his circumstances illustrate just how uncertain and difficult things could be during these dangerous times. He came to power in 52 BC following the murder of his father, who had ruled Cappadocia for twelve years. His grandfather Philo Romaeus had ruled Cappadocia for Rome for 30 years before his father came into power.

Ariobarzanes served Rome loyally in the years before Caesar entered Rome with his legions, even earning the gratitude of Cicero during his proconsulate in Cilicia. But civil war forced Ariobarzanes to choose sides.

After Caesar secured Rome and Pompey moved to Greece to meet up with his eastern legions, Ariobarzanes sided with Pompey and his occupying legions against Julius Caesar. When Caesar defeated Pompey at the Battle of Pharsalus in 48 BC, Ariobarzanes quickly and prudently switched his allegiance to Caesar. He was rewarded with additional territories.

But his good fortune was short lived. When Caesar was murdered in 44 BC, his assassins Brutus and Cassius fled east and took control of Cappadocia. Two years later, before their own defeat by Octavian and Antony, Cassius had Ariobarzanes put to death.

Ariobarzanes' coin is in the style of earlier Cappodician coins. It depicts the king on the front and Athena standing with shield and spear on the back, surrounded by Greek script. The legend on the back declares Ariobarzanes as king.

Cappadocia was and is renowned for an unusual landscape that contains a labyrinth of underground cities designed to provide its citizens with escape and safe haven from invaders. These underground cities contain traps and narrow passages that gave the Cappadocian's advantages in defending themselves. Early Christians used these underground hiding places to escape persecution before Christianity became accepted in the Roman Empire.

Coin details and provenance: Cappadocian Kingdom. Ariobarzanes III. 52 to 42 BC. Drachm. Obverse: Bust of Ariobarzanes facing right. Reverse: Athena standing left holding a spear and shield. The Greek legend on the reverse side of the coin reads as follows: ΒΑΣΙΛΕΩΣ ΑΡΙΟΒΑΡΖΑΝΟΥ ΕΥΣΕΒΟΥΣ ΚΑΙ ΦΙΛΟΡΩΜΑΙΟΥ . References: SG 7304. Acquired from Aegean Numismatics, Ohio in April of 2005.

Antioch

43 TO 42 BC

From what had been the western capital of the Seleucid Empire comes this curious coin of Roman Antioch issued just a couple of years after the murder of Julius Caesar. The portrait on the coin, surprisingly, is not of a Roman leader or client king. Instead, the portrait is of Philip Philadelphos, the last ruler of the Greek's Seleucid Empire some 40 years earlier. On the back, is the distinctly Greek image of Zeus sitting enthroned, similar in some respects to the reverse image found on many of Alexander the Great's coins.

Philadelphos and his brother Antiochus XI ruled Antioch and the Seleucid Empire jointly for three years after their father's death in 95 BC, when their reign was briefly interrupted by a coup engineered by their brother Antiochus XII. Philadelphos eventually reasserted control over the empire in 92 BC, but not until after his brother drowned in the Orontes River after a failed siege of Antioch. He ruled for nine years. In 83 BC, he was replaced by Tigranes the Great of Armenia.

The area did not come under Roman rule until 66 BC when Magnus Pompey defeated an aging Tigranes on the battlefield. After his defeat, Tigranes continued to rule Armenia as a Roman ally for another ten years.

The city of Antioch became a civitas libera, or free city, of Rome in 64 BC. Julius Caesar visited in 47 BC and confirmed its free status. The status accorded liberties to the city liberties that were not available to all Roman conquests. Its rights included freedom to tax and to mint its own coinage.

When this coin was issued, Antioch was embroiled with the rest of the Roman Empire in the civil war that followed the assassination of Julius Caesar, providing support for the forces of Octavian.

The city of Antioch was founded centuries earlier by Alexander's general Seleucus after Alexander's empire was divided following his death. The location was selected by ritual. Seleucus is said to have released an eagle, the bird of Zeus, with a piece of sacrificial meat. The city was situated on the site where the eagle landed with the offering. The city's name was chosen to honor Antiochus, the son of Seleucus.

Coin details and provenance: Roman Antioch, in the name of Philip Philadelphos 43 to 42 BC. Tetradrachm. Obverse: Head of Philip Philadelphos - the last king of the Selucid Kingdom - right. Reverse: Zeus seated left holding Nike in his out stretched hand and a scepter in his other; Greek legend around; KB in exergue (regnal year 22 or 43/42 BC). 14.04 grams. Acquired from Aegean Numismatics, Mentor, Ohio in August of 2009.

BRUTUS
42 BC

This is a replica of one of the rarest of Roman coins, the Eid Mar denarius issued by Caesar's assassin in 42 BC. It contains the only attested portrait of Marcus Junius Brutus. The original was minted in the field shortly before the Battle of Philippi, where the armies of Brutus and co-conspirator Gaius Cassius Longinus were defeated by the combined forces of Octavian and Marc Antony. Brutus and Cassius both died in the aftermath.

Two years earlier, on the Ides of March in 44 BC, Brutus and his fellow conspirators orchestrated a violent and bloody assassination of Julius Caesar. Sixty conspirators in addition to Brutus and Cassius participated in the plot. When Caesar arrived at the Senate that day, a mob of conspirators attacked him, stabbing him 23 times with their daggers in full view of the assembled Senate.

Brutus justified his brutal act as needed to save the Republic from destruction by Caesar. He likened it to the action his famous ancestor Lucius Junius Brutus took in 509

BC when he ousted Rome's last king Tarquinius Superbus to bring republican government to Rome.

On this famous coin, Brutus commemorates his role in the assassination and claims the deed was done to secure liberty for the Roman people. The image on the back shows a liberty cap between two daggers of the sort used to murder Caesar over the words "Eid Mar." On the front, the self-proclaimed champion of republican government oddly salutes himself as imperator (IMP), the same title that Julius Caesar had used.

Julius Caesar once said of Brutus that "it depends very much on what he wants; but what he wants, he wants utterly." According to the biographer Suetonius, a younger Caesar had seduced very many ladies of quality including the mother of Brutus, of whom it was said Caesar "loved above the others."

Based on their relative ages, however, Caesar would have been just 15 when Brutus was conceived. Nonetheless, many speculated that Brutus was the son of Julius Caesar. If true, then Brutus murdered a kinsman just as his famous ancestor did when he executed his sons for trying to restore the monarchy. Brutus died at the Battle of Philippi on October 23, 42 BC when, like Cassius, he took his own life.

Coin details and provenance: Replica Ides of March denarius of Marcus Junius Brutus. Original issued in 42 BC in Greece while on campaign. Obverse: Brutus portrait facing right, BRVT IMP L PLAET CEST. Reverse: liberty cap (Pileus) flanked by two daggers, EID MAR below.

CASSIUS
42 BC

This rare coin was minted by the assassin Gaius Cassius Longinus in the military mint of Smyrna that supported the troops of Brutus and Cassius before their fateful defeat by the forces of Octavian and Marc Antony at Philippi. The coin bears the images of Libertas, a jug and a curved war-trumpet known as a lituus.

Cassius, who served under Marcus Crassus in his Parthian campaign, was one of the few to survive the massacre of Rome's legions at Carrhae in 53 BC. The notoriety of his brave survival launch him on a distinguished military career that led to his appointment as governor of Syria. In 50 BC, he returned to Rome and was elected tribune of the plebs and sided with those opposed to Caesar.

Cassius commanded part of Pompey's fleet and destroyed a large number of Caesar's fleet off the coast of Sicily after Caesar took Rome. When Pompey was defeated at Pharsalus, Cassius headed to Africa but was intercepted by Caesar's legions and forced to surrender. He was made a general in

Caesar's army but returned to private life in Rome rather than fight against his former allies.

While in Rome, he became close to Cicero and a active conspirator in the plot to murder Julius Caesar. On the Ides of March in 44 BC, Cassius joined Brutus in leading the attack on Caesar on the Senate floor, striking Caesar in the face.

When Antony and Octavian later turned the Senate against the conspirators, Cassius headed east and amassed a large army. The next year he defeated the Roman legions of Caesar's general Dolabella and then marched on Egypt.

When Marc Antony joined forces with Octavian in November of 43 BC, Cassius joined Brutus and his army in Smyrna. The two conspirators led their armies successfully against the allies of Antony and Octavian in Asia and were proclaimed imperators by their legions when they rejoined their armies in Sardis a year later.

In 42 BC, they moved their armies to Philippi to await the combined armies of Antony and Octavian. In the two battles that followed, Cassius was routed by Antony and committed suicide believing he was defeated after mistaking some of Brutus' cavalry for forces of Antony. Cassius ordered his freedman to kill him. Co-conspirator Marcus Brutus, just days away from his own death, mourned him as the last of the Romans.

Coin details and provenance: Gaius Cassius Longinus and Publius Cornelius Lentulus Spinther. Military mint a Smyrna, summer of 42 BC. Silver denarius. Obverse: Diademed and draped bust of Libertas, C CASSI IMP LEIBERTAS. Reverse: Jug and lituus, LENTVLVS SPINT. 3.3 grams. 18 mm. References: Syd 1302, RCV 1447, BMC 78. Very scarce.

OCTAVIAN AT PHILIPPI
42 BC

This coin was struck in Macedonia in the autumn of 42 BC just before or after the battle of Philippi where the combined forces of Antony and Octavian defeated the legions of Brutus and Cassius. It was minted by Octavian, who, since learning the will of Julius Caesar had named him as heir with a common provision that he take Julius Caesar's name, referred to himself exclusively as Gaius Julius Caesar.

The coin bears the image of Mars on the front with the name of the new Caesar on the left side. The reverse shows two standards on either side of an Aquila, the legendary eagle who carried thunderbolts for Jupiter. The reverse also bears the legend SC, which required Senatorial consent.

Only 21 years of age when this coin was issued, Octavian had been just 18 when Julius Caesar died at the hands of Brutus, Cassius and their co-conspirators. Now, just three years later, the young man had avenged his adoptive father's assassination and become one of the most powerful men in Rome.

It had not been easy. When he arrived in Rome after the assignation, Marc Antony was consul, the conspirators had been forgiven by the Senate, and few took his aspirations seriously. Cicero met with him but refused to acknowledge his new name.

He quickly leveraged his testamentary adoption and borrowed funds to attract legionnaires from among Caesar's veterans, bringing 3,000 troops to Rome while he pressed his case with a reluctant Antony and Senate to confirm his inheritance and the honors earlier bestowed on Julius Caesar. With Senate approval, he later staged elaborate games commemorating Julius Caesar's victory over Pompey at Pharsalus during which a comet appeared in the sky. This came to be broadly interpreted as Julius Caesar ascending into heaven to live among the gods bolstering his adoptive son's earthly stature.

Within the year, a misstep by Antony in dealing with his Macedonian legions resulted in two legions switching allegiance to Octavian. With Antony gathering his legions in Brundisium for an anticipated march on Rome, the Senate became more accepting of Octavian. This made the young Caesar a force to be reckoned with.

Coin details and provenance: Octavian (Augustus). Military mint in Macedonia, autumn of 42 BC. AR silver denarius. Obverse: Helmeted and draped bust of Mars facing right, spear over shoulder, CAESAR III VIR R P C. Reverse: Legionary Aquila, surmounted by trophy flanked by two standards, SC legend. 3.1 grams. 20 mm. References: Syd 1320, Cr497/3, RCV 1537. Scarce. Acquired from Incitatus Coins & Antiquities, St. Johns, NL, Canada in December of 2014.

Victory over Brutus
27 TO 10 BC

This coin was minted more than 15 years after Octavian's and Anthony's victory over Brutus and Cassius at Philippi by veterans of the Praetorian Cohort. These former legionnaires had resettled near the site of their victory and had been granted the right to mint coins by Octavian, then Emperor Augustus.

The coin depicts a winged victory standing on a globe, representing the vastness of the Roman Empire and Augustus' dominion over it. To either side are legends identifying Augustus (AVG) and declaring victory (VIC). On the back are images of three legionary standards and a legend identifying the Praetorian Cohort who fought in the Battle of Philippi.

This was the great battle three years after Julius Caesar's death that established Octavian and Antony's control over the Empire's eastern provinces. In the tense days after Caesar's assassination, a shell shocked Senate had approved the conspirators actions to avoid further bloodshed. The assassins used their freedom to enlist more than 20 legions in Greece and Macedonia.

Three years after the assassination, the Senate reversed itself and declared the conspirators to be enemies of the State. This made military action against them by the legions of Octavian and Antony possible. But the declaration came reluctantly and only after the combined legions of Octavian, Antony and Lepidus marched on Rome and exterminated many of their adversaries, including prominent citizens like Cicero.

Leaving from Brundisium in September, Antony had to fight off raids as he shipped his legions to confront Brutus. Octavian had to ward of the navy of Sextus Pompey in the Adriatic. The young Caesar grew seriously ill during the voyage which held him back when they landed near Philippi while Antony forged ahead. Only ten days later was Octavian well enough to be carried with his legions to battlefield.

Fortunately, Brutus and Cassius had not yet initiated a full scale battle, instead being satisfied with small skirmishes while they enjoyed the higher ground. When battle did ensue, Antony was camped opposite the legions of Cassius while Octavian opposed Brutus. In two days of battle that culminated on October 23, 42 BC, first Cassius and then Brutus were defeated.

Coin details and provenance: Augustus. Minted between 27 and 10 BC by veterans of the Praetorian Cohort led by Augustus at Philippi in 42 BC. Bronze. Obverse: Victory standing facing left, legends VIC and AVG. Reverse: Three legionary standards, legends COHOR PRAEPHIL. 21.5 mm. 5.95 grams. References: BMC 23; Sear 32; SNG Cop. 306. Acquired from Sergey Nechayev Ancient Coins in December of 2014.

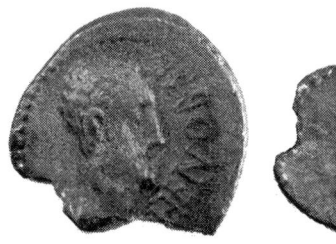

AHENOBARBUS
41 BC

This is the face of Lucius Ahenobarbus, Roman consul and imperator, placed on a coin by his son Gnaeus Ahenobarbus in 41 BC. Lucius allied with Magnus Pompey against Julius Caesar in the Senate and on the battlefield. In 49 BC, when the Senate removed Caesar from his command in Gaul, it was Lucius they appointed to succeed him. It was also Lucius who mounted the only resistance to Caesar as he approached Rome.

The two armies met at Corninium, north of Rome, where Lu-ius' 18,000 troops were surrounded by Caesar's legions. Lucius eventually surrendered after Pompey, in his hurry to retreat to Greece, failed to send aid. Lucius and his troops received clemency from Caesar in what was Caesar's first offering of clemency to his opponents.

After being released, Lucius traveled to Greece to join Pompey's resistance. He later died at the Battle of Pharsalus fighting for Pompey. He was reportedly struck down by Marc Antony as he tried to escape the battlefield.

Lucius' son and issuer of this coin, Gnaeus Ahenobarbus, served with his father at Corfinium and at the Battle of Pharsalus. He survived these engagements and Caesar's conquest of Rome. And, like many Pompey partisans, he was not executed for his associations.

Gnaeus followed Brutus and Cassius to Macedonia after Caesar's assassination and was among those later condemned to death as a conspirator by the Octavian-led Senate. He won an important naval battle at Philippi but became a pirate after Brutus and Cassius died.

After Philippi and pirating, Gnaeus reconciled with Marc Antony. When Antony and his fleet approached Brundisium in 40 BC, Ahenobarbus' "pirate" ships in the navy caused the town to close its port. Antony besieged the city and troops gathered on both sides for battle. Veterans of Caesar's legions on both sides intervened, brokering a settlement that created the Second Triumverate and avoided war.

Gnaeus Ahenobarbus remained with Antony, serving as a general in the camp of Antony and Cleopatra before the Battle of Actium. As matters deteriorated before the battle, however, troops who were disgruntled with Cleopatra's role in the battle planning pressed Gnaeus to replace Marc Antony. He refused and instead defected to Octavian. He died soon afterward.

Coin details and provenance: Gnaeus Domitius Ahenobarbus. 41 BC. Silver denarius from the region of the Adriatic or Ionian Sea. Obverse: AHENOBAR, bare head of Lucius Ahenobarbus right. Reverse: CN DOMITIVS IMP, trophy on prow right. 2.5 grams. 18mm. References: Cr519/2, Syd 1177; BMCRR (East) 94. RCV 1456. Acquired from Incitatus Coins & Antiquities, St. Johns, NL, Canada in October of 2005.

SEXTUS POMPEY
37 TO 36 BC

The youngest son of Magnus Pompey remained in Rome under the care of his stepmother, Cornelia Mettella, when his father fled to Greece to avoid Julius Caesar on his march to Rome. After Magnus Pompey was defeated at Pharsalas, Sextus traveled to Alexandria to join his father in Egypt and help him rebuild his legions. Sextus arrived, however, just in time to witness his father's assassination.

In the following years, Sextus joined Metellus Scipio, Cato the Younger and his brother Gnaeus Pompey in the African provinces to oppose Caesar. Their legions were defeated by Caesar in 48 BC at Thapsus, after which Scipio and Cato committed suicide.

Sextus and his brother Gnaeus lost again to Caesar three years later on the plains of Munda in Spain. The battle cost his brother his life but Sextus escaped to Sicily.

From there he consolidated a power base and built an army and navy to oppose the ambitions of Julius Caesar and later those of Octavian and Antony. He and his legions survived the assassination of Caesar and the formation of the Second Triumvirate by Octavian, Antony, and Lepidus.

Sextus' organizational and battlefield skills must have been considerable. His navy made it difficult for Octavian and Anthony's forces to travel to Pharsalus to engage with Brutus and Cassius. And he defeated Octavian's forces in 37 BC while defending Sicily and commanding the nearby seas.

But eventually the combined forces of Lepidus and Octavian and the naval acumen of Octavian's commander Marcus Agrippa brought an end to Sextus' ambitions. In 36 BC, with Octavian's forces approaching from Italy and Lepidus' legions growing in North Africa, Sextus suffered a crippling defeat to Agrippa in a naval battle off the northern coast of Sicily. Afterward, he fled east but was captured and executed by Marc Antony's forces.

This coin from Sextus, issued at the height of his power from his base in Sicily, reflects the source of the power that gave Octavian and others such trouble. On the front it depicts the sea god Neptune complete with trident. On the back is a trophy reminder of the many battles won by Sextus' navy. The trophy shows a warrior with arms composed of ships prows standing on an anchor.

Coin details and provenance: Sextus Pompey. 37 to 36 BC. AR denarius. Uncertain Sicilian mint. Obverse: Diademed and bearded head of Neptune, trident behind shoulder. Reverse: Naval trophy set on anchor, top trident visible above helmet, arms composed of the stern of a prow, heads of Scylly and Charybdis at base. 3.53 grams. 17 mm. References: Crawford 511/2a; RSC 1b. Acquired from London Coin Galleries, London, England in July 2016.

MARC ANTONY & OCTAVIA
39 BC

This coin commemorates the marriage of Marc Antony to Octavian's beloved sister Octavia in 40 BC. The marriage was arranged to cement a reconciliation between Rome's three triumvirs following Octavian's defeat of eight legions led by Antony's wife Fulvia against Rome. With the marriage came the Treaty of Brundisium that divided Rome into Africa (Lepidus), the West (Octavian), and the East (Antony).

Four years later in 36 BC, Antony abandoned the pregnant Octavia and their two daughters and traveled east to Antioch and the border with Parthia. From there he summoned Cleopatra, the mother of his twin boys, and began preparations for war against the Parthians.

Octavian, who had managed to exercise a degree of control over the popular and powerful Antony while Octavia was with him, struck back at Antony and set the stage for an eventual confrontation that would reunite Rome under one ruler. First, he increased his power by accusing fellow triumvir Lepidus of attempting rebellion.

Once Lepidus had been exiled, Octavian turned his expanded resources against Antony and played to the public dislike for Antony's abandonment of Octavia. He began attacking Antony publicly. One of his most effective accusations was the unforgivable charge that Antony had gone native, a reference to his assimilation into Egyptian ways and association with the Egyptian Queen Cleopatra.

Meanwhile, Antony invaded and conquered Armenia and distributed his conquests to his children by Cleopatra. He went on to declare Cleopatra Queen of Kings and Queen of Egypt. He also declared her son Caesarion as the legitimate son and heir of Julius Caesar.

This created an irreconcilable breach with Octavian, who began directing his invective directly against Cleopatra, eventually declaring war on the queen and making armed military confrontation inevitable.

This coin, issued to mark the marriage that brought a brief respite between Rome's two most powerful men, depicts Antony on the front and the beautiful Octavia on the back. Appropriately enough, Octavia appears atop a cista mystica, a basket used to hold snakes, between two intertwined serpents.

Coin details and provenance: Marc Antony. Circa 39 BC. Struck possibly in Pergamon AR cistophoric tetradrachm. Obverse: Head of Marc Antony right, lituus below. Reverse: Head of Octavia right, on cista mystica, on and between two serpents with heads erect. 11.59 grams. References: RSC 2. Commemorates the marriage of Antony and Octavia, Augustus' sister. Acquired from Nilus Coins, Austin, Texas in October of 2005.

Phraates IV
38 to 2 BC

The powerful King Phraates IV of Parthia came to power in 38 BC by murdering his father Orodes, his 30 brothers, and all of their families shortly after being named successor to the throne. While brutal in his methods, his approach to the throne was not unprecedented. His father had taken the throne by joining his brother to murder their father.

Phraates' coin depicts his crowned profile on the front with the signature royal Parthian wart on his forehead. On the reverse, Phraates sits before a standing Athena who presents him with a crown. The surrounding legend declares him king.

The Romans sent Marc Antony with his legions through Armenia to intervene after Phraates seized the throne. Anthony, however, unwisely pushed ahead of his supply line and Phraates destroyed his rear guard. The Romans lost 35,000 men before the campaign was over.

In 32 BC, while the Romans were fighting among themselves, Phraates was driven into exile by the Parthian ruler Tiridates. With the help of the Scythians, however, Phraates recaptured his throne. In the process, however, the fleeing Tiradates captured Phraates' son and turned him over to the Romans.

After Octavian's victory over Antony in 31 BC, Phraates had to deal with the Roman threat. Octavian, holding Phraates' son and desiring the return of the legionary standards lost to Parthia by Crassus years earlier, struck a deal with Phraates. In return for the lost standards, Phraates received back his son and an Italian slave to serve as his concubine.

Years later, Phraates made that slave his wife and named her Musa after a goddess. She bore Phraates a son named Phraatakes and was named Queen of Parthia. Many years later in 2 BC, Musa and her son Phraatakes would continue Parthian succession tradition by poisoning Phraates and ending his 36-year reign.

In an unusual twist, Phraatakes then married his mother. The marriage alienated Parthian nobility, however, and undermined his control. His reign lasted just six years.

Coin details and provenance: Parthian King, Phraates IV. 38 to 2 BC. AR tetradrachm. Seleucia on the Tigris mint (circa. S.E. 278-279 (=25-23 B.C.). Obverse: Diademed bust left, wart on forehead. Reverse: Phraates seated right on throne, facing Athena standing left before him, presenting diadem and holding scepter; year and month in exergue. 12.52 grams. References: Cf. Sellwood 52; cf. Shore 273. Toned, good VF, minor porosity. Acquired from Atlantis Ltd. in May of 2005.

Octavian Cut Coin
36 BC

It was common practice in ancient Rome to cut coins to make change, particularly in the provinces. Coins were cut for other reasons as well. Where a coin is irregularly cut like this one, it is possible that the coin was cut for another, uniquely Roman, purpose.

In ancient Rome, coins cut in half were frequently attached to abandoned babies. Immediately after birth, babies were traditionally placed at the father's feet by the midwife. The father then lifted the baby up to accept the child.

But if the father left the baby at his feet, the midwife would take the rejected child and dispose of it. Often, disposal meant leaving the baby on the streets at a place designated for such function such as the Columna Lactaria near the vegetable market adjacent to Rome's Forum.

The child could be taken by anyone and raised as they pleased. Slave traders sometimes collected abandoned babies.

In Rome, a cut coin was frequently attached to the child as a means of future identification. If the family later wanted to get the child back, for example if their financial circumstances improved or there was a change of heart, they could identify the child by matching the half of the coin they retained to the half left with the child. Compensation would be routinely required to secure the child's return.

There is no way of knowing if this coin was cut to serve this purpose but its large size and irregular cut would have made it a perfect candidate for such service. Matching up to its opposite would have been easy and made it possible to identify a wanted child.

The full coin itself was issued by Octavian and contains the busts of Julius Caesar and Octavian on the front with the prow of a ship with an elaborate superstructure on the reverse. On this cut example, only the head of Julius Caesar and the ship's superstructure can be seen.

Coin details and provenance: Octavian and Divus Julius Caesar. 36 BC. Halved dupondius. Vienna, Gaul mint. Obverse: Busts of Julius Caesar (missing) and Octavian above CAESAR and between DIVI IVLI and [DIVI.F.] Reverse: [C.I.V.] above Ship's prow with elaborate superstructure and mast. 6.76 grams. References: RPC 517; SIG 149. Acquired from Ingemar Wallin Mynthanel, Sweden in August of 2010.

Cleopatra as Aphrodite
Mid 30s BC

This coin comes from a Greece controlled by Cleopatra and Marc Antony in the years of the Second Triumverate just before Antony and Cleopatra would see their combined navies defeated by Octavian off the coast of Actium. The coin depicts the Greek goddess of love, beauty and procreation. It is believed to have been issued by Marc Antony and Cleopatra to pay their legions.

The choice of Aphrodite for the coin was appropriate for a queen whose rise to power within a Roman world began while she was in exile fighting for her survival in Cyprus. This same island that launched Cleopatra onto the world stage also housed one of the two principal cult sites dedicated to Aphrodite and was believed by the Greeks to have been the birth site of the goddess.

It is not hard to believe that the image was intended to honor the great queen who was worshiped as a goddess within her native Egypt. Most often she was portrayed as the Egyptian goddess Isis, who was worshiped as the ideal mother and wife, and goddess of children.

A remarkable woman by any account, Cleopatra was the last of the Greek Ptolemy dynasty that ruled Egypt for 300 years. She ruled the wealthiest empire in the Western world with the most advanced arts, the most impressive cities, and the most luxurious lifestyles for its ruling class.

She was also among the best educated rulers of her time, benefiting from being raised in a culture where women had more access to education than did their Roman counterparts. She could speak fluently in many languages and was the first Ptolemy able to speak to her Egyptian subjects in their native tongue.

Cleopatra was at the height of her power when this coin was issued. With Marc Antony at her side, she had been proclaimed Queen of Kings and Queen of Egypt, an empire that included Egypt and much of the Levant and Greece. Her son Caesarion had been proclaimed by Antony to be the legitimate son and rightful heir of Julius Caesar.

Cleopatra was also under vicious verbal attack from Octavian, who needed to sway popular opinion in Rome against Marc Antony as he prepared his legions for battle. His attacks against Cleopatra were meant to highlight Marc Antony's unforgiveable sin of adopting the extravagant and unacceptable lifestyle of the Egyptians.

Details and provenance: Achaea, Patrae. Mid-30s BC. Silver hemidrachm. Obverse: Head of Aphrodite right wearing stephane, resembling Cleopatra? Reverse ΔA/MACIAC and monogram within wreath. 16 mm. 2.32 grams. References: BCD 525; SNG Copenhagen 154. Acquired from Barry P. Murphy, Willow Street, Pennsylvania in April of 2010.

MARC ANTONY'S LEGIONS
32 TO 31 BC

This denarius was issued by Marc Antony to pay his legions before the Battle of Actium. The armies and navies of Cleopatra fought alongside Antony in this battle that marked the end of Antony's power and resulted in the consolidation of the Roman Empire under Octavian's rule.

The coin depicts a galley of the sort used by Marc Antony and Cleopatra in the battle of Actium, with its multiple oars, ramming device extending out of its prow and a mast with banners on the bow. On the back is the designation for the 11th legion with the legionary eagle between two standards.

On September 1, 31 BC, and after weeks of defections while Antony and Octavian jockeyed for advantage, Antony made the decision to fight by sea instead of marching against Octavian's land forces. That night he set fire to the ships he could not man. The bright blaze and smell of pitch from the burning war ships made it clear to both sides that the long stalemate was about to end.

The next morning, Antony launched his navy with ships full to the brim with fighting men. The ships headed out of Actium harbor to confront Octavian's navy. A ferocious sea battle ensued.

After considerable but inconclusive fighting, Cleopatra's ship, which had been in the rear, broke through Octavian's line to escape and head south. Antony's ship with 40 others followed, also breaking through the line.

The remainder of Antony's navy remained locked in a battle that would rage on long after the sails from Cleopatra's and Antony's ships disappeared from sight. Eventually, Octavian's marines, commanded by Marcus Agrippa, gained the upper hand and crushed the remaining ships in Antony's navy.

It is unclear whether this was a botched attempt to break Antony's navy free to regroup or, as some ancient sources suggest, a desperate triumph of love over good sense. That Antony understood the consequences, however, is clear. He brooded for days after the flight, sitting in the bow of Cleopatra's ship and speaking with no one.

Coin details and provenance: Marc Antony. 32 to 31 BC. Silver denarius. Struck at Patrae. Obverse: ANT AVG III VIR RPC, Galley facing right, mast with banners at prow. Reverse: LEG XI, Legionary eagle between two standards. 3.73 grams. 17.3 mm. References: Sear-1479var, Cr-544/14, Syd-1215, RSC-27. Acquired from Glenn W. Woods Numismatist, Dallas, Texas in December of 2005.

CAESARION

44 TO 30 BC

The teenager depicted on this coin is the son of Julius Caesar and Cleopatra. His profile is one of the few surviving depictions of a unique young man whose very existence helped fuel resentment toward Julius Caesar and conflict with Octavian. He appears on this coin as Cleopatra's nominal co-ruler of Egypt.

Caesarion was conceived during the intense months that followed Cleopatra's unconventional introduction to Caesar in 48 BC. As a young child, he lived in Rome with his mother after she was summoned there by Caesar. To Cleopatra, he must have seemed a perfect candidate to rule a combined Roman and Egyptian empire. In him was someone who was descended from both Julius Caesar and the Greeks of Alexander the Great.

After Caesar's assassination in 44 BC, Cleopatra returned to Egypt with her three year old son and named him co-ruler. There, Caesarion enjoyed a privileged upbringing as Cleopatra's anointed successor.

By the time Caesarion became a teenager, tensions had grown between Octavian and Marc Antony. In 34 BC, Marc Antony made armed conflict between the two rivals inevitable when he declared Caesarion to be Caesar's son and rightful heir, directly challenging Octavian's claim as Caesar's legal heir. To make matters worse, Antony granted eastern conquests to Caesarion and proclaimed him to be a god and King of Kings.

The combined armies of Antony and Cleopatra met Octavian on the field at Actium in 31 BC. After their defeat and retreat to Alexandria, Cleopatra began grooming Caesarion to become sole ruler of Egypt. When Octavian arrived in 30 BC to finish his conquest, she sent Caesarion to the Red Sea. After Cleopatra's suicide, however, Caesarion's guardians returned the boy to Alexandria and into the hands of Octavian's retainers.

The young Caesarion died shortly after, likely strangled to death on Octavian's order. For eighteen days before his death, however, Caesarion was the sole and last Greek ruler of Egypt.

Coin details and provenance: Cleopatra VII with Ptolemy XV (Caesarion). 44 to 30 BC. AR tetradrachm. Obverse: Diademed head of Ptolemy right wearing aegis. Reverse: PTOLEMAIOU BASILEWS around Eagle standing and facing left on thunderbolt, wings closed, palm over shoulder; date LI above crown of Isis left, PA right. 26 mm. 13.56 grams. References: Svoronos 1821, SNG Cop 418, Noeske - Paphos, I = 7, 74 BC. Acquired from Imperial Coins & Artifacts, New York, New York in June of 2011. Ex-Joseph C. Blazick collection.

OCTAVIAN, VICTORY AT ACTIUM
26 BC

This rare bronze was minted five years after the Battle of Actium to commemorate Octavian's decisive victory over the combined naval forces of Marc Antony and Cleopatra in 31 BC. The front shows Octavian in military dress holding a spear and resting his foot on the prow of a ship. The curile chair on the back of the coin signifies Octavian's position as commander and ruler.

The naval battle featured Marc Antony and Cleopatra aboard separate command ships with the Egyptian navy in the rear, rowing out of Actium Bay to meet Octavian's navy. Octavian's general and confidant Marcus Agrippa commanded his navy. After considerable but indecisive fighting, Cleopatra's ship advanced from the rear to break through Octavian's line and head south. Antony and 40 ships followed. Agrippa and Octavian's navy prevailed over the remaining ships.

This marked the end of Marc Antony's ability to resist Octavian. A broken man, both he and Cleopatra fled to Alexandria. From there, Antony traveled west to meet with four loyal legions in northern Africa, hoping to mount a defense against Octavian's inevitable attack. Cleopatra stayed in Alexandria and marshaled her resources there. Her plan was to flee east and establish a new kingdom there.

Both plans failed. Antony's legions deserted to Octavian and Cleopatra's attempt to move her warships overland to the Red Sea was thwarted by the Nabataeans, who burned her ships before they could be launched.

When Octavian and his forces eventually arrived in Alexandria, Antony had no legions and Cleopatra had built a towering mausoleum in Alexandria where she stored her valuables. She holed up there, knowing Octavian needed her wealth to pay for his wars and threatened to burn the building and its wealth.

Antony tried to kill himself with his sword after receiving a false message from Cleopatra's retainers that she had died. He was found lying in his own blood and was carried to Cleopatra's mausoleum and pulled by ropes up to Cleopatra's living quarters, where he died.

Later, Octavian's agents broke into Cleopatra's stronghold and captured the queen. They placed her under protective custody but, despite her guards, she managed to poison herself. She died in full ceremonial garb laid out on her bed.

Coin details and provenance: Augustus / Nonius Sulpicius IIviri Quinq. 26 BC. AE21 pella. Obverse: IMP DIVI F in field ACTIO in ex. Augustus in military dress right, foot on prow, holding spear. Reverse: NONIVS SVLPICIVS IIVIR QVINQ around curulis. 13.1 grams. 21.33 mm. References: RPC 1548. Acquired from Ancient Imports, Grand Marias, Minnesota in September of 2005.

MARCUS AGRIPPA

63 TO 12 BC

After serving as a cavalry officer under Julius Caesar at the Battle of Munda, Marcus Agrippa traveled east with Octavian to join Caesar's legions. The year was 45 BC and the two young men (they were 18 and 19) were traveling to join a planned invasion of Parthia.

On their way, they stopped in Apollonia to visit an astrologer named Theogenes who, according to Suetonius, predicted they would both have brilliant futures. They soon heard that their patron Julius Caesar had been assassinated and that the invasion of Parthia was cancelled.

Agrippa and Octavian returned to Rome and together, over the ensuing years, defeated Caesar's assassins and then the forces of Marc Antony to take control of the empire.

Marcus Agrippa was indispensable to Octavian. After taking over the navy, he succeeded in defeating the naval forces of Sextus Pompey off the coast of Sicily after multiple failed attempts by Octavian. He also commanded Octavian's forces at the pivotal battle at Actium against the navy of Marc Antony and Cleopatra.

After the battle, Agrippa married Octavian's niece Marcella. Ten years later, at Octavian's urging, he divorced his wife and married Octavian's daughter Julia.

When Agrippa unexpectedly predeceased Octavian in 12 BC, the Emperor was heartbroken. He honored his friend with a massive funeral and placed his remains in the tomb he had constructed for himself.

Octavian also took in Agrippa's children and raised them as his own. As later coins will reflect, Octavian did everything in his power to advance the prospects of Agrippa's two children, making them the heirs apparent to the Roman throne.

Coin details and provenance: Marcus Agrippa. 63 BC to 12 BC. AE. Memorial issue struck by Caligula. Obverse: Agrippa facing left, wearing rostral crown, M AGRIPPA L F COS III. Reverse: Neptune standing, head left, S C at sides. 10.3 grams. 27 mm. References: RCV 1812. Acquired from Incitatus Ancient Coins, St. Johns, NL, Canada and Antiquities in February of 2007.

AGRIPPA & AUGUSTUS
29 TO 10 BC

Close childhood friends Marcus Agrippa and Octavian are pictured here on a coin commemorating their victory over Antony and Cleopatra at the Battle of Actium. The symbolism on this coin would have been recognized by any Roman. Agrippa and Octavian appear back to back on the front, acknowledging their dual role in defeating the Egyptian menace of Antony and Cleopatra. The crocodile on the reverse symbolizes Egypt, now conquered and chained to a palm tree.

Both Agrippa and Octavian served as cavalry officers under Julius Caesar at the Battle of Munda in Spain. Afterward, Octavian and Agrippa were sent to Apollonia to serve with the Macedonian legions. It was there that they cemented their close friendship and learned of Caesar's assassination. When they returned to Rome, they discovered that Caesar had adopted Octavian in his will.

Marcus Agrippa became Octavian's most important general during the civil wars, delivering crucial victories for Octavian against Cassius and Brutus, Lucius Antonius, Fulvia, and Sextus

Pompey. His crowning glory, however, was his victory over the combined forces of Marc Antony and Cleopatra at Actium. By quick action, he managed to deliver a navy to the shores of Actium in time to trap Antony in the harbor. The resulting battle secured Octavian's place as Rome's only leader.

After the victory, Octavian enrolled all of Antony's 23 legions into his army and won their loyalty by declaring that the debased copper and silver alloy coins Antony had issued to them before the battle would be accepted as legal tender at full value throughout the empire. Antony's North African legions soon defected as well. Octavian now commanded all of Rome's legions and had no serious rival.

He later traveled to Alexandria with Agrippa to put an end to the civil wars and secure Egypt and her vast wealth for the newly unified Roman Empire. Agrippa continued to serve Octavian, delivering victories against the Aquitanian and the Germanic tribes. Until his unexpected death in 12 BC, Agrippa was designated as Octavian's heir to the Roman throne.

Coin details and provenance: Agrippa and Augustus. 29 to 10 BC. AE dupondius. Minted in Gaul colony of Nemausus (modern day Nimes in France). Obverse: Laureate heads of Augustus right and Agrippa left, with IMP above and DIVI F below. Reverse: Crocodile right, chained to a palm tree, with a comet above, and COL NEM across (the EM is off the flan). 12.73 grams. 24.9 x 25.5 mm. References: Sear-1730. The issue date is uncertain. Some references say 10 BC to 10 AD, but Sear (Roman Coins and Their Values) argues it was first issued in 28/29 BC but struck continuously over the next 30 or 40 years. Acquired from Ancient Imports, Grand Marias, Minnesota in August of 2006.

JUBA II
25 BC TO 23 AD

What happened to the children of the monarchs who were defeated by Roman forces? In 46 BC, the infant son of Juba I was taken to Rome and paraded in Caesar's African Triumph. This coin from a Mauritanian kingdom he would later rule as a Roman client-king shows Juba as a young man and Mauritanian king.

After his capture, Juba was not executed but, instead, remained in Rome to be raised in the household of Julius Caesar and then, later, Octavian. He was granted Roman citizenship and later wed to Cleopatra Selene II, the daughter of Marc Antony and Cleopatra. She had been captured after Antony and Cleopatra's defeat at Actium.

She too was raised by a prominent Roman family. In her case, it was Octavia, sister of Octavian and former wife of Marc Antony, who provided her with a home and an education.

Juba II became a lifelong friend of Octavian, accompanying him on military campaigns as a young man and fighting in the

Battle of Actium in 31 BC. After Octavian became emperor, he made Juba II his client-king in Numidia and then Mauretania.

When the royal couple moved to the Mauritanian capital they renamed it Caesarea in honor of Octavian. Once established, Juba and Cleopatra Selene attended to the arts and sciences in the Egyptian fashion that was her heritage. They installed public monuments and moved others from Alexandria to the Mauritanian capital.

They also constructed a grand library in the style of the one destroyed in Alexandria during the Egyptian civil war that matched Julius Caesar and Cleopatra against the armies of Ptolemy. Trade also flourished during Juba's reign, with the Mauritanians reestablishing the Phoenician art of extracting die from shell fish to produce purple stripes in senatorial robes.

The son of Juba II and Cleopatra Selene succeeded to the Mauritanian throne in 23 AD and ruled for 17 years. In 40 BC, however, he committed a fatal fashion faux pas. While visiting Rome on official business, he attended games at the Coliseum dressed as he would for a public event in his native Mauretania. His bright purple robe offended the erratic Caligula, who had him executed for his offense. After that, Mauretania became a Roman province.

Coin details and provenance: Juba II, Mauritanian Kingdom. 25 BC to 23 AD. AR drachm. Obverse: Diademed head right, REXIVBA. Reverse: Cornucopia and scepter. 2.54 grams. References: SNG Cop. 580; Mazard 241. Acquired from Atlantis Coins in November of 2004.

[5]
Afterwords

NOT EVERY IMPORTANT EVENT or influence of this era is recorded on an ancient coin. Here are a few other matters for your consideration.

Aristotle's Influence

Philip II began the search for Alexander's tutor when Alexander was 13 years old. He passed over Plato's successor at the Academy of Athens to offer the job to the 39-year-old Aristotle, who is imagined above (red gown) by the artist Raphael in the *School of Athens* fresco at the Vatican Museum. To attract Aristotle to the job, Philip gave him the Temple of the Nymphs at Mieza for a school and agreed to free the citizens of his hometown and rebuild their city.

Aristotle's temple became a boarding school for Alexander and many of the children of Macedonian royalty, some of whom, like Ptolemy and Cassander, would become Alexander's closest companions and generals. Aristotle tutored his pupils in philosophy, literature, morals, religion, logic, medicine and art.

Alexander took his training seriously and developed a passion for Homer and Greek arts. Alexander's formal studies ended after three years when Aristotle returned to Athens to start his own academy, the Lyceum. But Alexander continued, according to Plutarch, to thirst for learning through the rest of his life, reading extensively and conversing late into the night with scholars and scientists while he was on his military campaigns.

The influence of Aristotle had been profound. Throughout his adult life and military campaigns, Alexander carried with him a copy of Homer's epic poem, *The Iliad*, that had been personally annotated by Aristotle.

THE ROMAN SENATE

Pictured here in a 19th century fresco, Cicero attacks the conspirator Catalina who unsuccessfully plotted to murder Cicero and overthrow the Republic in 63 BC. At the time of this incident, the Republic had survived for almost 450 years. Within less than 40 years, the Republic would face civil wars that shifted the balance of power to a series of Roman emperors who continued Roman dominance in the region for another 500 years. Afterward, the European portion of the empire split off leaving an eastern Roman Empire headquartered in

Constantinople. This lasted for another 700 years until the Crusades, invading Muslims and then Mongols would finally displace the empire Rome began.

Governed by a constitution and series of checks and balances, the Republic provided the foundation for this lasting expansion of Roman influence and culture. In its first two centuries, the Republic expanded Rome's territory from the Italian peninsula to include most of the Mediterranean basin, making the Mediterranean Sea a Roman sea. The next century saw Rome dominate northern Africa, Greece, the Anatolian peninsula (Turkey) and much of southern France. From there, the Republic grew to include much of modern-day Spain, all of France and even Britain.

THE EGYPTIAN FACTOR

Cleopatra did not cause the civil wars that engulfed Rome after the assassination of Julius Caesar but she was a contributing factor. When Caesar brought her back from Egypt to live in Rome, she became another reason for skeptics to fear Caesar's intent. She was, after all, queen of an ancient empire now living as Caesar's paramour in a city whose republican government had only recently been overthrown.

She had been bold in 48 BC when she concealed herself in a sack to avoid spies so that she could meet Caesar in person after he arrived in Alexandria. And she would be bold again five years after his death, aligning herself with Marc Antony in his quest to emerge as the true heir to Caesar's legacy. She had born Caesar a son, named Caesarion, and would later bear the children of Marc Antony. With Antony, she would rule an eastern empire when Octavian, Lepidus and Antony divided the Roman Empire into separate zones of influence.

Her impact on Caesar had been immediate and physical. Observers said Caesar was instantly captivated with her when she emerged from her servant's rug. Antony's attraction to her would be equally strong. When politics dictated that he marry Octavian's sister Octavia, he complied and reduced the mounting tension between him and his principal rival. He even bore children with Octavia but eventually deserted her to head east and reunite with the wealthy Egyptian queen who could finance his campaign against Parthia.

In the end, his attentions to Cleopatra - naming her queen of his eastern empire and declaring her son Caesarion the rightful heir to Julius Caesar - made reconciliation with Octavian impossible. It also provided fodder for Octavian's propaganda war against him. Charging him with the sin of going native and abandoning the principals of all good Romans, Octavian turned popular opinion against Marc Antony. His ultimate victory would be sealed in 31 BC after pursuing Antony and Cleopatra to Alexandria, where they had fled after the Battle of Actium hoping to find refuge.

The image above from *The Death of Cleopatra* by Juan Luna 1881 depicts the self-inflicted death of Cleopatra after her capture by Octavian's agents. Under heavy guard, she nonetheless managed to sneak a poisonous asp into her quarters to use in her suicide. Marc Antony had taken his own life earlier after hearing, erroneously, that Cleopatra had died. Learning of his distress, Cleopatra had his wounded body hauled up into the tower where she was staying before he died.

Fulvia's Revenge

Depicted here in a painting by Pavel Svedomsky entitled *Fulvia With the Head of Cicero* is a moment from 43 BC recorded by Roman historian Cassius Dio. Fulvia, wife to Marc Antony and political power in her own right, admires the severed head of Cicero and the hairpins she has driven into his lifeless tongue.

Cicero had embarrassed Fulvia when he prosecuted her first husband P. Clodius Pulcher. In 62 BC, Pulcher had entered the house of Julius Caesar disguised as a woman to participate in the women-only ritual of Bona Dea. After being charged with incestum, Pulcher claimed he was away from Rome at the time. Cicero refuted the alibi in court, creating a life-long rift with Fulvia.

Twenty years later, after Fulvia's third husband Antony became powerful following Julius Caesar's assassination, Cicero became Antony's most outspoken critic. After Octavian arrived in Rome, Cicero actively attacked Antony in speeches from the Senate floor and eventually urged the Senate to declare Antony an enemy of the state.

When Antony and Octavian reconciled in 43 BC, Cicero found himself proscribed as an enemy of Rome. On December 7th he was murdered while fleeing the city. At Antony's instruction, his head and hands were placed on public display at the Forum.

[6]

Book II Preview: Imperial Rome

THIS IS THE FACE OF IMPERIAL ROME.[6] This is the man, formerly known as Octavian but now hailed as Caesar Augustus, who wrenched order from the chaos that followed the murder of Julius Caesar and, in so doing, imposed his will on Rome. This is what imperial power and empire looked like at the beginning of the first century – composed, thoughtful, youthful and unthreatening.

At least this is how Octavian chose to depict himself to the sometimes reluctant Republicans whose support he needed. Some scholars also believe this carefully crafted, and deliberately understated and nonmilitary image, is also an early examples of

---

[6] The silver denarius is from Caesar Augustus (formerly Octavian) and was minted in Lugdunum between 27 BC and 14 AD. Obverse: Head of Augustus, legend CAESAR AVGVSTVS. Reverse: Circular shield with inscription - S P Q R CL V - worn away. Acquired from Calgary Coin and Antique, Calgary, Alberta, Canada in April of 2006.

a dictator using art to deliberately misinform the public about his nature and intentions.

In his will, Julius Caesar named the 19 year-old staff officer Octavian as his sole heir. In the chaos that followed Caesar's bloody assassination, the young Octavian, with the assistance of Caesar's foremost lieutenant Marc Antony, entered the political and military fray to claim his bequest.

Born Gaius Octavian on September 23, 63 BC, Octavian took the name Gaius Julius Caesar Octavian in 44 BC after the murder of his great uncle. At the time of the assassination, Octavian had no official power. Only after marching an army on Rome and forcing the Senate to name him consul, did he establish himself as a power to be reckoned with.

Swearing vengeance to Mars against the conspirators who carried out Caesar's vicious murder on the Ides of March, Octavian successfully battled his adversaries and navigated the political minefield that was Rome at the time. All of the conspirators would be hunted down and die.

And eventually, after turning on and defeating Marc Antony and the forces of Cleopatra at the naval battle of Actium off the coast of Greece, Octavian would come to rule all of Rome. But this would not occur until 31 BC, after 12 years of strife that saw Rome divided into three smaller empires, with Octavian ruling the West, Marc Antony and his Egyptian queen Cleopatra ruling the East, and Lepidus ruling Africa.

The coins and stories that follow in this first section of Book II cover a period of two hundred years, from the imposition of imperial rule by Octavian Augustus just before the beginning of the first century AD to the beginning of the third century, when

Ancient Selfies | 317

the death of Emperor Septimius Severus ushered in a century of crisis for a faltering empire.

The great and the not so great would preside over Rome and adjacent kingdoms during this era. Roman Emperors Augustus, Tiberius, Caligula, Claudius, Nero, Vespasian, Titus, Domitian, Trajan, Hadrian, Pius, Verus, Aurelius and Commodus would each make their marks on the world stage during this period.

Vespasian, for one, would see his fortunes change dramatically with the advent of the First Jewish war in 66. Called out of relative obscurity to lead Rome's response to the Judean insurrection, Vespasian and his son Titus would put down the rebellion in violent fashion, culminating with the subjugation of the Jews and destruction of the Jewish Temple.

When the Roman Senate finally turned on Nero two years later, a quick succession of weak emperors gave Vespasian his chance to claim the role of emperor for himself....

.... AMONG THE COINS AND STORIES FEATURED IN BOOK II:

PHRAATACES & MUSA

The son who married his mother and ruled Parthia from 2 BC.

AZES II, COIN OF THE MAGI

The Eastern ruler who sent Gaspar to find the Christ child.

PONTIUS PILATE

The Roman prefect who sent Christ to the cross.

CLAUDIUS
The Roman emperor who stammered and slobbered.

NERO & POPPAE
He burned Rome and kicked the pregnant Poppae to death.

WIMA KADPHISES
First century Kushan king who ruled far to the east of Rome.

SEPTIMIUS SEVERUS
Rome's first African emperor from 200 AD.

JULIA AQUILIA SEVERA
The third century Vestal Virgin who became an empress.

JULIA MAMAEA
The first woman to openly rule Rome.

Maximinus I
Rome's eight foot tall "giant" emperor.

Constantine the Great
The emperor who reunified Rome in the fourth century.

Justinian
The sixth century emperor who codified Roman law, married a prostitute and survived the plague.

[7]

Appendix: Reading Material, Photo Credits and Index

ANGELA, ALBERTO. *A Day in the Life of Ancient Rome.* Europa Editions, New York, 2009.

ARNOLD, JOHN H. *History - A Very Short Introduction.* Oxford University Press. Oxford, 2000.

BAHAT, DAN, IN COLLABORATION WITH BEN-SHALOM, RAM. *Israel - 2000 Years, A History of People and Places.* Mantan Arts Publishers Ltd, 1999.

BERK, HARLAN J., RAM. *100 Greatest Ancient Coins.* Whitman Publishing, LLC, 2008.

CAESAR, JULIUS, *The Gallic War and Other Writings of Julius Caesar*. Moses Hadas translation. The Modern Library, Random House, Toronto, Canada, 1957.

CAHILL, THOMAS, *Desire of the Everlasting Hills - The World Before and After Jesus*. Nan A Talese, an imprint of Doubleday. 1999.

CAHILL, THOMAS, *Sailing the Wine Dark Sea - Why the Greeks Matter*. Nan A Talese, an imprint of Doubleday. 2003.

CARTLEDGE, PAUL, *Alexander the Great*. The Overlook Press, Woodstock and New York, 2004.

CARTLEDGE, PAUL, *Ancient Greece - A History in Eleven Cities*. Oxford University Press, Inc., New York, 2009.

DOLEAC, MILES, *In the Footsteps of Alexander – The King who Conquered the Ancient World*. Amber Books Ltd., New York, 2014.

CHARLES RIVER EDITORS, *The End of the Roman Republic: The Lives and Legacies of Julius Caesar, Cleopatra, Mark Antony, and Augustus*. Charles River Editors, Boston, 2012.

GODOLPHIN, F. R. B., Editor. *Great Classical Myths*, Random House (Modern Library Edition), New York, 1964.

GOLDSWORTHY, ADRIAN, Author. KEEGAN, JOHN, Series Editor. *Roman Warfare*, Smithsonian Books, U.S.A., 2005.

GOLDSWORTHY, ADRIAN, *Augustus First Emperor of Rome*, Yale University, New Haven, 2014.

GRANT, MICHAEL, *The Ancient Historians*, Barnes & Noble Books, 1970.

GRANT, MICHAEL, *Readings in the Classical Historians*, Charles Scribner's Sons, 1992.

GRANT, MICHAEL, *Roman History from Coins*, Cambridge University Press, 1968.

HAMILTON, EDITH. *The Greek Way.* W.W. Norton & Company, Inc., New York, 1991.

HAMILTON, EDITH. *The Roman Way.* W.W. Norton & Company, Inc., New York, 1991.

HERODOTUS, *The Histories*. Robin Waterfield translation. Oxford University Press, Oxford, New York, 1998.

HOLLAND, TOM, *Rubicon - The Last Years of the Roman Republic.* First Anchor Books Edition, March 2005.

HOLT, FRANK L. *Alexander the Great and the Mystery of the Elephant Medallions*, University of California Press, Berkeley and Los Angeles, 2003.

HOMER. *The Iliad.* Michael Reck translation. Harper Collins Publishers (Icon Edition), 1994.

HOMER. *The Odyssey*. Allen Mandelbaum translation. University of California Press, Berkeley, Los Angeles, New York, Oxford, 1990.

HOWGEGO, CHRISTOPHER. *Ancient History from Coins*. Rutledge Books, 2001.

JIMENEZ, RAMON L. *Caesar Against the Celts*. Castle Books, New Jersey, 1996.

JOSEPHUS, FLAVIUS. *The Works of Josephus*. William Whiston translation. Hendrickson Publishers, Inc., Peabody, Massachusetts, 2003.

KAGAN, DONALD. *The Peloponnesian War*. Viking, New York, 2003.

KAPUSCINSKI, RYSZARD. *Travels with Herodotus*. Alfred A. Knoff, New York, 2007.

KLAWANS, ZANDEER H. *Handbook of Ancient Greek and Roman Coins*. Whitman Publishing, LLC, Atlanta, 2003.

LABBERTON, ROBERT H. *An Historical Atlas - A Chronological Series of One Hundred and Twelve Maps from the Dawn of History to the Present Day*. Townsend Mac County, New York, 1884.

MARSH, W.B. & CARRICK, BRUCE. *365 - Great Stories from History for Every Day*. Fall River Press, New York, 2007.

MAYOR, ADRIENNE. *The Poison King - The Life and legend of Mithradates, Rome's Deadliest Enemy.* Princeton University Press, Princeton, 2010.

MEIER, CHRISTIAN. *Caesar – A Biography.* HarperCollins, United Kingdom, 1992.

NICOLSON, ADAM. *Why Homer Matters.* Henry Holt and Co., New York, 2014.

LIVY (TITUS LIVIUS). D. Spillan, A.M.M.D. translation. *The History of Rome.* Halcyon Classics Series, Halcyon Press, Alvin, Texas, 2010.

PARKER, PHILIP. *Eyewitness Companions - World History.* Dorling Kindersley Limited, United Kingdom, 2010.

PLATO. *Dialogs on Love and Friendship.* Benjamin Jowett translation. The Heritage Press, New York, 1968.

PLUTARCH. *Selected Lives.* The Dryden translation. The Franklin Library, Franklin Center, Pennsylvania, 1982.

ROMM, JAMES. *Herodotus.* Yale University Press, New Haven, London, 1998.

SAYLES, WAYNE G. *Ancient Coin Collecting.* Krause Publications, Ioal, Wisconsin, 2003.

SAYLES, WAYNE G. *Ancient Coin Collecting II, Numismatic Art of the Greek World*, Krause Publications, Ioal, Wisconsin, 1997.

SAYLES, WAYNE G. *Ancient Coin Collecting III, The Roman World - Polities and Propaganda*, Krause Publications, Ioal, Wisconsin, 1997.

SAYLES, WAYNE G. *Ancient Coin Collecting IV, Roman Provincial Coins*. Ioal, Wisconsin, 1999.

SAYLES, WAYNE G. *Ancient Coin Collecting VI, Non-Classical Cultures*. Krause Publications, Iola, Wisconsin, 1999.

SCHIFF, STACY. *Cleopatra, A Life*. Little, Brown and Company, New York, 2010.

STONE, I. F. *The Trial of Socrates*. Little Brown and Company, Boston, 1988.

STRASSLER, ROBERT B. *The Landmark Thucydides, A Comprehensive Guide to the Peloponnesian War*. The Free Press, Simon & Shuster, New York, 1996.

STRAUSS, BARRY. *The Battle of Salamis*, Simon and Schuster, New York, 2004.

Image Credits

All of the coins and their images are from the Ancient Selfies™ Collection. Other images in the book are either original to the author (A) or are public domain images sourced from Wikipedia.org (W):

Introduction

- Croesus on the Pyre, Louvre, Paris. (W)
- Alexander Mosaic from Pompeii at the Naples Archeological Museum. (A)
- Ancient Mosaic from the Roman Coliseum. (A)
- A fifth century AD manuscript page from *The Iliad*.(W)

The Ancients

- Raphael Imagines Aeneas Escaping a Burning Troy. Detail from the *Fire in the Borge* fresco at the Vatican Museum. (A)
- Persian Empire from *Labberton's Historical Atlas*.
- *The Death of Socrates* by Jacques-Louis David (1787). (W)

Greek Empire

- Temple of Athena at the Greek colony of Paestum. (A)
- Alexander the Great astride Bucephalus at the Battle of Isus. From the Alexander Mosaic from Pompeii. (A)
- The Diodach Kingdoms. (W)

Republican Rome First

- Bacchus, serpent Agathodaemon and Mt. Vesuvius from a fresco at the Naples Acheological Museum. (A)
- Ancient Gladiator Mosaic displayed at the Borghese Gallery in Rome. (A)
- Jupiter Empowers the Trojan Aeneas to Start a Roman Nation. Ceiling in the Borghese Gallery in Rome. (A)
- *Lictors Bring to Brutus the Bodies of His Sons* by Jacques-Louis David 1789. (W)
- Detail from *Intervention of the Sabine Women* by Jacques-Louis David 1799. (W)

Caesar's Legacy

- The Eventual Victor: Octavian as Augustus Wearing Civic Crown, Glyptothek, Munich. (W)
- *Cleopatra Before Caesar* by Jean-Léon Gérôme 1866. (W)
- *La Mort de César* by Jean-Léon Gérôme 1867. (W)

Afterwords

- Detail from the *School of Athens* fresco in the Vatican Museum by Raphael. (A)
- *Cicero Attacks the Conspirator Catalina*, 19th century fresco. (W)
- *The Death of Cleopatra* by Juan Luna 1881. (W)
- *Fulvia With the Head of Cicero* by Pavel Svedomsky. (W)

About the Author:

- Anubis and young admirer at the Vatican Museum. (A)

Index

'Abd' ashtart, 47
Actium, 114, 232-238, 293-306,
Aeneas, 12, 138, 199-200
Aeneid, 148, 199
Africanus, 104, 118, 145, 161-162
Agathocles, 61, 79-890, 101
Agripppa, 9, 232-238, 252, 296, 296, 299-304
Ahenobarbus, 8, 227, 233, 247, 283-284
Ajatashatru, 23-24
Alexander I, 31-32
Alexander III, 51, 56, 67-72, 176
Amazons, 16, 33-34, 73, 122
Apama, 83-84, 93
Antigonus, 85-87, 95-97
Antioch, 6, 83, 214, 237, 273-74
Antiochus I, 93, 107-08, 123
Antiochus IV, 127-28
Aphrodite, 235, 293-94
Arados, 43-44
Ariarathes, 183-184
Archimedes, 98
Aretes III, 207-08
Ariobarzanes, 271-72
Artaxeres, 55-46
Artemis, 73-74, 79-80

Athena, 39-42, 77, 85-88, 95-96, 132
Athens, 15-16, 28-30, 36, 39-42, 52, 67, 86, 308
Augustus, 9, 142, 199-200, 202, 228, 281-82
Babylon, 81, 85, 91, 122, 129
Bessus, 46, 83
Bimbasara, 16, 23-24
Blasio, 161-62
Bucephalus, 51, 58, 81
Buddha, 14, 16, 23-24
Caesarion, 72, 229, 232, 256, 258, 288, 294, 297-98, 311
Cappadocia, 271-72
Carthage, 29, 47, 60, 80, 101, 104, 117, 126, 149-52, 180-82
Cassander, 77-78, 86, 113, 308
Cassius, 201-02, 216, 219-20, 230-33, 241, 267, 269-276
Castulo, 105-06
Catalina, 309
Cato, 82, 233, 249-50, 265, 285
Celtiberians, 60, 125-26, 164
Celts, 5, 7, 53-54, 60, 62, 71, 125
Censorinus, 193-94
Children of Mars, 62, 101
Cinna, 189-91

Cicero, 98, 125, 197-98, 208, 223, 242, 250, 270-71, 278, 282, 312-13
Cleopatra I, 60, 123-24
Cleopatra VII, 229, 253-58, 293-98, 310
Cleopatra Selene, 206 262, 305-06
Clodianus, 6, 138, 185-86
Codomanus, 15, 45
Corinth, 29, 37, 41-42, 52, 152
Crassus, 6, 120, 135, 138, 142, 150, 186, 190-91, 213-16, 234, 252, 277, 290
Croesus, 3-4, 14-16, 20-22, 25, 27, 73, 112
Cupid, 141, 145, 167-68, 199-200, 248, 262
Cut Coins, 291
Cyrus, 3-5, 15, 22, 27-28, 112
Darius, 5, 15, 28-29, 32, 36, 45-46, 57, 68, 83, 177
Darsalas, 119-20
Delian League, 35, 39
Delphic Oracle, 51
Delsutor, 163
Demeter, 38, 73, 87, 128
Decimus Brutus, 8, 233, 240-42
Diadochi, 57, 60, 81, 95
Demetrius, 78 ,85-86, 93-96, 127, 131, 203-04
Dionysus, 73, 87, 176-77
Dyrrachion, 113
Ecbatana, 46, 57-59
Ephesus, 48, 73-74, 111
Epirus, 80, 97, 99-100, 113
Euclid, 92
Fish money, 18
Fulvia, 269-70, 287, 303, 312-13

Gaugamela, 57, 68, 81
Gaul, 94, 103, 160, 209-12, 227, 241-43, 247, 261, 283, 292, 304
Geminus, 153-54
Glabrio, 107
Gnaeus Pompey, 234, 263-64, 285
Gorgon, 83-84, 176, 179-82, 234
Gracchus, 154, 156
Hannibal, 8, 62, 71, 103-07, 117-18, 125-26, 150-51, 161-62
Halicarnassus, 22, 30, 121-22
Hasdrubal, 106-07, 117-18, 162
Heracles, 5, 31, 57-58, 67-73, 121-22
Herodotus, 3, 16, 21-22, 28-29, 33-40, 75, 111-12, 194
Herostratus, 73
Hieron, 61, 97-98
Homer, 8, 31, 60, 66, 69, 89-90, 119, 121, 164, 179, 195, 308-09
Hostilius Saserna, 244-46
Hydaspes, 68, 81
Ides of March, 231, 241, 267, 275, 278
Ilyrians, 52, 113, 190
Isis, 123-24, 293, 298
Janus, 157-58, 334, 252
Josephus, 48, 110
Juba I, 205-06, 220, 305
Juba II, 206, 262, 305-06
Jupiter, 79, 138, 157, 161-63, 165-70, 189, 191, 199, 207-08, 259, 279
Julius Caesar, 209-214, 217-22, 227-68
Juno, 161-62, 165-66
L. Julius Caesar, 167-68, 187
Last Pharaoh, 257-58

Lepidus, 198, 220, 231, 270, 282, 286-88, 311, 316
Library of Alexandria, 92, 174, 246
Limetanus, 195-96
Longinus, 201-02, 219-20, 275, 277-78
Lucius Brutus, 140, 221
Lysimachus, 59, 62, 76-78, 86-88, 99
Machiavelli, 61, 80
Magnus Pompey, 50, 72, 120, 139, 186-87, 191, 214, 217, 224, 228, 230, 234, 249-52, 263-64, 266, 274, 283-86
Mamertini, 5, 60, 62, 97, 101-02
Marc Antony, 8, 9, 61, 74, 114, 158, 160, 174, 187, 198, 202, 220, 228, 231-35, 258, 264, 268-70, 275-80, 283-84, 286-89, 293-301, 311-16
Marcus Brutus, 8, 140, 187, 221-22, 230, 233, 241-42, 278
Marius, 139-44, 166-70, 187-190, 223
Marsysas, 193-94
Marathon, 1, 28, 36, 50, 180
Masinissa, 106, 117-18
Mauretania, 5, 206, 220, 306
Medusa, 176, 181-82
Menander, 48, 62, 131-32
Mercury, 141, 195-96
Mesembria, 37-38
Milesians, 25-26
Miltiades, 35-36
Mithradates, 50, 72, 100, 129-30, 144, 170, 174-190, 215-17, 223
Monetas, 259-60
Moses, 110
Munda, 230, 234, 263-64

Natta, 149-50,
Nerva, 159-62
Nike, 103-04, 131-32, 176, 179-80, 269
Norbanus, 187-88, 190
Oath Scene, 155-56
Octavia, 287-88
Octavian, 228, 231,-35, 252, 258, 264, 269-306, 311-13
Odysseus, 195-96
Odyssey, 8, 60, 66, 89, 121, 195
Omphalos, 93-94, 107-08, 129-30
Orodes, 6, 138-39, 142, 215-16, 289
Pan, 49-50, 95-96
Panticapaeum, 49-50
Parthenon, 39, 86
Paullus, 140, 203-04
Peloponnesian War, 40-41, 52, 96
Perdiccas, 51, 92
Pergamon, 62-63, 87-88, 94, 153, 156, 173,-74, 185, 202, 288
Pericles, 40
Perseus, 150, 176, 181-82, 203-04
Philadelphos, 273-74
Pharsalas, 200, 206, 218, 285
Philetairos, 87-88
Philip II, 5, 7, 15, 17, 35, 38, 51-54, 67-68, 75-77, 81, 95, 155
Philippi, 231, 270, 275-84
Philometer, 124
Philus, 157-58
Phoenicians, 4, 15, 43-44, 47-48, 60, 107, 151-52, 306
Pharnaces, 50, 229
Phraates, 6, 50, 129, 215-16, 289-290
Pietas, 242, 246

Plato, 8, 16, 40, 90, 194, 308
Plutarch, 74, 90, 131, 174, 228, 220, 256, 309
Ptolemy, 5, 46, 59-61, 70, 72, 77-78, 83-86, 91--92, 94, 97-99, 123-24, 229, 245-46, 251-58
Punic War, 60-62, 97, 101-02, 117, 124-26, 149-51, 158-61
Pushkalavati, 131-32
Pyrrhus, 61, 78-80, 96-100, 113
Qin Shi Huangdi, 115-16
Quinctius, 163-64
Remi, 141, 209-10
Rubicon, 167, 219, 227-28, 241, 244-47, 250-51, 271
Rufus, 223-24, 261-62
Saba, 62, 109-10
Sabine War, 141, 171
Sabinus, 140, 171-72, 211-12
Samnite War, 143, 155
Sarmatians, 5, 16, 33-34, 49, 60
Saturn, 157, 248, 259
Scarus, 207-08
Seleucus, 59, 62, 77-78, 81-88, 93-95, 127, 274
Servile War, 154, 185
Seuthes, 75-76, 78
Sextus Pompey, 230, 234, 241, 252, 282, 285-86, 303
Sheba, 60, 64, 109
Silk Road, 130
Sol, 153-54
Sophocles, 16, 40
Sparta, 29, 35, 40-42, 100
Spartacus, 6, 119-20, 135-38, 185-86, 213-14, 216, 252
Sphinx, 105

Stratonice, 85, 93-94
Syphax, 117-18
Syracuse, 17 41-42, 79-80, 97-98, 101-02, 104,
Sythians, 50
Tanit, 6, 152
Tarquinius, 140, 221, 276
Terrentia, 197
Thales, 25-26
Themistocles, 29
Thermopylae, 30, 107-08
Thracians, 4, 35, 37, 49-50, 60, 62, 75-76, 119
Thrace, 6, 17, 37-38, 50, 77-78, 119-20
Triumph, 178, 191-92, 217-18, 229, 233, 244, 252, 261-62, 265, 305
Triumviri Monetales, 149, 153
Triumverate, 198, 220, 250. 268, 284, 293
Twelve Labors of Heracles, 121-122
Unelli, 211-12
Venus, 141, 167-68, 187-88, 197-200, 217-18, 233, 248, 261-62, 268
Vercingetorix, 7, 233, 243-44, 261-62
Vestal Virgin, 9, 191, 197, 201-02, 320
Veturius, 155-56
Viridovix, 211-12
Vote by Ballot, 139, 159-60
Vulcan, 167, 179, 259
Xerxes I, 29, 30, 32, 44
Zeus, 5, 51, 57-58, 61, 69-72, 75-86, 99-102, 108, 114, 121, 128, 175-76, 179, 181, 214, 273-74

ABOUT THE AUTHOR

Clinton Richardson is a student of history, lawyer, business advisor and author of two critically acclaimed books for entrepreneurs – *The Venture Magazine Complete Guide to Venture Capital* and *Richardson's Growth Company Guide 5.0 (fifth edition)*. This is his first history book. Clinton is a graduate of Albion College and Duke University School of Law. Please take your children to a museum.

COPYRIGHTS AND OTHER STUFF

Copyright © 2017 by Clinton Richardson as part of the Ancient Selfies™ series of publications. All worldwide rights reserved.

Reservation. No part of this publication may be reproduced, distributed or transmitted in any form or by any means without the prior written permission of the publisher, except for brief quotations embodied in critical reviews and noncommercial uses permitted by copyright law.

Credits: Coin images are from the private Ancient Selfies collection. Other images are from the author or public domain images courtesy of Wikipedia.

Accuracy: This book uses the actual coins commissioned by ancient rulers to illustrate our history. Hand stamped and made from dies engraved by artisans, these miniature works of art provide a unique first-person window into our past. Interpretations of history and coins are subject to bias and error.

Other books by the author include:

Richardson's Growth Company Guide 5.0 (Read Janus 2014 – 5th edition)
The Growth Company Guide (Pfeiffer & Co. 1993)
The Venture Magazine Compete Guide to Venture Capital (NAL 1987)

Clinton Richardson/Read Janus LLC
Atlanta, Georgia
clinton@readjanus.com

Ancient Selfies/ Clinton Richardson
ISBN 978-0-9912475-3-0

Made in the USA
Middletown, DE
25 July 2021